Lode and Placer Mining Claims

A Manual of Mining Law in the States and Territories of the United States

by Edward B. Howell
of the Butte Bar

with an introduction by Kerby Jackson

GOLD RUSH BOOKS

OREGON, USA

www.GoldMiningBooks.com

Introduction

It has often been said that "*gold is where you find it*", but even beginning prospectors understand that their chances for finding something of value in the earth or in the streams of the Golden West are dramatically increased by going back to those places where gold and other minerals were once mined by our forerunners. Despite this, much of the contemporary information on local mining history that is currently available is mostly a result of mere local folklore and persistent rumors of major strikes, the details and facts of which, have long been distorted. Long gone are the old timers and with them, the days of first hand knowledge of the mines of the area and how they operated. Also long gone are most of their notes, their assay reports, their mine maps and personal scrapbooks, along with most of the surveys and reports that were performed for them by private and government geologists. Even published books such as this one are often retired to the local landfill or backyard burn pile by the descendents of those old timers and disappear at an alarming rate. Despite the fact that we live in the so-called "Information Age" where information is supposedly only the push of a button on a keyboard away, true insight into mining properties remains illusive and hard to come by, even to those of us who seek out this sort of information as if our lives depend upon it. Without this type of information readily available to the average independent miner, there is little hope that our metal mining industry will ever recover.

This important volume and others like it, are being presented in their entirety again, in the hope that the average prospector will no longer stumble through the overgrown hills and the tailing strewn creeks without being well informed enough to have a chance to succeed at his ventures.

Kerby Jackson
Josephine County, Oregon
May 2018

CONTENTS.

NOTE.

This manual is primarily intended for the use of prospectors and miners. The author has sought, however, to make it useful to lawyers also by giving citations to decisions of the courts and of the Land Department. There has been no effort to give a full list of the decided cases, but only to give one or two leading cases, the latest adjudications so far as possible. Those desiring more citations or a fuller discussion of doubtful questions should consult Mr. Lindley's very excellent treatise on Mines, to which the author of this manual acknowledges himself indebted for many citations.

The order of the sections of the federal law as they occur in the Revised Statutes has been changed somewhat, and they have been grouped so far as possible according to subject. For convenience of reference, each group is given a paragraph number consecutive with the paragraph numbers of the text.

ABBREVIATIONS USED.

R. S.—Revised Statutes of the United States.

L. O. Reg.—Regulations of the General Land Office.

L. D.—Decisions of the Land Department.

Pac.—Pacific Reporter.

Fed.—Federal Reporter.

U. S.—United States Supreme Court Reports.

Op. Att. Gen.—Opinions of the Attorney General.

MINING LAWS

OF THE UNITED STATES.

INTRODUCTORY.

1. Scope of Mining Law.—Mining law, as the term is used in this book, relates to the legal authority under which title may be acquired to the mineral lands of the United States. As thus used, the term includes the mining laws of the United States, since these laws are the primary source of authority for the disposal of these lands. It includes also the decisions of the federal courts, since upon these courts devolves the duty of interpreting authoritatively and finally the mining laws of the United States. It includes the rules and decisions of the land department of the federal government, since the officials of this department must execute the land laws of the United States, and must give the first interpretation to these laws.

2. Jurisdiction of Land Department.—While the land department is a part of the executive branch of the federal government, yet it is often called upon to exercise functions essentially judicial. It has jurisdiction in many cases to take testimony and to decide as between rival claimants to the same tract, or as to the character of any specific tract, whether mineral or agricultural. When so acting it constitutes a real tribunal and its decisions are final, and will not be questioned by the courts except in cases where its officials have acted fraudulently or in excess of their lawful authority (1).

3. State Laws.—But mining law in the broad sense includes also the mining statutes of the states and territories in which mineral lands of the United States are situated. The act of congress under which title to mineral lands is acquired has delegated to the local legislatures of the states and territories, and even to the local organizations of miners in the several mining districts, the right to make regulations governing the location, manner of recording, and amount of work necessary to hold possession of mining claims. In pursuance of the authority thus given, the legislatures of most of the states and territories in which public mineral lands are situated have enacted statutes so fully covering these

---

(1) Johnson vs. Towsley, 13 Wall. 72; St. Louis Smelting Co. vs. Kemp, 104 U. S. 636; Kennedy vs. Dickie, 34 Mont. 205; Mineral Farm M. Co. vs. Barrick (Colo.), 80 Pac. 1055.

points that for many years past in those states miners have ceased to organize or enact rules, as they were accustomed to do in the early days of the mining industry.

4. Decisions of State Courts.—Within the limits of the authority delegated by congress, these state statutes are supreme (2). The decisions of the supreme courts of the various states and territories interpreting these statutes are the authoritative and final expression of their meaning, and these decisions constitute an important element of mining law.

5. Complexity of the System.—It will thus be seen that mining law in the broad sense is a complicated system of laws, derived from various sources of authority, each supreme within its own sphere. It well illustrates the complexity of the government under which we live,. a complexity which is so puzzling to foreign students of our government. But if anyone is puzzled to know just how far each of these spheres of authority extends, just to what extent, for instance, a state legislature may enact mining laws before it encroaches upon the authority of congress, or just how far the authority of the land department may go in any case before it trenches upon the domain of the courts, he need not be wholly discouraged, for there is no lawyer or judge but who encounters similar perplexities. But the number of questions thus left doubtful is being lessened year by year as the judicial interpretations of the law proceeds.

6. MINERAL LANDS RESERVED.

Sec. 2318, R. S. In all cases lands valuable for minerals shall be reserved from sale, except as otherwise expressly directed by law.—Act of July 4, 1866.

Sec. 2346, R. S. No act passed at the first session of the Thirty-eighth congress, granting lands to states or corporaitons to aid in the construction of roads or for other purposes, or to extend the time of grants made prior to the thirtieth day of January, eighteen hundred and sixty-five, shall be so construed as to embrace mineral lands, which in all cases are reserved exclusively to the United States, unless otherwise specially provided in the act or acts making the grant.—Act of Jan. 30, 1865.

7. Former Reservation of Mineral Lands.—In ancient times all mines of precious metals were reserved as the property of the crown. If they were operated by private persons, it was done under tribute to the king, and this tribute, the king's share, was termed the "royalty."

Following the ancient custom, the United States at the beginning adopted the policy of reserving its mineral lands

(2) Butte City Water Co. vs. Baker, 196 U. S. 119.

from sale. Where lands were granted for agricultural or other uses, known mines were reserved. The grants to the Pacific railroads, made more than a generation ago, expressly reserved all mineral lands except iron and coal lands.

Section 2318 of the Revised Statutes expresses the rule of the United States relative to its mineral lands. The sections immediately following set forth the exception to the rule, and give the express directions whereby lands valuable for minerals may be acquired. The first law providing for the sale of mineral lands was enacted in 1866. This law, as amended in 1872, still remains the law of the land.

8. Character of Land a Question of Fact.—Controversies frequently arise between mineral claimants, on the one side, and agricultural claimants or a railroad company on the other, as to the mineral or non-mineral character of land. The character of a given tract is always a question of fact, to be determined by the land department, and the decision of the land department is final (3).

8. Northern Pacific Grant.—In 1864, congress made a grant to the Northern Pacific railroad of twenty alternate sections on each side of its right-of-way. This amounted to a grant of all odd-numbered sections within a distance of forty miles on either side of the line of the railroad. Where lands thus granted had been lost to the railroad company through prior settlement or for other causes, the company was permitted to select in lieu thereof odd-numbered sections in a ten-mile strip on either side of the regular grant. The outer boundaries of these ten-mile strips are called the "indemnity" or "lieu" limits of the grant.

10. Mineral Land Commission.—For the purpose of assisting the land department in determining the mineral or non-mineral character of the lands to which the grant to the Northern Pacific attached, or of such lands as the company might select within the indemnity limits, congress passed a law in 1895 providing for the appointment of three commissioners in each land district of Montana and Idaho, whose duty it should be to examine all odd-numbered sections within the grant and indemnity limits of the Northern Pacific railroad, and to classify the same as mineral or non-mineral.

In determining the character of land, the commissioners were authorized to examine witnesses, and to reduce their testimony to writing. They were required to take into consideration the mineral discoveries in the vicinity, and the geological formation of the land. By the terms of the law, a mining location was prima facie evidence that the forty-acre tract upon which it is situated was mineral land. The register and receiver of the local land office were directed to publish the classification of lands made by the commission,

(3) Standard Quicksilver Co. vs. Habishaw, 132 Cal. 115.

and any person feeling aggrieved by the classification was given sixty days after the first publication within which to file his protest. This protest was heard and decided as other contests in the land office. In the absence of such a protest, the classification, when approved by the secretary of the interior, became final, except in case of fraud. But the final classification of a tract as mineral, while it operates to except the tract from the grant to the Northern Pacific railroad, does not prevent the land department from making such subsequent disposition of it as a fuller investigation of the facts in the case may show to be proper (4).

11. Method of Determining Character of Land.—It is not easy in all cases to determine whether any given piece of land should be classed as mineral or otherwise. It will be noted that only valuable mineral lands are reserved for sale (5). The land department has adopted the rule that the existence of mineral in such quantity as to render the land more valuable for mining than for agriculture must be shown in order to defeat an agricultural entry (6). Mere indications of mineral do not prove that the lands contain permanent valuable deposits. Nor does the fact that a mining location has been made indicate that the land is valuable for mineral. Nor can a tract be assumed to be mineral because it is situated in a mineral belt and is adjacent to numerous mining claims (7), although proof of such facts is admissible as tending to show the character of the land (8).

A controversy between two mining claimants of unpatented land is ordinarily determined by the courts under the special provision of the law relating to the filing of adverse claims(9). A controversy between an agricultural and a mining claimant is usually heard and determined by the officials of the land department. In the latter class of controversies, the mining claimant is nearly always the contestant, since the agricultural claimant initiates his right by making entry of the land in the local land office at the beginning of his occupation. By this entry the land is set apart for him, and a second application will not be permitted until the first one has been abandoned or cancelled. The mining claimant, on the other hand, initiates his right by locating his claim. He gives no notice to the land office until he is ready to apply for patent, which may be and often is several years subsequent to the location of the claim. Until such application is made, however, the land appears as unoccupied on the records of the land office.

However, agricultural claimants of land mineral in character will not be heard to plead special consideration on the

(4) 25 L. D. 446; Lynch vs. U. S., 138 Fed. 535.
(5) Merrill vs. Dixon, 15 Nev. 401.
(6) Morrill vs. Northern Pac. Ry. Co., 30 L. D. 475; Cf. Hunt vs. Steese, 75 Cal. 621.
(7) Lindley on Mines, Sec. 95.
(8) U. S. vs. Rossi, 133 Fed. 380.
(9) R. S., Sec. 2326.

ground that their entries were allowed by order of the general land office, and that they have settled upon and improved the land, where with full knowledge of the mineral classification of the land, and of rights asserted thereto under the mining laws, they procured the allowance of their entries without notice to the mineral claimants, and thereafter entered into possession against the protest of said claimants (10).

12. Subsequent Discovery of Mineral Cannot Defeat a Vested Agricultural Title.—After patent has issued for nonmineral land, the subsequent discovery of mineral inures exclusively to the benefit of the owner under the patent (11).

13. Procedure to Determine Character of Land.—For the procedure in controversies over the character of public lands see Land Office Regulations, 99 et seq. See also paragraph 161 infra for method of giving notice of hearing.

14. EXPLORATION AND PURCHASE OF MINERAL LANDS.

Sec. 2319 R. S. All valuable mineral deposits in lands belonging to the United States, both surveyed and unsurveyed, are hereby declared to be free and open to exploration and purchase, and the lands in which they are found to occupation and purchase, by citizens of the United States and those who have declared their intention to become such, under regulations prescribed by law, and according to the local customs or rules of miners in the several mining districts, so far as the same are applicable and not inconsistent with the laws of the United States.—Act of May 10, 1872.

Sec. 910 R. S. No possessory action between persons, in any court of the United States, for the recovery of any mining title, or for damages to any such title, shall be affected by the fact that the paramount title to the land in which such mines lie is in the United States; but each case shall be adjudged by the law of possession.—Act of Feb. 27, 1865.

15. Valuable Mineral Deposits.—Whatever is recognized by standard authorities as a mineral, whether metallic or otherwise, when found in quantity and quality sufficient to render the land more valuable on account thereof than for agricultural purposes, must be treated as subject to exploration and purchase under the mining laws (12). The term has been held to include alum (13), asphaltum (14), building

(10) 28 L. D. 349.
(11) Cleary vs. Skiffich, 65 Pac. 59.
(12) N. P. R. Co. vs. Sodeberg, 188 U. S. 534; 25 L. D. 233.
(13) 2 L. D. 707.
(14) 29 L. D. 269.

stone (15), borax (16), diamonds (17), gypsum (18), guano (19), fire clay (20), marble and slate (21), mica (22), soda and nitrate (23), petroleum (24), salt (25), coal (26), and other like substances.

The law seems to contemplate that if the deposit is metallic in character and in place it should be located as a lode claim; if metallic in character but found in gravel or other placer deposit, or if non-metallic, it should be located under the laws relating to placer claims.

16. Surveyed and Unsurveyed Lands.—A mining claim can be located upon either surveyed or unsurveyed land. The land department holds that upon unsurveyed lands a placer claim should be in rectangular form, with north-and-south and east-and-west boundaries (27).

17. Open to Exploration and Purchase.—The law permits the mineral to be explored and the land to be occupied with or without ultimate purchase. Exploration involves the privilege of working the mine and appropriating to the claimant's own use the ore or other mineral substance located. One who extracts such mineral substance before purchasing the land is not a trespasser (28).

18. Belonging to the United States.—If the land has already been disposed of by the United States, or expressly reserved from sale, as land upon a military or Indian reservation, it is not open to exploration and purchase (29). There is a special provision, however, permitting the prospecting, location and development of mining claims upon forest reserves (30).

19. Citizens of the United States and Those Who Have Declared Their Intention to Become Such.—A person born within the limits of the United States, whose father and mother were aliens domiciled within the United States, is a citizen of the United States (31). An alien woman becomes a citizen upon marrying a citizen of the United States (32), and minor children become citizens upon the naturalization of their father (33).

(15) Act of Cong., Aug. 4, 1892; L. O. Reg. 20.
(16) 2 L. D. 707.
(17) 14 Op. Atty. Gen. 115.
(18) 29 L. D. 181.
(19) 27 L. D. 95.
(20) 25 L. . 349.
(21) 29 L. D. 327.
(22) Lindley on Mines (2nd Ed.) 420.
(23) 2 L. D. 707.
(24) Act of Feb. 11, 1897; L. O. Reg. 21.
(25) Act Jan. 31, 1901.
(26) 31 L. D. 29.
(27) 34 L. D. 260. See infra, Sec. 125.
(28) Sullivan vs. Schultz, 22 Mont. 541.
(29) Lockhart vs. Johnson, 181 U. S. 520; Traphagen vs. Kirk, 30 Mont. 562.
(30) Act of June 4, 1897.
(31) U. S. vs. Wong Kim Ark, 169 U. S. 649.
(32) Kelly vs. Owen, 7 Wall. 496.
(33) Campbell vs. Gordon, 6 Cranch 176.

All aliens, excepting Chinese, may be naturalized after a residence of five years in the United States and one year in the state or territory where application for naturalization is made. But they must have declared their intention to become citizens at least two years prior to such application. An alien who is honorably discharged after serving in the army or navy of the United States occupies the status of one who has declared his intention to become a citizen (34), and so also does one who begins his residence in the United States at least three years next preceding his arriving at the age of twenty-one. After five years continuous residence, including the years of his minority, he may be admitted to citizenship without having made the prior declaration of intention, but at the time of his admission he must prove to the satisfaction of the court that for two years last past it had been his bona fide intention to become a citizen (35). Under the term "citizens" are included females as well as males, associations and partnerships composed of citizens, and corporations organized under the laws of any state or of the United States (36), but if more than 20 per cent of the stock is held by persons or corporations not citizens of the United States, then such holding incapacitates the corporation from acquiring or holding any real estate in any territory of the United States (37).

It has been held that a minor is a citizen within the meaning of the law, and may locate and hold mining claims (38).

20. Expatriation.—A citizen of the United States may lose his citizenship by emigrating to a foreign country with the intention of remaining, and by doing acts showing a determination and intention to transfer his allegiance (39).

21. Rights of Aliens.—The location of a mining claim by an alien is voidable, and not void, and is free from attack by anyone except the government (40), but if he seeks a patent for his claim, citizenship becomes a necessary and material fact to be alleged and proved (41). A location made by an alien is rendered valid by his subsequent grant thereof to a citizen (42); so also by his declaring his intention to become a citizen (43).

The act of congress of May 14, 1898, made a special provision in Alaska in favor of native-born citizens of the Dominion of Canada, who are thereby accorded the same rights as citizens of the United States and those who have declared their intention to become such citizens are accorded in British

(34) Act of July 26, 1894.
(35) R. S. 2167.
(36) McKinley vs. Wheeler, 130 U. S. 630.
(37) Act of March 3, 1887.
(38) Thompson vs. Spray, 72 Cal. 531.
(39) Juando vs. Taylor, Fed. Cas. No. 7558; (2 Paine 652).
(40) Manuel vs. Wulff, 152 U. S. 505; McKinley Creek Mining Co. vs. Alaska United Mg. Co., 183 U. S. 563.
(41) Lindley on Mines, Sec. 234.
(42) Stewart vs. Gold & Cop. Co. (Utah), 82 Pac. 475.
(43) Shea vs. Nilima, 133 Fed. 209.

Columbia and the Northwest Territory, provided, that no greater rights shall be thus accorded than are enjoyed in Alaska by citizens of the United States themselves.

22. Rights of Aliens After Patent.—After the United States has parted with the title to land, it becomes subject to the laws of the state in which the land is situated. The rights of aliens to hold and transmit such property are thereafter governed b ythose laws (44).

In Montana, the state constitution provides that aliens shall have the same right as citizens to acquire, hold, transmit and inherit mining property (45). The same right is given aliens by the laws of Washington (45), and Idaho, except that in the latter state alien Chinese are prohibited from acquiring real property (47). In California (48), Colorado (49), North Dakota (50), South Dakota (51), Utah (52), Wyoming (53), Oregon (54), and Nevada aliens may own, transmit and inherit all kinds of real estate, except that in Nevada (55), and Oregon (56) this privilege is withheld from alien Chinese.

23. Former Policy of the United States.—From the founding of the government it was the established policy of the United States to reserve from entry or sale all public lands containing "known mines." The miners who discovered gold in California in 1848 and succeeding years could not acquire title to their claims. Technically they were trespassers on the public domain, but their possessory rights were good as against anyone but the government, and the government pursued the policy of non-interference. Indeed, as early as 1865 congress enacted a law to the effect that no action in any court of the United States for the recovery of a mining claim should be affected by the fact that the paramount title is in the United States, thereby reversing the common law rule that the plaintiff in ejectment must show legal title. This law permitted the claimant of a mining claim, having a superior right of possession, to maintain an action in ejectment to recover his claim (57).

24. Miners' Rules.—The lack of any national law regulating mining rights led the miners of each district to organize and enact their own rules. These generally defined the manner of locating and recording mining claims, the extent of ground that might be located, and the amount of work

(44) Wilcox vs. McConnell, 13 Pet. 498. Lindley on Mines, 237.
(45) Const., Art. III, Sec. 25.
(46) Art. II, Sec. 33.
(47) Civil Code, Sec. 2555.
(48) Const., Art. I, Sec. 17.
(49) Const., Art. II, Sec. 27.
(50) Rev. Code 1899, Sec. 3277.
(51) Const., Art. VI, Sec. 14.
(52) Rev. Stats. 1898, Sec. 2847.
(53) Const., Art. L, Sec. 29.
(54) Hill's Annot'd Stats. 1892, Sec. 2988; Const., Art. I, Sec. 31.
(55) Cutting's Comp. Laws of Nevada, Sec. 2825.
(56) Const., Art. XV, Sec. 8.
(57) R. S., Sec. 910.

required to hold such claims, in default of which the claim would be deemed abandoned.

25. Mining Laws of the United States.—The first mining law was enacted by congress in 1866. It recognized the validity, within certain limits, of the local customs and rules of miners, and provided a method by which the title of the United States in mineral lands might be acquired. This was superseded by the law of May 10, 1872, which, with slight modifications, is still in force. This law has been so supplemented by state legislation as to leave little necessity or scope for rules of miners. It seldom now happens that the miners of any district deem an organization and enactment of rules either necessary or desirable, although the right to so organize and enact rules still remains. Such rules, when enacted, are void whenever they fall in disuse or are generally disregarded (58).

26. Necessity of Complying With Law.—There is no method of acquiring title to the mineral lands of the United States otherwise than by a compliance with the mining laws of the United States. Mere possession of the ground, no matter how complete or long continued, cannot inaugurate any title whatever. There is no such thing as adverse pos- of the United States. There is no such thing as adverse possession as against the United States (59). Mere possession of the ground cannot ripen into title, although possession continued for the period of the statute of limitations for actions to recover real estate creates the presumption of a valid location. (See Par. 131.)

27. LODE CLAIMS—SIZE.

Sec. 2320 R. S. Mining claims upon veins or lodes of quartz or other rock in place bearing gold, silver, cinnabar, lead, tin, copper, or other valuable deposits, heretofore located, shall be governed as to length along the vein or lode by the customs, regulations, and laws in force at the date of their location. A mining claim located after the tenth day of May, eighteen hundred and seventy-two, whether located by one or more persons, may equal, but shall not exceed, one thousand five hundred feet in length along the vein or lode; but no location of a mining claim shall be made until the discovery of the vein or lode within the limits of the claim located. No claim shall extend more than three hundred feet on each side of the middle of the vein at the surface, nor shall any claim be limited by any mining regulation to less than twenty-five feet on each side of the middle of the vein at the surface, except where adverse rights existing on the tenth day of May, eighteen hundred and seventy-two, render such limitation necessary. The end lines of each claim shall be parallel to each other.—Act of May 10, 1872.

(58) Jupiter M. Co. vs. Brodie M. Co., 11 Fed. R. 673.
(59) Gleeson vs. Martin Waite M. Co., 13 Nev. 455.

28. What Is a "Vein" or "Lode?"—The use of the terms "vein," "lode" and "ledge" in the mining law of 1872 would seem to indicate that it was the object of congress to avoid any limitation in the application of the law which a scientific definition of the term might impose. A "vein" is a seam or fissure in the earth's crust, filled with quartz or other rock in place, carrying gold, silver or other valuable metal. It may be thin or thick, rich or poor, provided it contains even the smallest quantities of the metals named in the statute (60). A "lode," in the broadest sense of the term, is any formation which a miner would follow in the expectation of finding ore. It is a zone or belt of mineralized rock lying within boundaries clearly separating it from the neighboring or country rock (61). A lode may and often does contain more than one vein (62). The quartz or other rock carrying the values is called the "matrix" or "gangue."

Veins usually penetrate the crust of the earth at a greater or less angle with the plane of the horizon. This angle is called the "dip." The "strike" of the vein is the line of intersection between the vein and the plane of the horizon. The "apex" of a vein is the edge nearest the surface. It may visibly outcrop or it may be deeply covered with alluvial or other deposits.

29. Walls.—The country rock immediately above the vein is called the "hanging wall," and that below, the "foot wall." The walls are only of importance as indicating the boundaries of the vein or lode (63). With well defined walls, very slight evidences of ore within such boundaries will prove the existence of the lode (64). But when the lode consists of a mineralized zone without distinct walls, its width is determined by the lines beyond which ore is not found (65). A deposit of ore in place without defined walls may be located as a lode claim, but when the locator seeks to mine such deposit beyond the vertical plane of his side lines he must follow it between definite wall boundaries. In such case it is the walls that determine the dip and strike of the vein.

A former statute of Montana required not only the discovery of the vein, but also of one well-defined wall (66). The discovery of a wall is no longer required.

30. Maximum Dimensions of Lode Claims.—Under the laws of the United States lode claims cannot exceed fifteen hundred feet in length along the vein or lode, and three hundred feet on each side of the middle of the vein at the surface. The locator may divide the distance claimed along the

(60) North Noonday M. Co. vs. Orient M. Co., 1 Fed. 522.
(61) Eureka Case, 4 Saw. 302; Iron S. M. Co. vs. Cheeseman, 116 U. S. 529.
(62) U. S. vs. Iron S. M. Co., 128 U. S. 680.
(63) Eureka Case, 4 Saw. 302.
(64) Iron S. M. Co. vs. Cheeseman, 116 U. S. 529.
(65) Bunker Hill and Sullivan Co. vs. Empire State-Idaho M. Co., 134 Fed. 268.
(66) Comp. Stats., Sec. 1479.

lode either way from the point of discovery in any proportion that he may choose. He cannot, however, place his discovery shaft upon an end line and make it serve as a basis for two locations (67). Where a posted notice of location in Colorado did not specify the distance claimed along the vein in each direction from the point of discovery, it was held that the claimant could hold 750 feet in each direction (68). The discovery shaft ordinarily marks the middle of the vein at the surface, and the shortest distance from the discovery shaft to either side line cannot in any case exceed three hundred feet (69). There is no requirement that the claimant trace the course of the apex throughout the length of his claim. In most cases this would be an exceedingly difficult task, and one wholly beyond the means of the claimant. In the actual work of surveying claims for patent, it is customary to assume the course of the vein by running a straight line through the discovery shaft approximating the direction of the apex, and to adjust the location of the side lines with reference to this line.

31. End Lines—End lines must be straight and parallel to each other, and when at right angles to the side lines may not exceed six hundred feet in length. Where the end lines cut the side lines obliquely they may exceed six hundred feet in length, but in no case can side lines be laid at a greater distance than three hundred feet from the central line of the lode (70).

32. Limitation of Maximum Dimensions.—Both the maximum width of lode claims permitted by the United States law may be cut down either by state legislation or by the rules of miners in any duly organized mining district. Since miners no longer follow the custom in the western states of organizing and adopting rules for such purposes, limitations by miners' rules may be practically disregarded. No state or territory has attempted to cut down the maximum length of lode claims, and only two states limit the width. In North Dakota the claimant may locate only one hundred and fifty feet on each side of the center of the vein, but counties may by majority vote increase or diminish this width (71). In Colorado the width of lode claims is limited to seventy-five feet on each side of the center of the vein in Gilpin, Clear Creek, Boulder and Summit counties, and to one hundred and fifty feet on each side of the center of the vein in all other counties of the state (72).

33. Discovery Essential.—Before there can be a valid lo-

(67) 16 L. D. 1; McKinstry vs. Clark, 4 Mont. 370.
(68) Erhardt vs. Boaro, 113 U. S. 527.
(69) Par. 5 L. O. Reg.; Taylor vs. Parentcan, 48 Pac. 505.
(70) 35 L. D. 22.
(71) Rev. Pol. Code 1895, Sec. 1427.
(72) Mills An. Stats., Sec. 3149.

cation there must be a discovery (73). A location without a discovery does not carry with it a grant from the government, and a discovery made upon land already appropriated by another is not a discovery within the meaning of the law (74). It will not support even such portions of the location as lie upon government domain. A notice posted upon mineral land before discovery is an absolute nullity (75). But a subsequent discovery upon the claim, made before adverse rights intervene, will render the claim valid as of the date when the discovery was made, the meaning of the law being that no location shall be considered complete until there has been a discovery (76). The discovery must be of a vein or lode. It is not enough to discover detached pieces of quartz, or mere bunches of quartz not in place (77).

34. What Constitutes Sufficient Discovery.—If the mineral character of the ground be conceded, as in contests between mining claimants, slight evidence of mineral values is sufficient to sustain a mining location (78). A discovery of a seam or vein similar in formation to seams or veins in the same district that by deep development have disclosed valuable ore bodies, is a sufficient compliance with the requirement of the law. The usual test is whether the vein contains mineral in sufficient quantity to justify the locator in expending his time and money in prospecting and developing the claim (80). But what may constitute a sufficient discovery to warrant the location of a mining claim may be wholly inadequate to justify the locator in claiming extralateral rights. A vein barren of mineral values is not such a discovery as justifies the locator in following it beyond the vertical plane of his side lines into ground belonging to another (81).

Where the mineral character of the ground is not conceded, as in contests between an agricultural claimant and a mining claimant, or between the claimant under a placer patent, or a townsite patent, and one claiming a "known" lode or mine upon the patented tract, a much higher showing of mineral values is required (82). In such cases it is usually required of the lode claimant to show that the lode or vein is of such a character as to add substantial value to the land in which

---

(73) King. vs. Amy-Silversmith M. Co., 152 U. S. 227; Hauswirth vs. Butcher, 4 Mont. 307.
(74) Upton vs. Larkin, 5 Mont. 600; Lockhart vs. Farrell (Utah), 86 Pac. 1077.
(75) Gemmell vs. Swain, 28 Mont. 331.
(76) Creede & C. C. M. & M. Co. vs. Uinta F. etc. Co., 196 U. S. 337.
(77) Jupiter M. Co. vs. Bodie C. M. Co., 11 Fed. 675.
(78) North Noonday M. Co. vs. Orient M. Co., 1 Fed. 522.
(79) Shoshone M. Co. vs. Rutter, 87 Fed. 801.
(80) Bonner vs. Meikle, 82 Fed. 697; McShane vs. Kenkle, 18 Mont. 208.
(81) Grand Cent. M. Co. vs. Mammoth M. Co., 83 Pac. 648.
(82) Steele vs. Tanana Mines R. Co., 148 Fed. 678.

it is situated, and to justify exploitation (83). If the mining claimant has had ample time and opportunity and has failed to show that valuable mineral deposits exist on the land, the land will be held non-mineral in character (84).

35. One Discovery, One Location.—A discovery must be treated as an entirety, and the basis of but one location. It cannot support two locations having a common end line that bisects the discovery shaft (85).

36. Locator Need Not Be the First Discoverer.—It is not necessary that the locator should be the first discoverer, but the vein must be known to him and claimed by him (86).

37. Possession Without Location.—On the public domain, a miner may hold the place in which he may be working against all others having no better right. But when he asserts title to land not occupied by him he must base his claim upon a valid location of the ground (87). Mere prior possession is not good as against a subsequent valid location (88). But undisputed possession continued for the period of the statute of limitations is equivalent to a valid location (89).

38. Overlapping Locations.—A locator may lay the lines of his claim upon or across a senior location for the purpose of acquiring rights not in conflict with the senior location (90). Upon the forfeiture of a senior location, the area in conflict does not revert to the United States, but becomes part of the junior location (91).

39. Parallelism of End Lines Necessary.—For the exercise of extralateral rights it is necessary that the end lines of the claim should be parallel (92). Hence it has been held that a triangular claim has no extralateral rights (93). A prospector will not lose his location, however, or forfeit his extralateral rights simply because in staking his claim he failed to make his end lines exactly parallel. He is permitted to make the necessary adjustment to render his end lines

(83) U. S. vs. Iron Silver M. Co., 128 U. S. 683; Brownfield vs. Bier, 15 Mont. 403; Casey vs. Thieviege, 19 Mont. 341; Pacific Coast Marble Co. vs. Nor. Pac. R. R. Co., 25 L. D. 233; Tam vs. Story, 21 L. D. 440.
(84) Brophy vs. O'Hare, 34 L. D. 596.
(85) 16 L. D. 1; McKinstry vs. Clark, 4 Mont. 370.
(86) Wenner vs. McNulty, 7 Mont. 30; Book vs. Justice M. Co., 58 Fed. 128; Erwin vs. Perego, 93 Fed. 612; Hayes vs. Lavignino, 17 Utah, 185.
(87) Zollars vs. Evans, 5 Fed. 172.
(88) Cosmos Exploration Co. vs. Gray Eagle Oil Co., 112 Fed. 4; Haws vs. Victoria Copper Co., 160 U. S. 303.
(89) See Section 2332; Altoona, etc., Co. vs. Integral, etc., Co., 114 Cal. 100.
(90) Del Monte M. & M. Co. vs. Last Chance M. & M. Co., 171 U. S. 83.
(91) Lavagnino vs. Uhlig, 198 U. S. 443; but see Lockhart vs. Farrell (Utah), 86 Pac. 1077; Nash vs. McNamara (Nev.), 93 Pac. 405.
(92) Parrot S., etc., Co. vs. Heinze, 25 Mont. 139. Iron S. M. Co. vs. Elgin M. Co., 118 U. S. 208; Del Monte M. Co. vs. Last Chance M. Co., 171 U. S. 55.
(93) Montana Co. vs. Clark, 42 Fed. 626.

parallel when he surveys his claim for patent, or at any earlier time that he may choose (94).

There is no requirement that side lines e parallel. But where the apex of a vein crosses both side lines whereby the side lines become end lines, it is doubtful if the claimant would have any extralateral rights whatever unless the side lines be parallel (95).

40. Location by Agent.—An agent may locate for the benefit of his principal, who may be either a person or a corporation. When an agent is employed to explore for and locate mining claims, the claims located are the property of the principal, even though the agent should locate them in his own name (96). The same principle applies where one member of a partnership formed for the discovery and location of mining claims locates in his own name. He holds the claim in trust for the partnership (97).

A mineral discovery on public land, made by an employe of one who has not entered thereon for the purpose of mining, belongs to the finder (98).

41. PROOF OF CITIZENSHIP.

Sec. 2321 R. S. Proof of citizenship, under this chapter, may consist, in the case of an individual, of his own affidavit thereof; in the case of an association of persons unincorporated, of the affidavit of their authorized agent, made on his own knowledge or upon information and belief; and in the case of a corporation organized under the laws of the United States, or of any state or territory thereof, by the filing of a certified copy of their charter or certificate of incorporation. —Act of May 10, 1872.

42. Affidavit of Citizenship.—The oath of one of the locators, accompanying the location certificate, is prima facie evidence of the fact of citizenship, and it will be deemed sufficient unless controverted (99). But proof by affidavit does not preclude other modes of proof (1).

This section also provides the method of proving the citizenship of the claimants when application is made for patent. (See paragraph 162. L. O. Reg., 66-70.)

43. MINING RIGHTS ON LODE CLAIMS.

Sec. 2322 R. S. The locators of all mining locations heretofore made or which shall hereafter be made, on any mineral

(94) Doe vs. Sanger, 83 Cal. 203; Doe vs. Waterloo M. Co., 54 Fed. 935.
(95) Lindley on Mines, Sec. 366.
(96) Book vs. Justice M. Co., 58 Fed. 106; Dunlap vs. Pattison, 42 Pac. 504.
(97) Hirbour vs. Reeding, 3 Mont. 13; Stevens vs. Grand Central Mining Co., 133 Fed. 28.
(98) Burns vs. Schoenfield, 1 Cal. App. 121; 81 Pac. 713.
(99) Hammer vs. Garfield M. Co., 130 U. S. 299.
(1) Thompson vs. Spray, 72 Cal. 531.

vein, lode, or ledge, situated on the public domain, their heirs and assigns, where no adverse claim exists on the tenth day of May, eighteen hundred and seventy-two, so long as they comply with the laws of the United States, and with state, territorial, and local regulations not in conflict with the laws of the United States governing their possessory title, shall have the exclusive right of possession and enjoyment of all the surface included within the lines of their locations, and of all veins, lodes, and ledges throughout their entire depth, the top or apex of which lies inside of such surface lines extended downward vertically, although such veins, lodes, or ledges may so far depart from a perpendicular in their course downward as to extend outside the vertical side lines of such surface locations.. But their right of possession to such outside parts of such veins or ledges shall be confined to such portions thereof as lie between vertical planes drawn downward as above described, through the end lines of their locations, so continued in their own direction that such planes will intersect such exterior parts of such veins or ledges. And nothing in this section shall authorize the locator or possessor of a vein or lode which extends in its downward course beyond the vertical lines of his claim to enter upon the surface of a claim owned or possessed by another.—Act of May 10, 1872.

44. Mining Claims as Property.—It has been repeatedly held by the supreme court of the United States that mining claims are property in the highest sense of the word, and may be sold (2), transferred, mortgaged and inherited without infringing the title of the United States, and that when a location is perfected it has the effect of a grant by the United States of present and exclusive possession (3). The law places no limitation upon the number of claims which a person may acquire by purchase, nor upon the number which he may include in a patent (4).

45. Right of Dower.—The wife of a locator has no dower interest in a mining claim prior to such time as the locator purchases the claim from the United States (5). Hence it is not necessary for the wife to join the locator in conveying an unpatented claim by deed.

46. Rights of Locator Within the Claim.—Within the lines of each location the owner has not only the right to the exclusive possession of the surface, but may be regarded as having full right to all mineral that may be found beneath the surface until some one can show clear title to it as a part of some lode or vein having its top or apex in other territory. In other words, there is a presumption of ownership in every locator as to the territory covered by his location

(2) L. O. Reg. 32.
(3) Manuel vs. Wulff, 152 U. S. 505.
(4) Smelting Co. vs. Kemp, 104 U. S. 651.
(5) Black vs. Elkhorn M. Co., 163 U. S. 450.

(6), and where other parties enter such territory, upon or underneath the surface, they are prima facie trespassers (7). The burden is upon them to show that they are rightfully there. The locator holds everything beneath the surface of his claim, subject only to the right of an adjoining claimant, who has the apex of a vein and has complied with the statute, to pursue the vein on its dip. If for any reason the adjoining claimant has lost this extralateral right, then the owner of the surface takes the vein (8).

47. Extralateral Rights.—By this term is meant the right of the locator of a valid claim to follow his vein on its dip beyond the vertical plane of the side line of his claim. No branch of mining law has given rise to more extensive litigation than the question of extralateral rights. We can here give only a brief outline of the present status of the law.

48. Possession of Apex Necessary.—Only such veins can be followed beyond the side lines as have their apex within the surface granted to the claimant. A patent cannot grant the vein and exclude the surface in which it apexes. It is void as to the portion of the vein so attempted to be granted (9).

It has been held that where the deposit located is a horizontal or "blanket" vein, the apex of the lode is co-extensive with the distance between the side lines of the location and every part or point of such apex within these limits is as much the middle of the vein, within the meaning of Sec. 2320 R. S., as any other part (16).

49. Parallelism of End Lines Necessary.—For the exercise of extralateral rights it is necessary that the end lines of the claim should be parallel. It is only within and between vertical planes passing through the end lines and extended in the direction of the dip that extralateral mining can be exercised. These planes must be parallel. If they diverge or converge, owing to non-parallelism of the end lines, they present a condition of things not contemplated by the statute, and one that would preclude the exercise of extralateral rights (10). It has been held that a triangular claim, having but one end line, has no extralateral rights (11).

50. Apex Crossing Both Side Lines.—For the exercise of the right to follow a vein beyond a side line, the direction of the apex should be along the course of the claim, and

(6) Doe vs. Waterloo M. Co., 54 Fed. 935; Duggan vs. Davy (Dak.), 26 N. W. Rep. 887; Min. Co. vs. Fitzgerald, 4 Mor. M. R. 385.
(7) Cheeseman vs. Shreve, 37 Fed. 36.
(8) A. C. M. Co. vs. Dist. Court, 25 Mont. 504; Montana Mg. Co. vs. St. Louis Mg. Co., 204 U. S. 204.
(9) M O. P. Co. vs. B. & M. Co., 20 Mont. 336.
(10) Iron S. M. Co. vs. Elgin M. Co., 118 U. S. 208.
(11) Montana Co. vs. Clark, 42 Fed. 626.
(12) Last Chance M. Co. vs. Tyler M. Co., 157 U. S. 683.

not transversely to it (12). Hence, where the apex crosses both side lines, it has been held that the side lines become end lines and terminate the claimant's rights in that direction (13). In that case if the claimant has any extralateral right it is to follow the vein on its dip under the end line (14).

51. Apex Crossing a Side Line and an End Line.—Where the apex crosses one end line and one side line, the claimant can follow his vein on its dip between the vertical plane of the end line crossed by the apex and a parallel plane drawn through the point where the apex crosses the side line (15).

52. Divided Apex.—When a wide apex crosses a side line obliquely, so that for a given distance it is partly within one claim and partly within another, the entire vein must be considered as apexing upon the senior location and the senior location takes the whole of it until it has wholly passed beyond its side lines (17).

53. Faulted Veins.—The faulting of a vein, whereby its continuity has been interrupted, does not prevent the claimant following upon its dip the displaced segment whenever found. But in such cases the identity of the displaced segment as a part of the original vein may become an important question of fact (18).

54. No Right to Make Extralateral Workings Outside the Vein.—The right given to a mining claimant to follow a vein upon its dip beneath a tract belonging to another does not give him a right to make mine workings outside of the vein. So the claimant has no right to run a horizontal tunnel or crosscut through territory belonging to another for the purpose of reaching the claimant's vein on its dip (19).

55. Group of Claims Under Common Ownership.—It would seem that questions of extralateral rights that might arise between claims held by different owners may be eliminated where the same claims are held in a group under common ownership. In the latter case the location of the interior lines of the group will not be regarded (20).

(13) King vs. Amy & S. Co., 152 U. S. 222.
(14) Empire M. & M. Co. vs. Tombstone M. & M. Co., 131 Fed. 339; 100 Fed. 910.
(15) Del Monte, etc., M. Co. vs. Last Chance M. Co., 171 U. S. 55.
(16) 29 L. D. 689.
(17) St. Louis M. Co. vs. Montana M. Co., 104 Fed. 664; Bullion, etc., M. Co. vs. Eureka Hill M. Co., 11 Pac. 515; Argentine Co. vs. Terrible Co., 122 U. S. 478; U. S. Mg. Co. vs. Lawson, 134 Fed. 769; Lawson vs. U. S. Mining Co., 207 U. S. 42.
(18) Pennsylvania Con. M. Co. vs. Grass Valley, etc., M. Co., 117 Fed. 509; Butte & Boston M. Co. vs. Societe, etc., Lexington, 23 Mont. 177; Lindley on Mines, Sec. 615.
(19) St. Louis M. Co. vs. Montana Mg. Co., 194 U. S. 235.
(20) Carson City, etc., Co. vs. North Star M. Co., 83 Fed. 658.

56. STATE AND DISTRICT REGULATIONS—MARK-INGS, RECORDS, ANNUAL LABOR, FORFEIT-URE TO CO-OWNER.

Sec. 2324 R. S. The miners of each mining district may make regulations not in conflict with the laws of the United States, or with the laws of the state or territory in which the district is situated, governing the location, manner of recording, amount of work necessary to hold possession of a mining claim, subject to the following requirements: The location must be distinctly marked on the ground so that its boundaries can be readily traced. All records of mining claims hereafter made shall contain the name or names of the locators, the date of the location, and such a description of the claim or claims located by reference to some natural object or permanent monument as will identify the claim. On each claim located after the tenth day of May, eighteen hundred and seventy-two, and until a patent has been issued therefor, not less than one hundred dollars' worth of labor shall be performed or improvements made during each year. On all claims located prior to the tenth day of May, eighteen hundred and seventy-two, ten dollars' worth of labor shall be performed or improvements made by the tenth day of June, eighteen hundred and seventy-four, and each year thereafter, for each one hundred feet in length along the vein until a patent has been issued therefor; but where such claims are held in common, such expenditure may be made upon any one claim; and upon a failure to comply with these conditions, the claim or mine upon which such failure occurred shall be open to relocation in the same manner as if no location of the same had ever been made, provided that the original locators, their heirs, assigns, or legal representatives, have not resumed work upon the claim after failure and before such location. Upon the failure of any one of several co-owners to contribute his proportion of the expenditures required hereby, the co-owners who have performed the labor or made the improvements may, at the expiration of the year, give such delinquent co-owner personal notice in writing or notice by publication in the newspaper published nearest the claim, for at least once a week for ninety days, and if at the expiration of ninety days after such notice in writing or by publication such delinquent should fail or refuse to contribute his proportion of the expenditure required by this section, his interest in the claim shall become the property of his co-owners who have made the required expenditures.—Act of May 10, 1872.

Provided, That the period within which the work required to be done annually on all unpatented mineral claims shall commence on the first day of January succeeding the date of location of such claim, and this section shall apply to all claims located since the tenth day of May, anno Domini eighteen hundred and seventy-two.—Act of Jan. 22, 1880.

That section two thousand three hundred and twenty-four of the Revised Statutes, be, and the same is hereby, amended so that where a person or company has or may run a tunnel for the purpose of developing a lode or lodes, owned by said person or company, the money so expended in said tunnel shall be taken and considered as expended on said lode or lodes, whether located prior to or since the passage of said act; and such person or company shall not be required to perform work on the surface of said lode or lodes in order to hold the same as required by said act.—Act of Feb. 11, 1875.

57. **District and State Regulations.**—By the provisions of section 2324, express permission is given to the miners of each mining district, and implied permission to the legislatures of states and territories in which public mineral lands are situated, to make regulations governing (a) the location, (b) manner of recording, and (c) amount of work necessary to hold possession of mining claims. District regulations are not of present importance in most of the states and territories. Statutory law, both federal and state, so fully covers the requirements of mining communities that the custom of the miners meeting and adopting a code of regulations has fallen into quite general disuse.

The third point above enumerated, upon which district and state regulation is permitted, i. e., concerning the amount of work necessary to hold possession, is not important except as regards the discovery work required in locating claims. After the location is made, the federal requirement is one hundred dollars' worth of labor or improvements each year. Local regulations cannot reduce the amount thus required, and, so far as the writer is informed, no greater amount is required in any mining district of the west by either statute or miners' regulations.

58. **Posting Notice of Location.**—The requirement is quite universal that the locator, as a first step toward making his location, shall post a notice of location at the point of discovery. As a rule state laws do not prescribe just how this notice shall be posted, leaving it to the judgment of the locator. Accordingly, locators sometimes tack the notice upon a neighboring tree, or to a post, or in a box, and even in some cases fold it and place it in a tin can which is placed in a conspicuous place in the top of a monument of stones or attached to a post (21). The laws of Arizona provide that the notice of location shall be posted upon either a conspicuous monument of stones not less than three feet in height, or upon an upright post, securely fixed, projecting four feet above the ground. These monuments would answer a similar requirement in Idaho, provided the post is at least four inches square.

(21) Donahue vs. Meister, 88 Cal. 121; Gird vs. California Oil Co., 60 Fed. 531.

59. Contents of Notice of Location.—The notice of location should in all cases contain the name of the claim, the name of the locator, or locators if there be more than one, and the date of location. Some states require the "date of discovery" (22). For practical purposes this must be regarded as equivalent to the date of location. A statement of the distance claimed along the vein or lode each way from the point of discovery and the width claimed on each side of the center of the vein should be also given in Arizona, Idaho, Montana, Nevada, North Dakota, South Dakota, Oregon, Utah and Washington. The course of the vein or lode should be given in Arizona, Nevada, Oregon, Utah and Washington. The location of the claim with reference to some natural object or permanent monument as will identify the claim should be stated in Arizona, Idaho, New Mexico, Oregon and Utah.

60. Form of Location Notice.—The following notice fulfils the requirements for the posted notice of location in all states and territories:

NOTICE OF LODE LOCATION.

Notice is hereby given that the undersigned locators, each of whom is a citizen of the United States or has declared his intention to become such citizen, did on the **15th** day of **January, 1908,** discover a lode or vein of rock in place bearing gold, silver, and other valuable metals, upon the unappropriated public domain of the United States in **Tidal Wave** mining district, county of **Madison**, state of **Montana**, and on the same day did locate, and do hereby locate, the said lode or vein as the **Treasury** Lode Mining Claim by posting this notice of location at the point of said discovery.

The general course of said lode or vein is **easterly** and **westerly**, along which the undersigned claim **500** feet in an **easterly** direction and **1,000** feet in a **westerly** direction from the point of discovery, and **300** feet on the **north** side and **300** feet on the **south** side of the middle or center of said lode or vein at the surface.

Measured from the discovery **shaft** of said claim as a starting point, the following natural objects and permanent monuments are distant as follows, to-wit: **The mouth of Coal Canyon** is distant **one mile** in a **westerly** direction; **the working shaft of the Ruby mine** is distant **350** feet in a **northerly** direction.

The undersigned hereby give notice of **their** intention to hold the said premises as a lode mining claim under the laws of the United States and of the state of **Montana.**

DANIEL HOLLAND,
ARTHUR BROWN,
Locators **and** Claimants.

---

(22) Sec. 3101 Rev. Stats. Idaho; Sec. 1430 Rev. Code N. Dak.; Grantham's An. Stats., Sec. 2660 S. Dak.; Sec. 2 Act of 1899, Washington. ec. 2538 Rev. Stats. Wyoming.

In certain states, the foregoing notice could be abridged if desired, though the surplusage is harmless. For instance, the first paragraph by itself constitutes a sufficient notice for posting in Alaska, California, Colorado and Wyoming, and the allegation of citizenship in that paragraph is not essential. The first two paragraphs are a sufficient notice for posting in Montana, Nevada, North Dakota, South Dakota and Washington.

Idaho requires two notices to be posted, the first at the date of the discovery and the second within ten days thereafter. The first two paragraphs of the foregoing form fulfil the requirements of the Idaho law for the first or preliminary notice, and the entire form is sufficient for the second and final notice. The latter notice should also be recorded within ninety days after the date of location, but before doing so the locator, or one of the locators, if there be more than one, must make and subscribe an affidavit, on or attached to the notice, hereinafter set forth. (See Par. 84.)

The foregoing form constitutes a sufficient certificate for record in Alaska, Arizona, California, Colorado, New Mexico, North Dakota, South Dakota, Utah, Washington and Wyoming.

61. Discovery Work.—All states and territories, excepting California and Alaska, require the performance of certain work as a part of the process of locating a mining claim. The usual requirement is a shaft at least ten feet deep at the point of discovery. The work is commonly termed "discovery work."

62. Object of Discovery Work.—The object in requiring discovery work is the same as in the case of annual labor. It is to require a showing of good faith on the part of the locator and to prevent purely speculative locations. The requirement for annual labor places a physical limit upon the number of claims which one miner can hold continuously, and a limitation of time during which he can hold a claim without improving it. But the requirement of the federal law concerning annual labor permits a locator to hold a claim more than a year, and in some cases nearly two years, before a forfeiture occurs on account of a failure to work the claim. It was found that many locations were made simply for the purpose of holding the ground for this limited period and without any intention of improving the claim. When the period had expired, the locators would promptly relocate the same ground either in their own names, or in the names of dummy locators,, and by continuing this process would hold possession without work year after year.

The requirement for discovery work prevents this purely speculative location of claims. It places a physical limit upon the number of claims which one man can successfully locate, and requires of the locator a demonstration of his good faith.

63. When Performed..... Each state and territory, excepting Alaska, California and New Mexico, prescribe a period within which the discovery work must be performed. This period is sixty days in Idaho, Montana, North Dakota, Oregon, South Dakota and Wyoming, ninety days in Arizona, Nevada, Utah and Washington, and three months in Colorado. If the discovery work is not performed within the time specified by law, it cannot be extended by renewing the notice posted upon the claim (23).

64. Ten-Foot Shaft.—Wherever a ten-foot shaft is required, it should be at least ten feet deep on the shallowest side, or, as the statute of Montana expresses it, "ten feet, vertically, below the lowest part of the rim of such shaft at the surface." In all cases the shaft must be sunk still deeper if necessary to disclose the vein, lode or deposit located.

65. Horizontal Dimensions of Shaft.—Most of the states do not prescribe any horizontal dimensions for the discovery shaft. But in Idaho the horizontal area of the shaft opening must be at least sixteen square feet. In Nevada it must be at least four by six feet. In Montana the amount of excavation in discovery work must be at least one hundred and fifty cubic feet, but if the vein is disclosed at a less vertical depth than ten feet, any horizontal extension of the discovery shaft, cut or tunnel will count as part of the amount of excavation required. So also in that case will excavation done elsewhere upon the claim, but in all cases there must be at least 75 cubic feet of excavation at the point of discovery.

66. Shaft Universally Sufficient.—The requirements of all the states and territories would be fulfilled by a shaft 4x6 feet horizontally and 10 feet in vertical depth below the lowest point of the rim of the shaft at the surface, provided that it discloses the vein. If not, it should be sunk deeper until it does disclose it.

67. Discovery Work Done in Tunnels, Crosscuts, Etc.—In many states there is an express statutory provision that any cut, crosscut or tunnel intersecting the vein at a depth of at least ten feet below the surface shall be regarded as the equivalent of the shaft. But where the statute requires a certain number of cubic feet of excavation in the discovery shaft, the cut, crosscut or tunnel used in lieu of a shaft should show an equivalent amount.

An express statutory provision making such a cut, crosscut or tunnel valid as discovery work exists in Arizona, Colorado, Idaho, Montana, Nevada, New Mexico, Oregon, Washington and Wyoming. Probably such a cut, crosscut or tunnel would be held valid as discovery work also in North Dakota and South Dakota even in the absence of such statutory provision.

---

(23) Ingemarson vs. Coffee (Colo.), 92 Pac. 903.

In California and Alaska there are no statutory requirements concerning discovery work, and none is required unless
required by the rules of the particular mining district in
which the claim is located.

68. Discovery Work on Relocated Claims.—Where the
location is of an abandoned or forfeited claim, the locator
may at his option perform his discovery work by sinking any
existing tunnel or cut ten feet further upon the vein. But
the amount of excavation should in all cases equal the discovery work required in a location upon virgin ground.

69. Marking Boundaries.—It is an imperative requirement
of the federal law that the location shall be marked upon the
ground so that its boundaries can be readily traced. State
legislation may add to this requirement, but it cannot subtract from it. Most of the states and territories have prescribed methods of marking boundaries. When these methods are observed, there is a presumption that the claim is
sufficiently marked. But if as a matter of fact the boundaries
thus marked cannot be readily traced, as for instance where
the ground is heavily timbered or very rugged or rough, the
claim is insufficiently marked (24), and the prudent locator
will employ additional means to define the boundaries, such
as setting additional stakes or blazing lines through timber.
A statute of Washington provides: "If any such claim be
located on ground that is covered wholly or in part with
brush or trees, such brush shall be cut and trees marked or
blazed along the lines of such claim to indicate the location
of such lines."

Locators in other states might well bear in mind this sug-
gestion of the Washington law.

70. When Marked.—Every state and territory excepting
California and Alaska prescribe a period after posting the
notice of location within which the boundaries of the claim
must be marked. This period is ten days in Idaho; twenty
days in Nevada; thirty days in Montana, Oregon and Utah;
sixty days in North Dakota, South Dakota and Wyoming;
three months in Colorado; and one hundred and twenty days
in New Mexico.

71. Posts as Monuments.—In all states and territories a
post is the standard monument, and among prudent locators
it is the kind most frequently used. Sometimes a mound of
earth or stone around the post is required. But whether expressly required or not, it is a wise precaution to support
each post by such a mound.

The state and territorial requirements concerning posts as
monuments are as follows:

In California and Alaska no markings are prescribed.

(24) Ledoux vs. Forrester, 94 Fed. 602; McCarthy vs. Phelan,
132 Cal. 404.

Arizona requires a post 4 feet long. No other dimensions are specified.

Colorado, North Dakota, South Dakota and Wyoming require a substantial post, hewed on the side or sides next the claim.

Idaho prescribes a post not les sthan 4 inches square standing 4 feet high above the ground, and hewn on the side facing the discovery.

New Mexico prescribes a substantial post, projecting at least three feet above the surface of the ground.

Oregon and Washington prescribe a substantial post not less than 4 inches square, projecting not less than 3 feet above the ground.

Montana and Nevada prescribe a post 4 feet 6 inches long, set one foot in the ground, and surrounded by a mound of earth or stone 4 feet in diameter by two feet in height. In Montana the post should be 4 inches "square," while Nevada prescribes a post 4 inches "in diameter."

It will be seen from the foregoing specification of statutory requirements that a post 4 inches square by 5 feet long, set one foot in the ground, blazed and marked on the side facing the discovery, and surrounded by a mound of earth or stone 4 feet in diameter by 2 feet in height, would fulfil the requirements of all the states and territories and would be universally valid.

72. Other Monuments Prescribed.—Other monuments permitted by the laws of the various states and territories are as follows:

Arizona—A pile of stones not less than 3 feet in height.

Idaho—A tree "so hewn as to readily attract attention."

Montana—(a) A tree at least 8 inches in diameter, blazed on four sides. (b) A stone at least 6 inches square by 18 inches in length in the ground, with a mound of earth or stone alongside at least 4 feet in diameter by 2 feet in height. (c) A boulder at least 3 feet above the natural surface of the ground on the upper side.

Nevada—(a) A blazed stump not less than 3 feet high surrounded by a mound. (b) A rock in place capped by small stones. (c) A stone not less than 6 inches in diameter by 18 inches in length, and set two-thirds of its length in the top of a mound of earth or stone, 4 feet in diameter by two and one-half feet in height.

Oregon—A substantial mound of stone, or earth and stone, at least 2 feet in height.

New Mexico—A substantial stone monument at least three feet above the surface of the ground.

Washington—A monument of stones not less than 3 feet high.

73. Monuments, Number and Markings.—In all cases there should be a monument set at each corner or angle of the claim, marked with the name of the claim and the designation of the corner either by number or cardinal point.

In addition to monuments at the corners of the claim, Idaho and Arizona require a similar monument to be placed at the point of discovery upon which the notice must be posted. Colorado, Oregon and Wyoming require similar monuments at the center of each side line, Arizona at the center of each end line, and New Mexico, North Dakota and South Dakota at the center of each end line and of each side line.

74. Corner Monuments on Ground Already Appropriated. —There is no provision of law forbidding corner monuments to be established on ground already appropriated and belonging to third parties. In locating contiguous claims this often occurs, and the validity of such monuments is in no way impaired thereby (25).

75. Effect of the Destruction of Monuments.—The locator, having once established the monuments required by law, is not charged with the duty of protecting them from destruction. His right cannot be divested by the obliteration or removal of the corner posts without his fault (26). But it is reasonable to suppose that there may be limits to this rule, and it is unsafe for a locator to conclude that he can continually neglect his corner monuments and permit them to fall into decay and become and remain completely obliterated without imperilling his rights. The prudent locator will use reasonable diligence in keeping his monuments in repair. Especially is this necessary where the location certificate does not describe the boundaries with accuracy.

Where there is a discrepancy between the calls of the location certificate and the monuments as actually placed upon the ground, the latter govern. The rule is that monuments control courses and distances (27). For this reason it is important that the posts and other monuments be protected and maintained.

76. Purpose of the Location Certificate.—The certificate of location is the permanent record of the claim. The federal statutes do not make mandatory the recording of the certificate of location (28), but, recognizing the prevailing custom in mining states to require mining locations to be recorded, congress provided that all records of claims must contain the name or names of the locators, the date of location, and such a description of the claim by reference to some natural object or permanent monument as will identify the claim (29). State laws can add to these requirements, but

(25) Del Monte M. Co. vs. Last Chance Co., 171 U. S. 55.
(26) Jupiter M. Co. vs. Bodie Cons. M. Co., 11 Fed. 666; Book vs. Justice M. Co., 58 Fed. 106.
(27) Garrard vs. Silver Peak Mines, 82 Fed. 578; Meyer-Clarke-Rowe Co. vs. Steinfield (Ariz.), 80 Pac. 400.
(28) Zerres vs. Vanina, 134 Fed. 610.
(29) Bonanza Con. M. Co. vs. Golden Head M. Co. (Utah), 80 Pac. 736.

cannot subtract from them. Hence a location certificate should comply with these federal requirements and also with the additional requirements of the state in which the claim is situated. When properly made and recorded in accordance with a law authorizing it to be recorded, the certificate furnishes constructive notice to the world, and is prima facie evidence of the facts which it properly recites (30). But a certificate recorded in a state which does not require it to be recorded constitutes neither notice nor evidence.

77. Identification of the Claim.—One of the most important requisites of such a certificate is that it shall contain such a description of the claim, located by reference to some natural object or permanent monument as will identify the claim. If the situation of the claim is so indefinitely or inaccurately described that the claim cannot be found, then the record affords no notice to any one.

78. Natural Objects and Permanent Monuments.—The natural object may consist of any fixed natural object in the immediate vicinity, such as a prominent boulder of unusual size or shape, the confluence of streams, the point of intersection of well-known gulches, ravines or roads, prominent buttes, hills, etc. (31). The permanent monument may be a conspicuuous stone monument constructed for the purpose, a prominent post or stake firmly planted in the ground (32), well-known shafts or tunnels on neighboring claims, an adjoining claim whose location is generally known, or, what is best of all, a corner of the United States land survey. It is no objection to a permanent monument that it is on the claim itself. In each case the question whether the object chosen is such a natural object or permanent monument as serves to identify the claim is a question of fact for the jury (33).

The distance from the discovery shaft or other initial point on the claim to two or more such natural objects or permanent monuments should be given with as great accuracy as possible. Such objects or monuments as lie in directions nearly at a right angle to each other from the starting point should be chosen. This is called "tieing the claim."

The laws of Idaho require the references to natural objects and permanent monuments to be made from the discovery monument as the initial point. Montana and Nevada require the location of the discovery shaft to be stated in the location certificate. Making the point of discovery the initial point for the reference to natural objects and permanent monuments fixes not only the location of the claim, but also the location of the discovery shaft, and constitutes a compliance

(30) Strepy vs. Stark (Colo.), 5 Pac. 111; Jantzen vs. Arizona Cop. Co. (Ariz.), 20 Pac. 93.
(31) L. O. Reg. 9.
(32) Jupiter M. Co. vs. Bodie M. Co., 11 Fed. 673; Flavin vs. Mattingly, 8 Mont. 242.
(33) Dillon vs. Bayliss, 11 Mont. 171.

not only with the special requirements of Idaho, Montana and Nevada, above mentioned, but also with the laws of all the states and territories and of the United States relative to fixing the locus of the claim.

In Wyoming, if the claim is situated upon surveyed land, the reference in the certificate of location should be to section or quarter-section corners (34).

79. Reference to Adjoining Claims.—An adjoining mining claim is presumed to be a well known natural object or permanent monument until the contrary appears, and a reference to such adjoining claim or claims is a sufficient compliance with the law.

80. Rule for Interpreting Location Certificates.—With just how much accuracy the references to natural objects and permanent monuments must be stated in the location certificate is not set forth in the statute. It is a rule generally adopted by courts that location notices and statutes prescribing their contents will be liberally construed, and a substantial compliance with the statute is sufficient (35). Where the location has been made in good faith the locator is not, as a rule, held to great exactness in the directions and distances given (36). If by reasonable construction in view of the surrounding circumstances the language employed in the description will impart notice to subsequent locators, it is sufficient (37). Unless the description of the location of the claim contained in the location certificate is impossible or hopelessly uncertain, its sufficiency is a question of fact and not of law (38).

81. State Requirements.—All states and territories require the certificate of location to state the name of the claim, the name of the locator, or locators if there be more than one, the date of location and such a description of the claim located with reference to some natural object or permanent monument as will identify the claim. A location certificate failing to state all of these things would be void.

A statement of the course of the lode, "as near as may be," must be given in Arizona, Colorado, Montana, Idaho, Nevada, North Dakota, Oregon, South Dakota, Utah, Washington and Wyoming.

Nevada makes mandatory a statement of the dimensions and location of the discovery shaft, and the location and description of each corner with the markings thereon.

Montana requires the location of the discovery shaft to be given, and further provides: "The locator and claimant.

---

(34) Sec. 2546 Rev. Stats. Wyo.; Shothower vs. Hunter, 88 Pac. 36.
(35) Hammer vs. Garfield M. Co., 130 U. S. 291; Shothower vs. Hunter (Wyo.), 88 Pac. 36.
(36) Walton vs. Wild Goose M. & T. Co., 123 Fed. 209.
(37) Farmington Gold M. Co. vs. Rhymey Gold, etc., Co., 20 Utah, 363; Duryea vs. Boucher, 67 Cal. 141.
(38) Eilers vs. Boatman, 111 U. S. 356; Dillon vs. Bayliss, 11 Mont. 171.

at his option, may also set forth, in such certificate of location, a description of the discovery work, the corner monuments and the markings thereon, and any other facts showing a compliance with the provisions of this law." Such certificate of location, duly verified, is prima facie evidence of all facts properly recited therein.

82. Form of Certificate of Location.—The following form of certificate of location, while fuller than required by the laws of some of the states, has the merit of fulfilling the requirements of the laws of all the states and territories:

CERTIFICATE OF LOCATION OF THE **TREASURY** LODE MINING CLAIM.

KNOW ALL MEN BY THESE PRESENTS, That the undersigned, each of whom is a citizen of the United States, or has declared his intention to become such, did, on the **15th** day of **January, 1908,** discover a vein or lode of rock in place, bearing gold, silver, and other valuable metals, and on the same day did locate and claim the same as the **Treasury** Lode Mining Claim, by posting a notice of location conspicuously at the point of discovery, containing the name of said claim, the names of the undersigned as locators, the date of said location, and the approximate dimensions of said claim intended to be appropriated.

This claim is situated in **Tidal Wave** Mining District (unorganized), in the County of **Madison,** State of **Montana.** The adjoining claims are as follows, to-wit: On the north, the **Ruby** lode claim; on the northeast, the **Stand Fast** lode claim; on the south, the **Rich Quick** lode claim; on the west, **no known** lode claim.

Measured from the discovery **shaft** of this claim as a starting point, the following natural objects and permanent monuments are distant as follows, to-wit: **The mouth of Coal Canyon** is distant **about 1 mile** in a **westerly** direction; **the working shaft of the Ruby mine** is distant 350 feet in a **northerly** direction.

With reference to legal subdivisions of the public survey said claim is situated as follows, to-wit: Measured from the discovery **shaft** of said claim the section corner common to sections **4, 5, 8 and 9,** T. **1 S.,** R. **6. W,** is distant **1,867** feet in a **N. 89 deg. 67 min. W.** direction.*

The course of said vein or lode is **easterly and westerly** along which the undersigned claim **500** feet in **an easterly** direction and **1,000** feet in a **westerly** direction from the center of the discovery **shaft,** together with surface area **300** feet on the **north side** and **300** feet on the **south** side of the center of said vein, comprising a tract **600** by **1,500** feet in size.

Subsequent to the date of said location, to-wit, on the **14th** day of **February, 1908,** the undersigned did distinctly mark said location on the ground so that its boundaries could be readily traced, in the following manner, to-wit:

Beginning at the **N. W.** Corner No. 1, which is a **post 4x4 inches by 5 feet in height, set one foot in ground, blazed on the side facing discovery, marked "N. W. Corner Treasury Lode,"** surrounded by a mound of stone 4 feet in diameter by 2 feet in height, and running thence, first course: Direction, **southerly,** distance **600** feet, to **southwest** corner No. 2, which is a **fir tree 1 foot in diameter, blazed on the side facing discovery and marked "S. W. Corner Treasury Lode;"** and running thence second course: Direction, **easterly,** distance 1,500 feet, to the **southeast** corner No. 3, which is a **post 4x4 inches by 5 feet long, set one foot in ground, blazed on side facing discovery, marked "S. E. Corner Treasury Lode,"** and surrounded by a mound of earth 4 feet in diameter by 2 feet in height; and running thence third course: Direction, **northerly,** distance **600** feet, to the **N. E.** corner No. 4, which is a **post 4x4 inches by 5 feet in height, set one foot in ground, blazed on side facing discovery, marked "N. E. Corner Treasury Lode,"** and surrounded by a mound of earth and stone 4 feet in diameter by 2 feet in height; and running thence fourth course: Direction, **westerly,** distance 1,500 feet, to corner No. 1, the place of beginning.

Within 60 days after posting said notice of location the undersigned performed the following discovery work, to-wit:

At the point of discovery dug a **shaft** of the following dimensions, to-wit: **4x6 feet horizontally by 10 feet deep below the lowest point of the collar of said shaft,** constituting in all 240 cubic feet of excavation, and said work has disclosed at the point of discovery the vein or lode located.

The undivided interest in the above described location, claimed by each of the undersigned, is indicated by the fraction set after each name.

DANIEL HOLLAND   ¾
ARTHUR BROWN   ¼
Locators and Claimants.

*The reference to a corner of the public survey is required only in Wyoming when the claim is upon surveyed land.

83. Verification of Location Certificate in Montana.— Montana requires the certificate of location to be verified before some officer authorized to administer oaths by the locator, or by one of the locators, if there be more than one, or by an authorized agent. In the case of a corporation, the verification may be made by any officer thereof, or by an authorized agent. When the verification is made by an agent, the fact of the agency shall be stated in the affidavit.

The following form of affidavit is sufficient in Montana:

STATE OF MONTANA,
County of.. } ss.

...., being duly sworn, on oath says: That he is.. the locator.... and claimant.... whose name................................ signed to the foregoing Certificate of Location; that he has.............................read the said Certificate and knows the contents thereof, and that the matters and things therein stated are true of his own knowledge.

Subscribed and sworn to before me this...........................day of..............................., A. D. 190.......

Notary Public in and for the County of.........................., State of Montana.

84. Verification of Location Certificate in Idaho.—In Idaho, the following form of verification, to be sworn to by one of the locators and attached to the certificate, is provided by statute:

STATE OF IDAHO, County of............................... } ss.

I, ..., do solemnly swear that I am a citizen of the United State (or have declared my intention to become such), and that I am acquainted with the mining ground described in this notice of location, and herewith called the..............................ledge, lode or claim; that the ground and claim therein described or any part thereof has not, to the best of my knowledge and belief, been located according to the laws of the United States and of this state, or if so located, that the same has been abandoned or forfeited by the reason of the failure of such former locators to comply in respect thereto with the requirements of said laws, and that I have opened new ground to the extent or depth of ten feet, as required by the laws of Idaho.

(Signature) ....

Subscribed and sworn to before me this...........................day of..............................., A. D. 190.......

(Signature) ....

85. Certificate Recorded, When.—All states and territories, excepting California, provide by statute a period after the posting of the notice of location within which the certificate of location should be recorded. This period is thirty days in Utah, sixty days in Montana, North Dakota, Oregon, South Dakota, and Washington, and three months in Colorado and New Mexico.

In Alaska, the certificate of location must be filed for record within ninety days from the discovery of the claim described in the notice. Where the claim is situated in an established recording district, the certificate should be filed with the recorder thereof, otherwise with the clerk of the division of the court having supervision over the recording division in which the claim is situated.

In California, the statute permits the filing of the certificate, but no time is prescribed for doing so. The whole matter is left to district regulation. If no such regulation exists in the district where the claim is situated, then no record is required.

86. Effect of Tardy Compliance With Law.—Sometimes locators mark the boundaries of their claim, perform their discovery work and record their certificates of location, but fail to do some or all of these acts within the time prescribed by law. The effect of this tardy compliance with the law is not to render the location invalid, but to expose it, during the period of delinquency, to the danger of a relocation by third persons (39). If the act required is finally performed before adverse rights have accrued, the location is as valid as if the performance had been within the period prescribed by law (40). Arizona is a possible exception to this statement of the law. The statute in that state seems to make a timely compliance with the law essential to the validity of the location (41).

87. Penalty for Non-Compliance With Law.—The laws of most of the states and territories as to what a certificate of location shall contain are in terms mandatory. It often happens that a location certificate wholly fails to state one or more of the matters required by the law to be stated. It is important to consider what effect, if any, such an omission has upon the validity of the location.

The laws of Nevada expressly provide that "any record of the location of a lode mining claim which shall not contain all the requirements named in this section shall be void." Among these requirements are "the dimensions and location of the discovery shaft or its equivalent, sunk upon the claim," and "the location and description of each corner, with the markings thereon." Under a former statute in Montana making the same requirements as the Nevada law it was found that very few location certificates complied with the letter of the law, and a series of decisions by the supreme court of Montana strictly interpreting the law created such havoc in mining circles and invalidated so many locations otherwise good, that it finally resulted in the amendment of the law (42).

The present law in Montana concerning location certificates makes mandatory certain things and permissive certain other things. It makes mandatory a statement of the name of the lode and of the locator, the date of location, the reference to natural objects or permanent monuments, the direction and distance claimed along the lode each way from the discovery and the width claimed on each side of the center of the vein. It also permits, as we have already seen, the incorporation in the certificate of certain other matters pertaining to discovery work and marking of boundaries. As an incentive to care and completeness in such certificates,

---

(39) Brockbank vs. Albion M. Co. (Utah), 81 Pac. 863.
(40) Preston vs. Hunter, 67 Fed. 996; Strepy vs. Stark, 7 Colo. 614; Lockhard vs. Leeds (N. Mex.), 63 Pac. 51.
(41) Sec. 3225 R. S. Ariz.
(42) Dolan vs. Passmore, 34 Mont. 277; Purdum vs. Laddin, 23 Mont. 387; Hahn vs. James, 29 Mont. 1; Wilson vs. Free-Men, 29 Mont. 470; Mares vs. Dillon, 30 Mont. 117.

it makes a certificate, duly verified and recorded, prima facie evidence of the facts properly recited therein. This law saves in this manner the rights of the unlettered miner who is unable to make an elaborate certificate, but who has made a valid discovery, has properly marked the boundaries of his claim, and has complied with the main requisites of the law relating to location certificate. But the Montana law further safeguards the rights of the first locator by providing that "no defect in the posted notice or recorded certificate shall be deemed material, except as against one who has located the same ground, or some portion thereof, in good faith and without notice. Notice to an agent, who makes a location in behalf of another, shall be deemed notice to his principal, and notice to one of several co-claimants shall be deemed notice to all." Under this provision, it is impossible for a man, who covets his neighbor's mining claim, to deprive him of it by picking a flaw in the recorded certificate.

The statute of Arizona, after providing for the recording of the location certificate, performing discovery work and marking the boundaries, proceeds with the following forfeiture clause:

"The failure to do all the things enumerated in this section in the time and space specified shall be construed into an abandonment of the claim, and all right and claim thereto of the discoverer and locator shall be forfeited."

The statute of Colorado is mandatory as to certain essential requirements of the location certificate. Section 4 of the act of Feb. 13, 1874, is as follows:

"Any location certificate of a lode claim which shall not contain the name of the lode, the name of the locator, the date of location, the number of lineal feet claimed on each side of the discovery shaft, the general course of the lode, and such description as shall identify the claim with reasonable certainty, shall be void."

North Dakota and South Dakota each have a section identical with the one last quoted (43).

The act of October 14, 1898, of the state of Oregon has the following forfeiture clause:

"Section 10. Any and all locations or attempted locations of quartz mining claims within the state subsequent to the thirty-first day of December, 1898, that shall not comply and be in accordance with the provisions of this act shall be null and void."

Section 2548 of the Revised Statutes of Wyoming is as follows:

"Any certificate of the location of a lode claim which shall not fully contain all the requirements named in the preceding section (relative to contents of location certificate), together with such other description as shall identify the lode or claim with reasonable certainty, shall be void."

___

(43) Sec. 1429 Rev. Code N. Dak.; Sec. 2659 Grantham's Annot. Stats. S. Dak.

In states that have no express forfeiture provisions, courts hold divergent views as to the effect of a non-compliance with the requirements of the law. It is a general principle of the common law that forfeitures are not favored (44). The supreme court of California in an early case held that the failure to comply with any rule or regulation of a mining district would not work a forfeiture unless the rule so provided (45). The same principle applies to a state statute making requirements of a locator. The principle thus laid down has become the settled law in California (46), and has also been followed by the supreme court of Arizona (47). The supreme court of the United States in a recent case expressly withheld a ruling on this question (48).

In King vs. Edward, 1 Mont., 235, the supreme court of Montana refused to follow the ruling of the California supreme court, and held in effect that the rules of miners and state statutes prescribing the method of making a mining location, are conditions precedent to a valid location, and that the law implies a forfeiture if any of them are not complied with. But the effect of this decision has been modified by the Montana statute last above quoted.

In Nevada it has been held that a failure to comply with the laws of the state, or with the rules of the mining district in which the claim is situated, works a forfeiture of the claim, whether the laws or rules provide for forfeiture for non-compliance or not, and in such case the mining claim becomes subject to location by any qualified locator (49).

88. Forfeiture; Abandonment.—The failure of a locator of a mining claim to perform the requisite annual labor subjects the claim to relocation, and a peaceable entry may be made for that purpose, even though the claim is occupied by the original locator (50). The right of the original locator to perform the required amount of work after such failure depends upon his beginning the work before the relocation, and completing the same with reasonable diligence (51). A forfeiture is complete when there has been no performance or resumption of annual labor, and another person enters with intent to locate (52).

When a mining claim is abandoned by the locator, it is thereupon immediately subject to relocation. Abandonment is a question of intention (53). Leaving the claim in a neglected condition does not of itself prove

(44) Jupiter M. Co. vs. Bodie Con. M. Co., 11 Fed. 666.
(45) McGarrity vs. Byington, 12 Cal. 426.
(46) Emerson vs. McWhirter, 133 Cal. 510.
(47) Johnson vs. McLaughlin, 1 Ariz. 493; but see Zerres vs. Vanina, 134 Fed. 610.
(48) Yosemite G. M. & M. Co. vs. Emerson, Oct. Term, 1907.
(49) Sissons vs. Sommers, 24 Nev. 379; 55 Pac. 829.
(50) Goldberg vs. Bruschi, 146 Cal. 708.
(51) DuPrat vs. James, 65 Cal. 555; Hirschler vs. McKendricks, 16 Mont. 212.
(52) Cunningham vs. Pirrung (Ariz.), 80 Pac. 329.
(53) Moffatt vs. Blue River Gold Ex. Co. (Colo.), 80 Pac. 139.

abandonment (54). But if a claimant leaves his claim with the intention of never returning and of never asserting any further right of ownership over it, he thereby abandons it, and the claim thereupon becomes subject to relocation. The intention once formed and acted upon is as absolute if it exists for a minute or a second as though it continued for years. The burden of proving abandonment rests upon the party alleging it (55).

89. Relocation.—A mining claim forfeited or abandoned may be relocated in the same manner as an original location is made. For discovery work a new shaft may be sunk, or an old shaft deepened ten feet. The corner monuments of the former claim may be adopted by repairing them or reconstructing them (56).

In Arizona the certificate must state that the claim is located as forfeited or abandoned property. To mention the former location in this way is to acknowledge its original validity (57). It would seem to be a hardship to compel one making an adverse location to do this. Furthermore, it is questionable whether this requirement does not conflict with the provisions of the federal law which expressly says that upon a failure to perform annual labor, "the claim or mine upon which such failure occurred shall be open to relocation in the same manner as if no location of the same had ever been made." In other words, the forfeited claim can be relocated in precisely the same manner as any other part of the unappropriated government domain.

The supreme court of Arizona has held that the rule does not apply where the subsequent locator bases his right on the contention that the prior location was invalid, but in such case it limits the issue to the one question as to whether the prior locator ever had a valid location (58).

The supreme court of the United States in a recent case has held that one who relocates a mining claim on the theory that the annual labor has not been performed cannot thereafter justify his act on the ground that the original locator had not complied with the local rules of miners in making his location (59).

89a. Relocation or Amended Location by Original Claimant.—The statutes of most of the mining states provide that if at any time the locator of a mining claim shall apprehend that his original certificate was defective for any reason, he may amend his certificate or relocate his claim, provided that it does not interfere with the existing rights of others. But the right to so amend exists independently of statutory

(54) Integral Quicksilver Co. vs. Altoona Q. Co., 75 Fed. 379.
(55) Stone vs. Geyser Co., 52 Cal. 315; Omar vs. Soper (Colo.),
     18 Pac. 448. Trevaskis vs. Peard, 44 Pac. 246.
(56) Brockbank vs. Albion M. Co. (Utah), 81 Pac. 863.
(57) Wills vs. Blain, 4 N. M. 378; 20 Pac. 798.
(58) Cunningham vs. Pirrung (Ariz.), 80 Pac. 329.
(59) Yosemite G. M. & M. Co. vs Emerson, Oct. Term, 1907.

regulation (59½). If the original location was so imperfect as to be void, it cannot be amended so as to cut out intervening rights.

The statutes of Montana make a distinction between a relocation and an amended location. Under an amendment, a new location certificate can be filed, and any change in the boundaries can be made which does not involve a change in the discovery. But if the point of discovery is changed, new discovery work must be performed as well as a new certificate filed, and this constitutes a relocation. Such amended location or relocation cannot be construed as an abandonment of any right acquired by the original location except as to such portions of the previous location as are omitted from the boundaries of the claim as so amended or relocated. As to the portion of the ground included in both the original location and the location as amended or relocated, the claimant may rely on either the original location or the location as amended or relocated, or on both, unless the original discovery should be in some portion of ground which has been abandoned by the relocation, in which case he must rely on the relocation alone.

89b. AMENDED CERTIFICATE OF LOCATION— FORM.

JUNO LODE MINING CLAIM.

Know all men by these presents, that on the 1st day of January, 1895, Robert Elmore and George Davenport did discover a vein or lode of rock in place, bearing gold, silver, manganese and other valuable metals, in Wigwam mining district (unorganized), Madison County, State of Montana, and on the same day did locate and claim said vein or lode, by virtue of the laws of the United States and of the State of Montana, as the Juno lode mining claim, and within thirty days thereafter did distinctly mark said location upon the ground so that its boundaries could be readily traced, and did dig a shaft at the point of discovery of the following dimensions, to-wit, 4x6x10 feet, and did file in the office of the county clerk of said county a location certificate of said lode mining claim, which is recorded in Book 10 of Lode Locations, page 56, records of said county.

The undersigned, who are the above named locators, or the successors in interest of said locators, do make and file this amended certificate of location for the purpose of perfecting said location and of correcting and making more specific the description of said location and claim in said original location certificate contained, and of taking in adjoining territory open to location, without waiver, however, of any right or rights which the undersigned may severally have by reason of said

(59½) Thompson vs. Spray, 72 Cal. 528; Empire State M. Co. vs. Bunker Hill M. Co., 131 Fed. 604; Tonapah and Salt Lake M. Co. vs. Tonapah M. Co., 125 Fed. 395.

original certificate of location, which is hereby referred to and made a part hereof.

The general course of said vein or lode is easterly and westerly, along which the undersigned claim 300 feet in an easterly direction and 1,200 feet in a westerly direction from the point of discovery, together with surface 300 feet on the north side, and 300 feet on the south side of the center of said vein.

The location of said claim is distinctly marked on the ground so that its boundaries can be readily traced, viz.:

Beginning at the southeast corner No. 1 of this claim, which is a post marked "S. E. Cor. No. 1 of the Juno Lode," thence 600 feet in a northerly direction to the northeast corner No. 2 of this claim, which is a post marked "N. E. Cor. No. 2 of the Juno Lode;" thence 1,500 feet in a westerly direction to the northwest corner No. 3 of this claim, which is a post marked "N. W. Cor. No. 3 of the Juno Lode;" thence 600 feet in a southerly direction to the southwest corner No. 4 of this claim, which is a post marked "S. W. Cor. No. 4 of the Juno Lode;" thence 1,500 feet in an easterly direction to the place of beginning.

All corner posts used in marking the above boundaries are severally at least 4 inches square by 5 feet long, set 1 foot in the ground and surrounded by a mound of earth or stone 4 feet in diameter by 2 feet in height.

At the point of discovery said locators and claimants have dug a shaft the dimensions of which are 4 by 6 feet and 18 feet in depth, in which is disclosed a well-defined vein, crevice or deposit of ore at a vertical depth of at least ten feet below the lowest point of the rim or collar of said discovery shaft at the surface, and measured from said discovery shaft the following natural objects and permanent monuments are distant as follows, to-wit: Wigwam creek is distant 1,500 feet in a southerly direction; Madison river is distant 2 miles in an easterly direction.

The adjoining claims are as follows, to-wit: On the northeast the Bulldog lode mining claim; on the southeast the Black Prince lode mining claim; on the south the Madison (patented) lode mining claim.

The undivided interest in the above described location claimed by each of the undersigned is indicated by the fraction set after each name.

ROBERT ELMORE   ½
WILLIAM DAVENPORT   ¼
JENNIE DAVENPORT   ¼
                    Locators and Claimants.

In Montana and Idaho the amended location certificate should be verified in the same manner as an original certificate of location. (Par. 83, 84.)

90. Annual Labor and Improvements.—The laws of the United States require not less than one hundred dollars' worth of labor to be performed or improvements to be made upon all mining claims during each year beginning with the first day of January suceeding the date of the location. Work performed for the purpose of complying with this law is called "assessment work." Neither a rule of miners nor a state statute can authorize a less annual expenditure than one hundred dollars (60). Nor can district or state regulations establish an arbitrary rate of wages for annual labor in disregard of the current rate of wages in the same locality. The test is the worth or value of the labor or improvements. "One hundred dollars' worth" of labor in one community may mean more days' work and more hours per day than in another community (61). While the amount of money paid for the work is an important element in establishing the fact that the annual labor has been fully performed, yet it is not conclusive of that fact (62). The labor must be really and actually of the value of one hundred dollars (63). The fact that the work has not been paid for does not impair its validity as annual labor (64).

91. Where Owner Is Wrongfully Deprived of Possession. —Where the owner is forcibly deprived of possession of his claim, his failure to perform annual labor thereon is not a ground of forfeiture (65).

92. When Requirement for Annual Labor Ceases.—While the statute in terms requires the performance of annual labor upon the claim "until a patent has been issued therefor," yet it has been held that where the claimant has properly applied for a patent, paid the price required by law, and obtained a receiver's receipt, he has a complete equitable right to the land. The delay in the actual issuance of the patent will not impose any further burden upon him, hence there is no obligation upon him to do any further annual work (66). So where the right to a patent has fully accrued by the making of the requisite amount of improvements and the prosecution of a proper application for patent, but the entry of the claim is delayed by the filing of an adverse claim, the land department has held that there is no further obligation upon the claimant to do annual labor, provided he prosecutes his application for patent with diligence after the adverse claim has been disposed of (67).

But where a receiver's receipt has been obtained by fraud, the claimant is not relieved from the necessity of doing the assessment work (68).

(60) Sweet vs. Webber, 7 Colo. 443.
(61) Penn vs. Oldhauber, 24 Mont. 287.
(62) Stolp vs. Treasury Gold M. Co., 38 Wash. 619; McCormick vs. Parriott (Colo.), 80 Pac. 1044; Whalen Con. Copper M. Co. vs. Whalen, 127 Fed. 611.
(63) Woody vs. Bernard, 69 Ark. 579.
(64) Coleman vs. Curtis, 12 Mont. 301.
(65) Trevaskis vs. Peard (Cal.), 44 Pac. 246. Field vs. Tanner (Cal.), 75 Pac. 916.
(66) Benson, etc., Co. vs. Alta M. Co., 145 U. S. 428.
(67) The Marburg Lode, 30 L. D. 202; L. O. Reg. 55.
(68) Murray vs. Polglase, 23 Mont. 401.

93. Application for Patent Not Obligatory.—So long as the locator complies with the statutory requirements and performs the hundred dollars' worth of work in each year, he is entitled to hold and enjoy possession of his claim against all the world, subject only to the paramount sovereignty of the United States. He may never apply for a patent, yet, so long as he does the acts required by this section, he may hold and enjoy his claim (69).

94. Terms "Work" and "Improvements."—The terms "work" and "labor" relate to manual work in prospecting or mining excavation. The term "improvements" has reference to any structures or machinery put in place for the purpose of developing the property and extracting the minerals contained in it (70).

95. Annual Labor on Claims Held in Common.—Upon a group of claims held by one owner or one set of co-owners, the annual labor for all may be performed upon any one claim. The expenditure of labor or money must equal in value that which would be required on all the claims if they were separate or independent. The claims must be contiguous, and the labor or improvements must benefit each claim of the group (71).

96. What Expenditure Will Count.—The labor is not required to be applied in any particular manner so that it is unquestionably devoted to the claim. It may be in digging, erection of works for mining, in placing machinery, or in buildings on the claim necessary for its working. It has been held that a road built to the claim is labor performed and improvements made upon the claim within the meaning of the law (72). Where mining property was idle and the improvements thereon were valuable, the work of a watchman in protecting the same from deterioration, loss or danger, has been held to count for annual labor (73). But a watchman's services will not count where he is employed simply to protect the claim against trespassers (74).

Work done outside the claim, if done in reasonable proximity thereto and for the purpose of draining or developing the claim, is as available for holding the claim as if done within the boundaries of the claim itself (75), and it is immaterial whether the land upon which such work is done is vacant or occupied, patented or unpatented, except in so far

(69) Gillis vs. Downey, 85 Fed. 487.
(70) Power vs. Sla., 24 Mont. 243.
(71) Chambers vs. Harrington, 111 U. S. 353; Power vs. Sla, 24 Mont. 243; Little Dorrit G. M. Co. vs. Arrapahoe G. M. Co., 30 Colo. 431.
(72) Mt. Diablo M. Co. vs. Callison, 5 Saw. 439.
(73) Lockhart vs. Rollins (Ida.), 21 Pac. 415.
(74) Altoona, etc., Co. vs. Integral, etc., Co., 114 Cal. 100; Gear vs. Ford, 88 Pac. 600.
(75) Mt. Diablo M. Co. vs. Callison, 5 Saw. 439. Book vs. Justice Co., 58 Fed. 117.

as that fact may throw light on the intention of the party doing the work (76).

97. What Will Not Count.—Material brought upon the mine and not used, or taken away after slight use, will not count (77). So, also, a house built for the use of miners 200 feet from the claim (78). Traveling expenses in going to and from the claim will not count (79), nor will work done by third parties and bought in (80). Taking samples and making assays will not count as annual labor (81).

98. When Made.—The period within which the annual labor must be performed commences on the first day of January succeeding the date of location, and for this purpose the date of location is the date of posting the notice of location. The discovery work required by state laws to be done when location is made cannot count as part of the annual labor required by the United States law. The former is an additional requirement and is part of the process of location.

The locator has the whole of each year in which to represent his claim, and a relocation made before the full time has elapsed is void. In such case the relocator is a mere trespasser, and his relocation is not cured by a subsequent default by the original locator (82).

99. Affidavit of Annual Labor.—All of the states and territories excepting Oregon, North Dakota and South Dakota, have enacted laws providing for the filing of affidavits showing the due performance of annual labor. The law does not require such affidavits of annual labor to be recorded. It merely authorizes it. The provision for recording is designed to enable the owner to better preserve his proof, and for this purpose the record is made prima facie evidence of the facts authorized to be stated therein. A failure to record an affidavit does not work a forfeiture of the claim, and the facts may be proven by other testimony (83). The affidavit must be filed within the time required by the state law and the requirements of the law otherwise complied with in order that it shall constitute prima facie proof of the facts it recites.

100. Affidavit of Annual Labor; By Whom Made.—In all states and territories the affidavit may be made by the owner or by the person or persons who performed the work. In Alaska, Arizona, California, Colorado, Idaho, Nevada, New Mexico, Washington, and Wyoming the affidavit may be made by anyone cognizant of the facts.

(76) Godfrey vs. Faust (S. D.), 105 N. W. 460.
(77) Honaker vs. Martin, 11 Mont. 98.
(78) Remington vs. Baudit, 6 Mont. 138.
(79) Duprat vs. James, 65 Cal. 555.
(80) Little Gunnell G. M. Co. vs. Kimber, 1 Mot. M. R. 536.
(81) Bishop vs. Baslley, 28 Or. 119.
(82) Belk vs. Meagher, 104 U. S. 279.
(83) Book vs. Justice M. Co., 58 Fed. 106.

101. Affidavit; When Filed.—The periods within which the affidavit of annual labor must be filed for record vary greatly in different states. Some states specify a period after the close of the year for which the work is due, while others specify a period after the completion of the work.

The periods specified for filing such affidavit after the close of the year during which the annual labor was due are as follows: California and Washington, thirty days; Idaho and Oregon, sixty days; Alaska, ninety days; Arizona, three months; Colorado, six months.

The periods specified for filing such affidavit after the completion of the work are as follows: Montana, twenty days; Utah, thirty days; Nevada and Wyoming, sixty days.

102. Affidavit—Where Filed; Form.—The affidavit should be filed with the county recorder of the county in which the claim is situated in Arizona, California, Colorado, Idaho, Montana, New Mexico and Wyoming; with the county auditor in Washington; with the mining district recorder in Nevada, and with the county recorder and duplicate with the mining district recorder in Utah.

The following form fulfils the requirements of the laws of all states and territories relative to the affidavit of annual representation, to-wit:

STATE OF.............................., ⎫
County of............................, ⎬ ss.

...., being duly sworn, each for himself deposes and says: That he is a citizen of the United States and more than twenty-one years of age, resides at............................, in the county of........................, state of..............................., and is personally acquainted with the......................................mining claim, situated in........................... mining district, in the county of....................................., state of ...., the certificate of location of which is recorded in Book........................, page......................, of the records of....................mining locations of said county; that between the....................day of..................................., 190......, and the ....day of................................., 190......, and as annual labor for said year 190......, at least..............................dollars' worth of work and improvements were done and performed upon said claim (not including the location or discovery work performed upon said claim); that said work was performed upon the following dates, to-wit:........................ ....; that said work and improvements were performed for the purpose of complying with the laws of the United States pertaining to annual labor, and were done by and at the instance and expense of.., owner.... of said claim; that besides the work performed and improvements made by said owner.... in person, the sum of...dollars was actually paid by said owner.... in wages or otherwise to.. ...., each of whom was employed in the performance of said work and the making of said improvements upon said claim.

That the total number of days' work so performed was ...., and the character and value of said improvements are as follows, to-wit:..

....

....

That the number of cubic feet of earth or rock removed in performing said work is..

....

Subscribed and sworn to before me this................................day of................................, 190........

....

Notary Public in and for................................county, State of................................

(My commission as Notary Public expires on the................................ day of................................190........)

103. Effect of Failure to Perform Annual Labor.—A default in the performance of annual labor renders the claim open to relocation in the same manner as if no location of the same had ever been made, but as between the locator and the United States the failure to do annual labor does not work a forfeiture. It is the location by a new claimant that terminates the right of the original locator (84). When the new claimant in such case has initiated his claim by posting his notice of location, and while he is duly performing the acts required by law to perfect his location, his rights cannot be affected by any re-entry or resumption of work by the original locator (85).

104. Resumption of Work.—If an original locator fails to perform his assessment work during any year, but thereafter resumes work upon the claim in good faith before any adverse rights have intervened, he thereby preserves his right to the claim (86). But after such resumption there must be a diligent effort to complete the assessment work so begun (87).

105. Relocation to Avoid Assessment Work.—In Utah it has been held that a locator of a mining claim, who has allowed his location to lapse by his failure to perform the necessary annual labor thereon, may make a relocation or new location covering the same ground (88). It may well be doubted if this decision is in harmony with the law of the United States. The provision of the latter law permitting the original owner to resume work at any time subsequent to his default in assessment work, provided adverse rights

(84) Beals vs. Cone, 27 Colo. 501.
(85) Little Gunnell M. Co. vs. Kimber, 1 Mor. M. R. 536; Sec. V, Chap. 16, Laws of 1907, Mont.
(86) Buffalo Zinc, etc., Co. vs. Crump, 70 Ark. 525.
(87) Hirschler vs. McKendricks, 16 Mont. 211.
(88) Warnock vs. DeWitt, 11 Utah 328.

have not accrued, would seem to provide the only proper
method whereby the original locator can preserve his claim.
A relocation of a claim made for the purpose of avoiding
the performance of annual labor would seem to be an evasion
of the requirement for annual labor. A relocation made for
this purpose is expressly forbidden by statute in Montana (89).

106. Relocation While Original Locator Is in Possession.
—It is a general rule that no right can be initiated, on government land which is in the actual possession of another,
by a forcible, fraudulent or clandestine entry thereon for the
purpose of locating it as a mining or other claim (90). But
where the first location was void, or where the first locator
has forfeited the claim by non-performance of annual labor,
an entry thereon for the purpose of locating the ground may
be made by other persons if the same can be made peaceably.

Where the original locators were engaged in doing the
annual assessment work on a claim on the 31st of December,
and left their tools on the claim with the intention of resum-
ing work the next day, which they did, their possession and
work was held to be continuous, and one who located the
claim during the night was held to be a trespasser and acquired no rights (91). The same rule prevailed where the
31st day of December was Sunday, and the original locators,
having worked on Saturday, the 30th, left their tools on the
claim and resumed work on Monday, January 1st (92).

107. Delinquent Co-Owners.—The federal statute provides
that where one of several co-owners of a claim has failed to
contribute his proportion of the expenditure required for
assessment work, the co-owners who have performed the
work or made the improvements may, at the expiration of
the year, give the delinquent co-owner personal notice in
writing or notice by publication in the newspaper published
nearest the claim, at least once a week for ninety days. If
at the expiration of ninety days after such notice the delinquent co-owner fails or refuses to contribute his proportion
of the necessary expenditure, his interest in the claim becomes the property of the co-owners who have made the required expenditure.

108. Statute Strictly Construed.—This statute is one of
forfeiture and must be strictly construed (93). Where the
co-owner against whom the notice is published is in fact not
in default, the notice will not divest him of his title (94).
The same is true where the co-owner publishing the notice

(89) Sec. VII, Chap. 16, Laws 1907.
(90) Nevada Sierra Oil Co. vs. Home Oil Co., 98 Fed. 673.
(91) Willett vs. Baker, 133 Fed. 937.
(92) Fee vs. Durham, 121 Fed. 468.
(93) Turner vs. Sawyer, 150 U. S. 585.
(94) Brundy vs. Mayfield, 15 Mont. 201.

has not in fact done the alleged work or made the alleged expenditure (95).

109. The Notice.—The expenditure for several years may be included in one notice to a co-owner. And if that co-owner. be dead, a notice addressed to the deceased, "his heirs, administrator and to all whom it may concern," has been held a sufficient notice to all parties interested, whether they are minors, heirs or lienholders (96).

110. Stockholder in Corporation Not Co-Owner.—A stockholder in a corporation which owns a mining claim in whole or in part is not a co-owner within the meaning of the law, and cannot avail himself of the provisions of this section to declare a forfeiture of the interests of other stockholders, or of other co-owners in the claim where the corporation holds only an undivided part thereof (97).

111. Time of Publication.—The phrase "for at least once a week for ninety days" means "at least once a week during ninety days." The first publication is sufficient for the week beginning on that day, the second publication is sufficient for the week beginning on that day, and so on until the ninety day period has been fully covered. No publication is required after the ninetieth day (98).

112. Record of Forfeiture to Co-Owner.—While the law provides a method by which the undivided interest in a claim of a delinquent co-owner becomes the property of the co-owner who has performed the annual labor for the whole claim, it prescribes no method by which the transfer of interest thus brought about may be made a matter of record. Such a record is important, however, in tracing the chain of title to any mining claim in which such a forfeiture of interest has occurred. To supply this deficiency in the law, it has been customary to file in the office of the county recorder a copy of the notice together with an affidavit of the person who served the notice, whether personally or by publication, showing the time, place, and manner of service, and an affidavit of the co-owner who made the expenditure showing that the period allowed by law for the delinquent co-owner to redeem his interest has fully expired without payment having been made. This record, consisting of the notice and the two affidavits, should show a full compliance with the law, and when recorded constitutes at least prima facie evidence of a transfer of the interest of the delinquent owner to the co-owner who has made the expenditure (99).

In Arizona and Nevada it is provided by statute that the co-owner giving notice may file a copy of the notice, with an

(95) Delmoe vs. Long, 88 Pac. 778.
(96) Elder vs. Horseshoe M. Co., 194 U. S. 248.
(97) 35 L. D. 54.
(98) Elder vs. Horseshoe M. Co., 194 U. S. 248.
(99) L. O. Reg. 15.

affidavit attached showing due service, in the office of the county recorder of the county in which the mining claim is situated. If the delinquent co-owner contributes his proportion of the expenditure within ninety days after the service of the notice, then the co-owner to whom the payment is made must give him a receipt showing the payment and referring specifically to the claim by name and the book and page where the location certificate is recorded, and also naming the year for which the contribution is made. The recording of this receipt has the effect of showing a redemption from the delinquency described in the notice to co-owner (1).

113. DESCRIPTION OF LODE CLAIMS.

Sec. 2327 R. S. The description of vein or lode claims, upon surveyed lands, shall designate the location of the claim with reference to the lines of the public surveys, but need not conform therewith; but where a patent shall be issued for claims upon unsurveyed lands, the surveyor general, in extending the surveys, shall adjust the same to the boundaries of such patented claim, according to the plat or description thereof, but so as in no case to interfere with or change the location of any such patented claim.

114. Description of Lode Claims.—The regulations of the land office give specific instructions as to the proper method of marking the boundaries of mining claims and describing the same when they are surveyed for patent. The reader is referred to these regulations as contained in the Appendix. (L. O. Reg., 129 et seq.)

115. APPLICATIONS UNDER FORMER LAWS.

Sec. 2328. Applications for patents for mining claims under former laws now pending may be prosecuted to a final decision in the general land office; but in such cases where adverse rights are not affected thereby, patents may issue in pursuance of the provisions of this chapter; and all patents for mining claims upon veins or lodes heretofore issued shall convey all the rights and privileges conferred by this chapter where no adverse rights existed on the tenth day of May, eighteen hundred and seventy-two.

This section was applicable to the condition of things existing at the time of the enactment of the law in 1872. It was intended to preserve the rights of claimants under the law of 1866, and to permit such claimants to have the benefit of the new law also where adverse rights did not exist.

116. TUNNEL CLAIMS—RIGHTS.

Sec. 2323 R. S. Where a tunnel is run for the development of a vein or lode, or for the discovery of mines, the owners

(1) **Statutes Nevada, 1897, p. 106; Revised Stats. Arizona, Secs. 3245-3247.**

of such tunnel shall have the right of possession of all veins or lodes within three thousand feet from the face of such tunnel on the line thereof, not previously known to exist, discovered in such tunnel, to the same extent as if discovered from the surface; and locations on the line of such tunnel of veins or lodes not appearing on the surface, made by other parties after the commencement of the tunnel, and while the same is being prosecuted with reasonable diligence, shall be invalid; but failure to prosecute the work on the tunnel for six months shall be considered as an abandonment of the right to all undiscovered veins on the line of such tunnel.— Act of May 10, 1872.

117. **Tunnel Rights.**—A miner may run a tunnel for discovery purposes as well as for development purposes (2). While prosecuting his work with reasonable diligence, he has an inchoate right to every vein which his tunnel will intersect, unless the same has been appropriated by a valid location made prior to the commencement of the tunnel (3). And the same rule prevails where the second locator has gone so far as to apply for and obtain a patent for his claim. The tunnel claimant is under no obligation to adverse such application prior to the time that he has discovered the vein in controversy in his tunnel. His right to the vein is not affected by the issuance of a patent to another under such circumstances (4).

When the vein is discovered in the tunnel, the tunnel claimant should mark the boundaries of a claim covering his discovery and record his certificate of location in the same manner as if the discovery had been made upon the surface.

118. **Right of Way.**—A tunnel location gives the locator no right of way for his tunnel through any prior valid location or ground held under private ownership (5).

119. **Method of Locating a Tunnel Claim.**—The regulations of the Land Office, paragraphs 16, 17 and 18 infra, give very full directions as to the method of locating a tunnel claim.

120. **PLACER CLAIMS—SIZE; LANDS VALUABLE FOR BUILDING STONE, SALT DEPOSITS, PETROLEUM, ETC.**

Sec. 2329 R. S. Claims usually called "placers," including all forms of deposit, excepting veins of quartz, or other rock in place, shall be subject to entry and patent, under like circumstances and conditions, and upon similar proceedings, as are provided for veins or lode claims; but where the lands have been previously surveyed by the United States, the entry

---

(2) Fissure M. Co. vs. Old Susan M. Co., 22 Utah 438.
(3) Calhoun G. M. Co. vs. Ajax G. M. Co., 182 U. S. 507.
(4) Uinta T. & M. Co. vs. Ajax Gold M. Co, 141 Fed 563; Creede
    & Cr. Creek M. & M. Co. vs. Uinta, etc., Co., 196 U. S. 337.
(5) Calhoun G. M. Co. vs. Ajax G. M. Co., 182 U. S. 507.

in its exterior limits shall conform to the legal subdivisions of the public lands.—Act of July 9, 1870.

Sec. 2330 R. S.   Legal subdivisions of forty acres may be subdivided into ten-acre tracts; and two or more persons, or associations of persons, having contiguous claims of any size, although such claims may be less than ten acres each, may make joint entry thereof; but no location of a placer claim, made after the ninth day of July, eighteen hundred and seventy, shall exceed one hundred and sixty acres for any one person or association of persons, which location shall conform to the United States surveys; and nothing in this section contained shall defeat or impair any bona fide preemption or homestead claim upon agricultural lands, or authorize the sale of the improvements of any bona fide settler to any purchaser.—Act of July 9, 1870.

Sec. 2331 R. S.   Where placer claims are upon surveyed lands, and conform to legal subdivisions, no further survey or plat shall be required, and all placer mining claims located after the tenth day of May, eighteen hundred and seventy-two, shall conform as near as practicable with the United States system of public land surveys, and the rectangular subdivisions of such surveys, and no such location shall include more than twenty acres for each individual claimant; but where placer claims cannot be conformed to legal subdivisions, survey and plat shall be made as on unsurveyed lands; and where by the segregation of mineral lands in any legal subdivision a quantity of agricultural land less than forty acres remains, such fractional portion of agricultural land may be entered by any party qualified by law, for homestead or preemption purposes.—Act of May 10, 1872.

That any person authorized to enter lands under the mining laws of the United States may enter lands that are chiefly valuable for building stone under the provisions of the law in relation to placer mining claims: Provided, That lands reserved for the benefit of the public schools or donated to any state shall not be subject to entry under this act.—Act of Aug. 4, 1892.

That all unoccupied public lands of the United States containing salt springs, or deposits of salt in any form, and chiefly valuable therefor, are hereby declared to be subject to location and purchase under the provisions of the law relating to placer mining claims: Provided, That the same person shall not locate or enter more than one claim hereunder.—Act of Jan. 31, 1901.

That any person authorized to enter lands under the mining laws of the United States may enter and obtain patent to lands containing petroleum or other mineral oils, and chiefly valuable therefor, under the provisions of the laws relating to placer mineral claims: Provided, That lands containing such petroleum or other mineral oils which have heretofore been filed upon, claimed, or improved as mineral, but not yet patented, may be held and patented under the provisions of this act the same as if such filing, claim, or improvement were subsequent to the date of the passage hereof.—Act of Feb. 11, 1897.

That where oil lands are located under the provisions of title thirty-two, chapter six, Revised Statutes of the United States, as placer mining claims, the annual assessment labor upon such claims may be done upon any one of a group of claims lying contiguous and owned by the same person or corporation, not exceeding five claims in all: Provided, That said labor will tend to the development or to determine the oil-bearing character of such contiguous claims.—Act of Feb. 12, 1903.

121. **Placer Claims.**—The term "placer claim" primarily refers to all forms of valuable mineral deposits not in place, as, for instance, gravel beds containing grains or nuggets of gold, platinum, copper or other metals, or precious stones, such as sapphires, rubies and diamonds.

The scope of the law relating to placer claims has been greatly extended, however, so that many forms of deposit may be located as placer that cannot be recovered by washing and that are as much "in place" as any vein or lode could be. For instance, lands that are chiefly valuable for building stone may be located under the placer laws. So also may be lands chiefly valuable for petroleum, natural gas, saline springs or salt deposits. But where saline springs or salt deposits are located, the same person is not permitted to locate or enter more than one claim.

122. **Requisites of Placer Location.**—It is necessary that a placer claim should have a discovery (6). The location should be marked on the ground by the same kind of monuments as lode claims. Where state statutes require the posting of a notice of location, the performance of discovery work and the recording of a certificate of location in the case of lode claims, the same requirements should be observed in the case of placer claims, unless the latter are expressly excepted from the operation of the law.

123. **Size of Claims.**—If not limited by state or district regulations, placer claims may be of any size up to 160 acres, but if the claim exceeds 20 acres in area, there must be as many locators as there are multiples of twenty acres, or parts thereof. For instance, it would require an association of at least two persons to locate a placer claim of forty acres, of at least five persons to locate a claim of ninety acres, and of at least eight persons to locate a claim of one hundred and sixty acres. A placer location in excess of the · size authorized by law is void as to the excess (7).

(6) Nevada Sierra Oil Co. vs. Miller, 97 Fed. 681; Steele vs. Tanana Mines R. Co., 148 Fed. 678.
(7) Price vs. McIntosh, 1 Alaska, 291; L. O. Reg. 19.

124. "Dummy" Locators Not Allowed.—The policy and object of this law are to limit the quantity of placer land which may be located by one person in a single claim to twenty acres. If he seeks to enter more than this acreage in a single location, he must show that he acquired the excess by purchase from other bona fide locators whose locators were made in conformity with the same statutory requirement. For this reason contracts by which sham locators permit their names to be used as locators by friends for the purpose of securing the entry of more placer land than they were entitled to by the law are void (8).

125. Conformity to Public Survey.—On surveyed lands placer claims should conform to the divisions of the public survey. The smallest legal subdivision that may be appropriated by a placer location is a rectangular tract of ten acres. Rectangular tracts of five acres will not be permitted to be carved out of larger subdivisions (9).

Upon unsurveyed lands the rectangular form of the claim and the conformity to the subdivisions of the public survey should be preserved so far as possible. The claim should be of lawful dimensions with east-and-west and north-and-south boundary lines (10).

To this rule requiring conformity to the subdivisions of the public survey and east-and-west and north-and-south boundary lines, the land department has made an exception in favor of gulch placers enclosed by precipitous hills destitute of mineral values. In such cases it is permitted to include only the gulch and have the boundary lines follow the bases of the abutting hills (11).

126. Requisites for Location by Association.—Where a placer location in excess of twenty acres is made by the proper numbers of qualified locators, it is nevertheless a single location, requiring but a single discovery (12), and the same amount of annual labor to represent and the same value of improvements to patent as other single locations (13).

127. Discovery Work on Placer Claims.—There are no statutory provisions requiring the performance of discovery work upon placer claims in Alaska, Arizona, California, Colorado, New Mexico, Oregon, North Dakota, South Dakota, Utah or Wyoming.

In Montana the same amount of discovery work is required upon placer as upon lode claims. The discovery shaft or cut must be deep enough to disclose the valuable deposit located, and the total amount of excavation must equal 150

(8) Mitchell vs. Cline, 84 Cal. 409; Durant vs. Corbin, 94 Fed. 383; Gird vs. California Oil Co., 60 Fed. 531.
(9) Roman Placer Mining Claim, 34 L. D. 260.
(10) Laughing Water Placer, 34 L. D. 56; L. O. Reg. 23, 28.
(11) Woods Placer Mining Co., 32 L. D. 363.
(12) Miller vs. Chrisman, 140 Cal. 440; Reins vs. Raunheim, 28 L. D. 526. Union Oil Co., 25 L. D. 351.
(13) McDonald vs. Montana Wood Co., 14 Mont. 88.

cubic feet, at least one-half of which must be at the point of discovery.

In Idaho at least 100 cubic feet of excavation is required. In Nevada it must be "twenty dollars' worth of labor." In Washington the locator or locators must perform ten dollars worth of labor for each twenty acres or fraction thereof and within 60 days after discovery file with the auditor of the county in which the claim is situated an affidavit showing the due performance of the work, describing it.

128. Annual Labor Upon Placer Claims.—The same amount of annual labor must be performed upon a placer as upon a lode claim (14). The federal law makes no distinction in the size of a claim, whether placer or lode. The owner of a small claim must perform the same amount of annual labor thereon as the owner of a large one. A state law which permits a twenty-acre placer claim to be represented by the expenditure of twelve dollars in labor or improvements, is in conflict with the law of the United States.

129. Form of Notice of Placer Location.—The following form is sufficient for the posted notice upon a placer claim in all states and territories, to-wit:

NOTICE OF PLACER LOCATION.

Notice is hereby given that the undersigned locator...., each of whom is a citizen of the United States or has declared his intention to become such citizen, did on the **1st** day of **January, 1908,** discover a valuable deposit of gold, **sapphires** and other minerals having a commercial value, upon the unappropriated public domain of the United States, in **Yogo** Mining District, County of **Fergus,** State of **Montana,** and on the same day did locate and claim, and do hereby locate and claim, the said deposit as the **Fortuna** Placer Mining Claim by posting this notice of location at the point of said discovery.

The area of said claim is **20 acres** and its dimensions are **40x80 rods.**

Measured from the discovery **cut** of said claim as a starting point, the following natural objects and permanent monuments are distant as follows, to-wit:

Buck's saw mill is distant **one mile** in a **northerly** direction; **the mouth of Wolf Gulch** is distant **1,500 feet** in a **westerly** direction.

The undersigned hereby gives notice of **his** intention to hold said premises as a placer mining claim under the laws of the United States and of the State of **Montana.**

SAMUEL JAYNES,

Locator.... and Claimant.....

The same notice is a sufficient notice or certificate for record in Alaska, Arizona, California, Colorado, Idaho, North

---

(14) L. O. Reg. 25.

Dakota, South Dakota, Oregon, Washington and Wyomnig, but in Idaho the certificate should be verified before filing by the same statutory affidavit as is required in the case of a lode claim. (See Paragraph 84.)

130. Certificate of Placer Location for Record.—The following form is a sufficient certificate for record in all states and territories, without exception, to-wit:

CERTIFICATE OF LOCATION OF THE YELLOW BOY PLACER MINING CLAIM.

Know all men by these presents, that the undersigned, each of whom is a citizen of the United States, or has declared his intention to become such, did, on the **19th** day of **February, 1908,** discover a placer deposit bearing gold and other minerals having a commercial value, and on the same day did locate and claim the same as the **Yellow Boy** Placer Mining Claim, by posting a notice of location conspicuously at the point of said discovery, containing the name of said claim, the names of the undersigned as locators, the date of said location, and the approximate dimensions of such claim intended to be appropriated.

This claim is situated in **Summit Valley** Mining District (unorganized),in the County of **Silver Bow,** State of **Montana.** The adjoining claims are as follows, to-wit:

On the north, the **Yellow Streak Placer** claim; on the east, the **Blue Streak Placer** claim; on the southwest, the **Futurity Lode** claim.

Measured from the discovery **shaft** of this claim as a starting point, the following natural objects and permanent monuments are distant as follows, to-wit: **The junction of Bear and Silver Bow creeks** is distant 860 feet in a **westerly** direction; the ¼ Sec. Cor. between Secs. 4 and 7, T. 3 N.. R. 8 W. is distant 1,165 feet in a **northwest** direction.

Subsequent to the date of said location, to-wit, on the **5th** day of **March, 1908,** the undersigned did distinctly mark said location on the ground so that its boundaries could be readily traced, in the following manner, to-wit:

Beginning at the **N. W.** Corner No. 1, which is a **post 4x4 inches by 5 feet long, blazed on side facing discovery,** set one foot in ground, surrounded by a mound of stone 4 feet in diameter by 2 feet in height, and marked "N. W. Cor. Yellow Boy Placer," and which is distant 625 feet in a northwesterly direction from the point of discovery, and running thence first course: Direction, **easterly,** distance 2,640 feet, to the N. E. Corner No. 2, which is a post 4x4 inches by 5 feet long, set one foot in the ground, marked "N. E. Cor. Yellow Boy Placer," and surrounded by a mound of stone 4 feet in diameter by 2 feet in height, and running thence second course: Direction, **southerly,** distance 2,640 feet, to the S. E. Corner No. 3, which is a post 4x4 inches by 5 feet long, set 1 foot in the ground, marked "S. E. Corner Yellow Boy Placer," surrounded by a mound of earth and stone 4 feet in diameter by 2 feet in height, and running thence third course: Direction, westerly, distance 2,640 feet, to the S. W. Corner No. 4, which is apost 4x4 inches by 5 feet long, set one foot in ground, marked "S. W. Cor. Yellow Boy Placer," and surrounded by a mound of earth 4 feet in diameter by 2 feet in height, and running thence fourth course: Direction, northerly, distance 2,640 feet to Corner No. 1, the place of beginning, containing an area of 160 acres more or less.

Within sixty days after posting said notice of location the undersigned performed the following discovery work, to-wit:

At the point of discovery dug a shaft of the following dimensions, to-wit: 5x5 feet to bedrock, a distance of 12 feet. constituting in all 300 cubic feet of excavation, and said work has disclosed at the point of discovery a valuable deposit of gold bearing gravel.

The undivided interest in the above described location, claimed by each of the undersigned, is indicated by the fraction set after each name.

THOMAS LUMBARD,	⅛
JAMER MAYER,	⅛
ALEX MITCHELL,	⅛
ROBERT MILLER,	⅛
FRED L. HUFF,	⅛
DANIEL HICKEY,	⅛
ANDREW GANNON,	⅛
FRANK CRAWFORD,	⅛

Locators and Claimants.

In Idaho and Montana, the foregoing certificate should be verified in the same manner as a certificate of lode location. (See Paragraphs 83, 84.)

131. STATUTE OF LIMITATIONS ON MINING CLAIM.

Sec. 2332 R. S. Where such person or association, they and their grantors, have held and worked their claims for a period equal to the time prescribed by the statute of limitations for mining claims of the state or territory where the same may be situated, evidence of such possession and working of the claims for such period shall be sufficient to establish a right to a patent thereto under this chapter, in the absence of any adverse claim; but nothing in this chapter shall be deemed to impair any lien which may have attached in any way whatever to any mining claim or property thereto attached prior to the issuance of a patent.—Act of July 9, 1870.

132. Title by Occupation and Possession.—This section was enacted to meet cases where applicants for patent have been in possession of their claims for the period of the statute of limitations, but are unable to make full proof of their rights to the patent as required by the previous provisions of the law. To excuse these defects in title congress has

authorized the land office to overlook them where there is no adverse claimant (15). It applies to lode claims as well as placers (16).

Where possession has continued for the period covered by the statute of limitations before the adverse right exists, the title acquired is equivalent to a valid location under the laws of congress, and, it would seem, may thereafter be asserted even against an adverse claimant (17).

For the method of proving possessory rights in the land office, see L. O. Reg., 74-77.

133. PATENTS FOR MINING CLAIMS.

Sec. 2325 R. S. A patent for any land claimed and located for valuable deposits may be obtained in the following manner: Any person, association, or corporation authorized to locate a claim under this chapter, having claimed and located a piece of land for such purposes, who has, or have, complied with the terms of this chapter, may file in the proper land office an application for a patent, under oath, showing such compliance, together with a plat and field notes of the claim or claims in common, made by or under the direction of the United States surveyor general, showing accurately the boundaries of the claim or claims, which shall be distinctly marked by monuments on the ground, and shall post a copy of such plat, together with a notice of such application for a patent, in a conspicuous place on the land embraced in such plat previous to the filing of the application for a patent, and shall file an affidavit of at least two persons that such notice has been duly posted, and shall file a copy of the notice in such land office, and shall thereupon be entitled to a patent for the land, in the manner following: The register of the land office, upon the filing of such application, plat, field notes, notices, and affidavits, shall publish a notice that such application has been made, for the period of sixty days, in a newspaper to be by him designated as published nearest to such claim; and he shall also post such notice in his office for the same period. The claimant at the time of filing this application, or any time thereafter, within the sixty days of publication, shall file with the register a certificate of the United States surveyor general that five hundred dollars' worth of labor has been expended or improvements made upon the claim by himself or grantors; that the plat is correct, with such further description by such reference to natural objects or permanent monuments as shall identify the claim, and furnish an accurate description, to be incorporated in the patent. At the expiration of the sixty days of publication the claimant shall file his affidavit, showing that the plat and notice have been posted in a conspicuous place on the claim during such period of publication. If no adverse claim shall

---

(15) McCowan vs. Maclay, 16 Mont. 234.
(16) Lavignino vs. Uhlig, 26 Utah 1.
(17) Altoona Quicksilver M. Co. vs. Integral Q. M. Co., 114 Cal. 105; Upton vs. Santa Rita M. Co., 89 Pac. 275.

have been filed with the register and the receiver of the proper land office at the expiration of the sixty days of publication, it shall be assumed that the applicant is entitled to a patent, upon the payment to the proper officer of five dollars per acre, and that no adverse claim exists; and thereafter no objection from third parties to the issuance of a patent shall be heard, except it be shown that the applicant has failed to comply with the terms of this chapter.—Act of May 10, 1872.

Provided, That where the claimant for a patent is not a resident of or within the land district wherein the vein, lode, ledge, or deposit sought to be patented is located, the application for patent and the affidavits required to be made in this section by the claimant for such patent may be made by his, her, or its authorized agent, where said agent is conversant with the facts sought to be established by said affidavits: And provided, That this section shall apply to all applications now pending for patents to mineral lands.—Act of Jan. 22, 1880.

Sec. 2. That applicants for mineral patents, if residing beyond the limits of the district wherein the claim is situated, may make any oath or affidavit required for proof of citizenship before the clerk of any court of record, or before any notary public of any state or territory.—Act of April 26, 1882.

134. **Obtaining Patents.**—It does not come within the purpose of this book to give minute directions as to the method of obtaining a patent. The locator who desires to secure a patent will wisely secure the services of an attorney versed in such work and of a United States deputy mineral surveyor, who will be able to advise him as to the various steps necessary to be taken (18). The procedure is outlined very fully in the land office regulations. The following, however, is a summary of the process:

135. **Application for Order of Survey.**—This application is made to the surveyor general, and must be accompanied by a certified copy of the notice of location, and a fee of from $25 to $30, the fee varying somewhat in different states. The surveyor general thereupon issues an order of survey and forwards the same to the deputy mineral surveyor whom the claimant has designated. These orders are numbered consecutively for the entire state. The survey number of a claim fixes its location in the state (19).

136. **Survey.**—On receipt of the order for survey the deputy mineral surveyor makes the survey, marks the corners and forwards to the surveyor general copies of the plat, field notes and an affidavit of $500 improvements. If approved by the surveyor general, he returns to the claimant or his attorney a transcript of the field notes and two copies of the

(18) L. O. Reg. 34 et seq.
(19) L. O. Reg. 72.

plat, one to be posted on the claim, together with a notice of claimant's intention to apply for patent, the other to be forwarded with the application for patent to the register of the local land office.

137. Application for Patent.—The mineral application is then made by forwarding to the register of the local land office the following documents:

(1) Proof by affidavit of two disinterested persons that the plat and notice of intention to apply for patent have been posted on the claim.

(2) Copy of the official plat.

(3) Transcript of field notes.

(4) Application for patent.

(5) Affidavit of $500 improvements.

(6) An affidavit of the citizenship of each claimant; or, in case of a corporation, a certified copy of the certificate of incorporation.

(7) Agreement of publisher to hold the claimant alone responsible for cost of publication.

(8) Two copies of the notice to be published.

(9) Certified copy of the notice of location.

(10) An abstract of title showing title to the claim in the claimant.

(11) Ten dollars for cost of filing in the land office.

If these papers are approved, the register signs the notice for publication, and returns it to the local paper for publication.

138. Mineral Entry.—After the expiration of sixty days, if no adverse claim has been filed, the claimant makes his mineral entry by furnishing to the register (a) proof by affidavit that the plat and notice have remained posted on the claim during this period; (b) proof of publication by affidavit of the publisher; (c) statement of fees and charges and affidavit of claimant that the same have been paid; (d) supplemental abstract to date; (e) application to purchase at the government price; (f) money sufficient to pay for the land at the rate of $5 per acre or fraction of an acre in case of lode claims, and $2.50 per acre or fraction thereof in case of placer claims. Upon the receipt of these in proper form the receiver's receipt should at once issue.

139. Improvements Necessary to Patent.—Five hundred dollars' worth of labor must be expended or improvements made upon the claim before it can be entered for patent. This expenditure must have been made by the claimant or his predecessors in interest (20). Where an abandoned claim has been relocated, improvements made by the former owner cannot be set up by the new claimant as a basis for a patent (21).

(20) L. O. Reg. 25.
(21) Yankee Lode Claim, 30 L. D. 289; Russell vs. Wilson Creek Con. M. & M. Co., 30 L. D. 322, Cf. Sec. 97 supra.

140. Improvements on Claims Patented in a Group.— Where a group of contiguous claims, held by one person or in common by an association of persons, capable of being worked at one point by a general system which develops all of the claims, the work done at such point is as effective for the purpose of obtaining patent as if done upon each of the several claims. All of the claims may be included in one application and in one patent (22). Two claims having only one corner in common are not contiguous within the meaning of the law (23). The total expenditure must amount to at least $500 for each claim in the group sought to be patented.

141. Application for Patent.—The application for patent must be verified by the oath of the applicant if he is a resident of or within the land district in which the land is situated. This verification may be made before any officer authorized to administer oaths within such land district (24). An application sworn to by the applicant outside of the land district but within the state in which the land is situated does not comply with the law and gives the land office no jurisdiction (25). A verification made by an agent when the applicant himself is within the land district where the land is situated is also void (26). If the applicant is not a resident of or within the district the application may be verified by his duly authorized agent.

If a corporation is the applicant, it should by resolution of its board of directors appoint some one of its officers as its agent to sign and verify the application and any other necessary papers. A certified copy of this resolution should accompany the application.

142. Notice of Application for Patent.—During a period of sixty days the notice of application for patent must be given concurrently in three distinct ways,—it must be posted on the claim and in the land office, and be published in a newspaper to be designated by the receiver of the land office (27).

The posting in the land office is done by the register, who subsequently makes a certificate to the fact. The posting on the claim is done by the applicant or his agent. The fact that the notice was posted must be established by the affidavit of two disinterested witnesses. After the sixty days have expired, the fact that the notice remained posted during all of said period in a conspicuous place on the claim must be established by the affidavit of the claimant himself. A

(22) St. Louis Smelting, etc., Co. vs. Kemp, 104 U. S. 649.
(23) Hidden Treasure, etc., Mine, 35 L. D. 485.
(24) Paragraph 162 infra.
(25) North Clyde Quartz Claim and Mill Site, 35 L. D. 455.
(26) Crosby and other Lode Claims, 35 L. D. 434.
(27) Tilden vs. Intervenor M. Co., 1 L. D. 572; Great Western Lode, 5 L. D. 510.

failure to post in a conspicuous place will invalidate the notice and make a new notice necessary (28).

The register of the land office in which application is made designates the newspaper in which the notice should be published. In the exercise of his discretion he may designate a newspaper that he regards best for the purpose of giving the greatest publicity to the claim, even though it may not be the paper nearest to the land (29). If published in a daily paper, it should appear in sixty-one consecutive issues. If published in a weekly, it should appear in nine consecutive issues. In both cases the first day of issue is excluded in counting the sixty-day period (30).

143. Effect of Patent.—The dignity and character of a patent from the United States is such that the holder of it cannot be called upon to prove that everything has been done that is usual in the proceedings had in the land office, nor can he be called upon to explain irregularities or even improprieties in the process by which the patent was procured (31). In a court of law, the patent is conclusive of all matters within the jurisdiction of the land department (32). A patent cannot be collaterally attacked. It can only be impeached or set aside by a direct action brought in a court of equity for that purpose (33), and in that manner only during a period of six years from the date of its issuance, after which period it becomes unassailable on any ground whatever. A patent void on its face, however, may be impeached collaterally at any time (34).

144. Failure to Adverse.—A failure to adverse an application for patent is a waiver of all rights (35), and it will be assumed that no adverse rights exist and that the applicant is entitled to a patent (36).

145. Protest.—If, however, "the applicant has failed to comply with the terms of this chapter," a protest may be filed even after the expiration of the sixty-day period of publication, and a hearing had before the officers of the land department. At such hearing, the protestant cannot prevail by showing his own superior right to the ground, but he rather appears as a citizen of the United States to show that the laws have not been so complied with as to entitle the applicant to a patent (37).

146. Transfer of Title Pending Application for Patent.—A transfer of title by an applicant for a patent to a mining

(28) Ferguson vs. Hanson, 21 L. D. 336.
(29) Bretell vs. Swift, 17 L. D. 558.
(30) Par. 45, L. O. Reg.
(31) U. S. vs. Marshall Silver M. Co., 129 U. S. 589.
(32) St. Louis Smelting, etc., Co. vs. Kemp, 104 U. S. 646.
(33) Cowell vs. Lammers, 21 Fed. 200.
(34) Paire vs. Wells, 6 Colo. 409.
(35) Nesbitt vs. Delmar's Nevada G. M. Co., 24 Nev. 273.
(36) Lily M. Co. vs. Kellogg, 74 Pac. 518.
(37) Wight vs. Dubois, 21 Fed. 695.

claim during the pendency of the application has the effect of making him the trustee for the transferee. Upon the issuance of the patent the title passes to the transferee immediately by operation of law (38).

147. ADVERSE CLAIMS.

Sec. 2326 R. S. Where an adverse claim is filed during the period of publication, it shall be upon oath of the person or persons making the same, and shall show the nature, boundaries, and extent of such adverse claim, and all proceedings, except the publication of notice and making and filing of the affidavit thereof, shall be stayed until the controversy shall have been settled or decided by a court of competent jurisdiction, or the adverse claim waived. It shall be the duty of the adverse claimant, within thirty days after filing his claim, to commence proceedings in a court of competent jurisdiction, to determine the question of the right of possession, and prosecute the same with reasonable diligence to final judgment; and a failure so to do shall be a waiver of his adverse claim. After such judgment shall have been rendered, the party entitled to the possession of the claim, or any portion thereof, may, without giving further notice, file a certified copy of the judgment roll with the register of the land office, together with the certificate of the surveyor general that the requisite amount of labor has been expended or improvements made thereon, and the description required in other cases, and shall pay to the receiver five dollars per acre for his claim, together with the proper fees, whereupon the whole proceedings and the judgment roll shall be certified by the register to the commissioner of the general land office, and a patent shall issue thereon for the claim, or such portion thereof as the applicant shall appear, from the decision of the court, to rightly possess. If it appears from the decision of the court that several parties are entitled to separate and different portions of the claim, each party may pay for his portion of the claim with the proper fees, and file the certificate and description by the surveyor general, whereupon the register shall certify the proceedings and judgment roll to the commissioner of the general land office, as in the preceding case, and patents shall issue to the several parties according to their respective rights. Nothing herein contained shall be construed to prevent the alienation of a title conveyed by a patent for a mining claim to any person whatever.—Act of May 10, 1872.

If, in any action brought pursuant to section twenty-three hundred and twenty-six of the Revised Statutes, title to the ground in controversy shall not .be established by either party, the jury shall so find, and judgment shall be entered according to the verdict. In such case costs shall not be allowed to either party, and the claimant shall not proceed

(38) Shothower vs. Hunter (Wyo.), 88 Pac. 36; L. O. Reg. 71.

in the land office or be entitled to a patent for the ground in controversy until he shall have perfected his title.—Act of March 3, 1881.

The adverse claim required by section twenty-three hundred and twenty-six of the Revised Statutes may be verified by the oath of any duly authorized agent or attorney in fact of the adverse claimant cognizant of the facts stated; and the adverse claimant, if residing or at the time being beyond the limits of the district wherein the claim is situated, may make oath to the adverse claim before the clerk of any court of record of the United States or the state or territory where the adverse claimant may then be, or before any notary public of such state or territory.—Act of April 26, 1882.

148. Purpose of Adverse Claim.—The purpose of this section is to provide a method by which rival mining claimants to the same tract of land can litigate their controversy in the courts instead of the land office. As a rule, controversies over other kinds of land are heard and decided by officers of the land department. The filing of an adverse claim is a procedure intended for mining claimants only (39). If the adverse claimant is asserting a right under a land grant, or any other law except the mining law, his proper procedure is to file a protest (40).

149. When Filed.—To be effectual, an adverse claim must be filed within the sixty-day period of publication of the notice of application for patent (41). The adverse claimant is not excused for a failure to do this because a foot-note to the published notice states erroneously the date when the sixty-day period will expire (42), nor because the adverse claim was delayed in the mail or on its way to the land office (43). The land office is without authority to extend the time.

150. Stay of Proceedings.—The filing of an adverse claim has the effect of staying all proceedings in the land office upon the application for patent except the completion of the publication of notice and the making and filing of the necessary proof thereof (44). This stay of proceedings, however, is conditional upon the adverse claimant's beginning an action upon the adverse claim in a court of competent jurisdiction within thirty days, and thereafter prosecuting the same with reasonable diligence to a final judgment. A failure to so prosecute an adverse suit is deemed a waiver of the adverse claim. The intent of the law is that the diligent miner, who has complied with the law, should not be retarded in his

(39) Creede, etc., C. M. & M. Co. vs. Uinta T. M. & T. Co., 196 U. S. 337.
(40) Grand Canyon Ry. Co. vs. Cameron, 34 L. D. 495.
(41) Hamilton vs. Southern Nev. G. & S. M. Co., 33 Fed. 562.
(42) Draper vs. Wells, 25 L. D. 550.
(43) Gross vs. Hughes, 29 L. D. 467, 470.
(44) L. O. Reg. 78-88.

efforts to obtain a patent by the institution of adverse suits that are negligently prosecuted. But the application for relief should be made to the court in which the suit is pending and not the land office (45). The officers of the land department cannot assume that the adverse claim has been waived because there have been delays in the court (46).

151. **The Adverse Suit.**—The form of the action is not provided for by the statute, and, apparently, an action at law or in equity would lie as either might be appropriate, an action to recover possession when the plaintiff is out of possession, and a suit to quiet title when he is in possession. In the former case, the parties are entitled to a jury as a matter of right, and in the latter they are not (47).

In states where actual possession of the land is by statute made an immaterial question in such actions, as in Montana (48), any form of action that will determine the right of possession is appropriate.

The supreme court of Arizona has held that an adverse suit is neither an action at law, nor, strictly speaking, one in equity, but a special statutory proceeding having for its object the guidance of the land officers in determining which, if either, of the contesting parties is entitled to the patent. The same court in the same case holds that if the original complaint in an adverse suit fails to state a cause of action, an amended complaint cannot be filed after the expiration of the thirty-day period allowed by law for commencing the action (49).

In Montana an insufficient complaint may be amended after the thirty-day period has expired (50).

152. **Court Determines Right of Possession Only.**—In adverse suits the court does not determine who is entitled to the patent, but simply who is entitled to the possession of the ground in controversy. All other facts constituting an applicant's right to a patent are within the jurisdiction of the land department (51).

153. **Where Neither Party Shows Title.**—Adverse suits are peculiar in one respect in that it is within the province

(45) Cone vs. Jackson, 12 Colo. App. 461; 55 Pac. 940; McEvoy vs. Herman, 25 Fed. 539; Rose vs. Richmond M. Co. (Nev.), 27 Pac. 1105.
(46) Deeney vs. Mineral Creek M. Co. (N. M.), 67 Pac. 724.
(47) Perego vs. Dodge, 163 U. S. 165. The rule in ejectment suits that the plaintiff must show legal title in himself has been modified by Section 910 of the Revised Statutes of the United States, which is as follows: "Sec. 910. No possessory action between persons, in any court of the United States, for the recovery of any mining title, or for damages to any such title, shall be affected by the fact that the paramount title to the land in which such mines lie is in the United States; but each case shall be adjudged by the law of possession."
(48) Code Civ. Pro. Mont., Sec. 1322.
(49) Keppler vs. Becker (Ariz.), 80 Pac. 334.
(50) Woody vs. Hinds, 30 Mont. 189.
(51) Clipper M. Co. vs. Eli M. Co., 194 U. S. 233; Upton vs. Santa Rica M. Co. (N. M.), 89 Pac. 275.

of the jury to render a neutral verdict and to find that neither party has shown title to the land. This changes the common law rule in actions involving the title to land which requires that plaintiff shall recover on the strength of his own title and not on the weakness of defendant's title, and places an equal burden upon each party to show his own title (52).

154. Effect of the Judgment.—The officers of the land department are governed by the judgment (53). The prevailing party may file a certified copy of the judgment roll with the register of the land office, together with a certificate of the surveyor general that the requisite $500 worth of labor or improvements have been expended or made, and the description required in other cases, and thereupon without giving further notice he may make entry of the tract which the judgment of the court has shown that he is entitled to.

If the applicant has prevailed he can proceed to enter his entire claim as originally applied for. If he has lost, he can nevertheless enter the remainder of his claim after excluding the controverted area, provided the remainder of the claim includes his discovery. If either party's discovery is included in the area in controversy, the loss of this area is the loss of the entire claim.

155. KNOWN LODE WITHIN PLACER CLAIM.

Sec. 2333 R. S. Where the same person, association, or corporation is in possession of a placer claim, and also a vein or lode included within the boundaries thereof, application shall be made for a patent for the placer claim, with the statement that it includes such vein or lode, and in such case a patent shall issue for the placer claim, subject to the provisions of this chapter, including such vein or lode, upon the payment of five dollars per acre for such vein or lode claim, and twenty-five feet of surface on each side thereof. The remainder of the placer claim, or any placer claim not embracing any vein or lode claim, shall be paid for at the rate of two dollars and fifty cents per acre, together with all costs of proceedings; and where a vein or lode, such as is described in section twenty-three hundred and twenty, is known to exist within the boundaries of a placer claim, an application for a patent for such placer claim which does not include an application for the vein or lode claim shall be construed as a conclusive declaration that the claimant of the placer claim has no right of possession of the vein or lode claim; but where the existence of a vein or lode in a placer claim is not known, a patent for the placer claim shall convey all valuable mineral and other deposits within the boundaries thereof.—Act of May 10, 1872.

(52) Murray Hill M Co. vs. Havenor, 24 Utah 78.
(53) Richmond M. Co. vs. Rose, 114 U. S. 585; Last Chance M.
    Co. vs. Tyler M. Co., 157 U. S. 693.

156. Lodes Within Placer Claims.—If a lode is known to exist within the boundaries of a placer claim at the time when patent is applied for, a statement of that fact should be made in the application (54), otherwise it will be conclusively presumed that the placer claimant has no right to the lode.

The time at which the lode must be known in order to be excepted from the grant of a placer patent is the date of the application for patent (55). If a lode is discovered subsequent to that date, the placer patent will convey good title to the same.

157. What Is a "Known Lode."—Not every crevice in the rocks, nor every outcropping on the surface which suggests the possibility of mineral, or which on subsequent exploration develops ore of great value, can be adjudged a known vein or lode within the meaning of the statute (56). In order to meet that designation the lodes or veins must be clearly ascertained, and be of such extent as to render the land more valuable on that account, and to justify their exploitation (57).

It is not necessary that such a lode should have been located prior to the time of application for placer patent to make it a known lode. It is enough that it be known to the applicant or known to the community generally, or else disclosed by workings and obvious to any one making a reasonable and fair inspection of the premises for the purpose of obtaining title from the government. Where, however, the lode has been properly located and recorded and the title is held by third parties, it is known to exist within the meaning of the law, and a placer application covering such a lode and making no mention of it, originates no title adverse to the lode claimant (58). It is not even necessary for the lode claimant to adverse the placer application, though it would be advisable to do so.

As no title to a known vein not included in the placer application can be conveyed by a placer patent, a fee simple to all such known lodes continues to reside in the United States until it parts with the same in accordance with law. It may be located as other veins or lodes. The placer grantee can never acquire title to such lode by adverse possession, since the statute of limitations does not run as against the United States.

158. Patent for Known Lode.—Whenever it is ascertained by inquiry instituted by the land department, or determined by a court of competent jurisdiction, that a lode exists within the boundaries of the land covered by a placer patent, and

(54) L. O. Reg. 26.
(55) Iron Silver Co. vs. Mike & Starr Co., 143 U. S. 402.
(56) Noyes vs. Clifford, 94 Pac. 842.
(57) Migeon vs. Montana Central Ry. Co., 77 Fed. 249.
(58) Noyes vs. Mantle, 127 U. S. 348.

that such lode was known to exist at the date of the application for such patent, a patent will issue for the lode claim if the law has been in other respects fully complied with (59). If the lode claim was a valid subsisting location at the date of placer location, patent will issue for the full width of surface rightfully claimed. If the lode location was made after the placer location, patent will issue for surface twenty-five feet wide on each side of the lode (60).

Before the placer claimant applies for patent he should search his claim diligently to discover if lodes exist therein, and if they do, he should state the fact in his application, and make it include an application for the lodes as well. When a valuable lode is developed in placer ground for patent, there is always the danger that adverse claimants will attempt to show that the lode was known to exist at the date of the placer application. This danger constitutes an infirmity in such patents which should be guarded against by diligent examination of the ground in the presence of witnesses before patent is applied for.

159. Status of Lodes Within Placers Prior to Application for Patent.—Until the placer claimant applies for patent he holds all veins and lodes, whether known or unknown ,by virtue of his placer location. Any person going upon his claim against his will for the purpose of prospecting for unknown lodes is a trespasser. It is only when the claimant applies for a patent and fails to segregate and make separate application for the known lode that it becomes open to location by others (61).

160. APPOINTMENT OF U. S. DEPUTY MINERAL SURVEYORS.

Sec. 2334 R. S. The surveyor general of the United States may appoint in each land district containing mineral lands as many competent surveyors as shall apply for appointment to survey mining claims. The expenses of the survey of vein or lode claims, and the survey and subdivision of placer claims into smaller quantities than one hundred and sixty acres, together with the cost of publication of notices, shall be paid by the applicants, and they shall be at liberty to obtain the same at the most reasonable rates, and they shall also be at liberty to employ any United States deputy surveyor to make the survey. The commissioner of the general land office shall also have power to establish the maximum charges for surveys and publication of notices under this chapter; and, in case of excessive charges for publication, he may designate any newspaper published in a land district where mines are situated for the publication of mining notices

(59) South Star Lode, 20 L. D. 204.
(60) North Star Lode, 28 L. D. 41; Mt. Rosa M. Co. vs. Palmer, 56 Pac. 176; Daphne Lode Claim, 32 L. D. 513; Noyes vs. Clifford, 94 Pac. 842.
(61) Clipper M. Co. vs. Eli M. & L. Co., 194 U. S. 220.

in such district, and fix the rates to be charged by such paper; and, to the end that the commissioner may be fully informed on the subject, each applicant shall file with the register a sworn statement of all charges and fees paid by such applicant for publication and surveys, together with all fees and money paid the register and the receiver of the land office, which statement shall be transmitted, with the other papers in the case, to the commissioner of the general land office.—Act of May 10, 1872.

161. **Method of Securing Appointment; Right to Locate Mining Claims.**—For method of securing appointment, bond and duties of a U. S. deputy mineral surveyor, see L. O. Regulations 90, 93, 94, 115 et seq. For a full discussion of the nature of the office and of the right of a U. S. deputy mineral surveyor to locate and hold mining claims, see Hand vs. Cook (Nev.), 92 Pac. 3, where it is held that he has such right.

162. AFFIDAVITS—VERIFICATION.

Sec. 2335 R. S. All affidavits required to be made under this chapter may be verified before any officer authorized to administer oaths within the land district where the claims may be situated, and all testimony and proofs may be taken before any such officer, and, when duly certified by the officer taking the same, shall have the same force and effect as if taken before the register and receiver of the land office. In cases of contest as to the mineral or agricultural character of land, the testimony and proofs may be taken as herein provided on personal notice of at least ten days to the opposing party; or, if such party cannot be found, then by publication of at least once a week for thirty days in a newspaper, to be designated by the register of the land office as published nearest to the location of such land; and the register shall require proof that such notice has been given.

Sec. 2. That applicants for mineral patents, if residing beyond the limits of the district wherein the claim is situated, may make any oath or affidavit required for proof of citizenship before the clerk of any court of record, or before any notary public of any state or territory.—Act of May 10, 1872.

Concerning method of proving citizenship see paragraph 41.

163. INTERSECTION AND UNION OF VEINS.

Sec. 2336 R. S. Where two or more veins intersect or cross each other, priority of title shall govern, and such prior location shall be entitled to all ore or mineral contained within the space of intersection; but the subsequent location shall have the right of way through the space of intersection for the purposes of the convenient working of the mine. And where two or more veins unite, the oldest or prior location shall take the vein below the point of union, including all the space of intersection.—Act of May 10, 1872.

164. Intersection of Veins.—Veins may intersect on thei strike or on their dip.. Two veins may have parallel apexe and yet may so vary in the angle of their downward cours into the earth as to intersect or unite. If they unite, th senior location takes the consolidated vein below the poin of union. If they merely intersect, so that the identity o each vein is preserved beyond the point of intersection, thei each claimant can continue to follow his own particular vein As to the space of intersection, the senior location will take the ore found therein, but the junior locator will have a right-of-way through it for the purpose of reaching the lowei section of his vein (62).

An intersection upon the strike occurs in the case of lodes that cross on the surface. The supreme court of the United States in the case of Del Monte M. Co. vs. Last Chance M. Co., 171 U. S. 55, has recognized the right of a junior locator to lay the lines of his claim across a senior location. So a location upon a cross lode may be so made that the claim is bisected by the intervening territory of a senior location. In such case it has been held that the prase in the statute, "space of intersection," refers to the intersection of the claims and not of the veins. Through this space of intersection of the claims the senior location takes the mineral, but the junior locator has a right-of-way for the joint operation of the two ends of his claim (63).

165. Priority—How Determined.—In respect of conflict· ing mining claims, the priority is determined by the order in which they were located. The issuance of a patent for the area between their overlapping boundaries does not necessarily determine the question of priority where such question was not put in issue and litigated during the patent proceedings (64).

166. MILL SITES.

Sec. 2337 R. S. Where non-mineral land not contiguous to the vein or lode is used or occupied by the proprietor of such vein or lode for mining or milling purposes, such non-adjacent surface ground may be embraced and included in an application for a patent for such vein or lode, and the same may be patented therewith, subject to the same preliminary requirements as to survey and notice as are applicable to veins or lodes; but no location hereafter made of such non-adjacent land shall exceed five acres, and payment for the same must be made at the same rate as fixed by this chapter for the superficies of the lode. The owner of a quartz mill or reduction works, not owning a mine in connection there-with, may also receive a patent for his mill site, as provided in this section.—Act of May 10, 1872.

(62) Bunker Hill and Sullivan M. & C. Co. vs. Empire State-
    Idaho M. & D. Co., 134 Fed. 268.
(63) Calhoun Gold M. Co. vs. Ajax Gold M. Co., 27 Colo. 1; S.
    C. 182 U. S. 499.
(64) U. S. M. Co. vs. Lawson, 134 Fed. 769.

167. Mill Sites.—An entry of non-mineral land for mill site purposes, not exceeding five acres in area, is permissible in two classes of cases, viz: 1. Where non-mineral land not contiguous to the vein or lode is used or occupied by the proprietor of such vein or lode for mining or milling purposes. 2. Where the land is actually occupied by a quartz mill or other reduction works, and the owner thereof does not own a mine in connection therewith (65).

168. Mill Site Appurtenant to Lode Claim.—It should not be contiguous to the lode claim, but it should be made use of or occupied in connection therewith (66). The object of the requirement of law that such mill sites be non-adjacent to the lodes is to prevent the acquisition of mineral land as mill sites. But it is the practice of the land department to allow the patent of a mill site contiguous to the side of a lode claim where its non-mineral character is shown, and even where the mill site adjoins the end of the lode claim patent has been granted where it has been shown that the lode does not extend beyond the end line of the lode claim.

Where a mill site is patented in conjunction with a lode claim, five hundred dollars' worth of improvements is sufficient to patent both. But where the mill site is patented separately, five hundred dollars' worth of improvements must be shown thereon.

169. Quartz Mill Sites.—The second class of mill sites are those which are claimed and patented by reason of their being in actual use for quartz mills, reduction works, or some necessary mining or milling purpose.

170. Manner of Locating.—A mill site is located in the same manner as a placer claim, with the exception that no discovery or discovery shaft is necessary, and on surveyed land it need not conform to the public survey. Only non-mineral land can be taken as a mill site. The law does not allow land to be acquired for merely speculative purposes under the mill site law (67).

171. EASEMENTS.

Sec. 2338 R. S.—As a condition of sale, in the absence of necessary legislation by congress, the local legislature of any state or territory may provide rules for working mines, involving easements, drainage, and other necessary means to their complete development; and those conditions shall be fully expressed in the patent.—Act of July 26, 1866.

172. Reservation of Easements.—The apparent intent of this section is to reserve to the various states and territories the right to enact laws providing for rights of way over the

---

(65) Burns vs. Clark, 133 Cal. 634; Cleary vs. Skiffich, 28 Colo. 362.
(66) Hartman vs. Smith, 7 Mont. 29.
(67) L. O. Reg. 61-65.

surface for roads or pipe-lines, or beneath the surface for tunnels or drifts whereby mines may be better drained or ventilated, or better means of escape for workmen provided or means provided for the common operation of segregated properties owned by the same person or company. With the reservation contained in this section expressed in the patent as a condition of the sale, it would seem the the patentee is precluded from objecting that the taking of a right-of-way for such purpose is a taking of private property for private uses. Yet in California it has been held that this section contains no reservation of a right-of-way to be made available by state legislation for such purposes where private persons or companies are to reap the benefit (68).

173. VESTED RIGHTS IN WATER AND WATER DITCHES.

Sec. 2339. Whenever, by priority of possession, rights to the use of water for mining, agricultural, manufacturing, or other purposes, have vested and accrued, and the same are recognized and acknowledged by the local customs, laws, and the decisions of courts, the possessors and owners of such vested rights shall be maintained and protected in the same; and the right of way for the construction of ditches and canals for the purposes herein specified is acknowledged and confirmed; but whenever any person, in the construction of any ditch or canal, injures or damages the possession of any settler on the public domain, the party committing such injury or damage shall be liable to the party injured for such injury or damage.—Act of July 26, 1866.

Sec. 2340. All patents granted, or preemption or homesteads allowed, shall be subject to any vested and accrued water rights, cr rights to ditches and reservoirs used in connection with such water rights, as may have been acquired under or recognized by the preceding section.—Act of July 9, 1870.

174. USE OF TIMBER UPON MINERAL LANDS.

All citizens of the United States and other persons, bona fide residents of the State of Colorado, or Nevada, or either of the Territories of New Mexico, Arizona, Utah, Wyoming, Dakota, Idaho, or Montana, and all other mineral districts of the United States, shall be, and are hereby, authorized and permitted to fell and remove, for building, agricultural, mining, or other domestic purposes, any timber or other trees growing or being on the public lands, said lands being mineral, and not subject to entry under existing laws of the United States, except for mineral entry, in either of said states, territories, or districts of which such citizens or persons may be at the time bona fide residents, subject to such rules and regulations as the secretary of the interior may

---

(68) Amador Queen M. Co. vs. Dewitt, 73 Cal. 484.

prescribe for the protection of the timber and of the undergrowth growing upon such lands, and for other purposes: Provided, The provisions of this act shall not extend to railroad corporations.

Sec. 2. That it shall be the duty of the register and the receiver of any local land office in whose district any mineral land may be situated to ascertain from time to time whether any timber is being cut or used upon any such lands, except for the purposes authorized by this act, within their respective land districts; and, if so, they shall immediately notify the commissioner of the general land office of such fact; and all necessary expenses incurred in making such proper examinations shall be paid and allowed such register and receiver in making up their next quarterly accounts.

Sec. 3. Any person or persons who shall violate the provisions of this act, or any rules and regulations in pursuance thereof made by the secretary of the interior, shall be deemed guilty of a misdemeanor, and, upon conviction, shall be fined in any sum not exceeding five hundred dollars, and to which may be added imprisonment for any term not exceeding six months.—Act of June 3, 1878.

Upon all unappropriated mineral lands not within a forest reserve, timber may be cut for domestic use, which is held to mean any beneficial use within the state where the timber is situated.

175. Cutting Timber on Mining Claims.—After patent, the owner of a mining claim can make any disposition of the growing timber thereon that he chooses. Before patent, the United States has such interest in the land as authorizes it to control, either by civil or criminal proceedings, the cutting of timber on a mining claim (69).

Within forest reservations, the owner of a valid mining location can cut timber upon his claim for actual mining purposes in connection with that particular claim, but for no other purpose. Miners, prospectors and settlers within the limits of a forest reservation, however, may secure a permit to cut timber free of charge to the extent of a stumpage value not exceeding $20 per year for mining, prospecting, firewood, fencing, buildings, and other domestic purposes (70). A permit to cut timber to the extent of $50 stumpage value may be obtained by making application to the nearest forest ranger. If larger amounts are wanted, they can be purchased of the government through the forest supervisor. The timber so purchased should not be cut or removed until permission has been granted by a forest officer, but in great emergencies, when a forest officer cannot be reached and serious loss would result from delay, one may take what timber is actually needed and report to the forest ranger afterwards (71).

(69) Teller vs. U. S., 113 Fed. 273.
(70) Regulation 19, The Use Book.
(71) Regulation 11, The Use Book.

MISCELLANEOUS SUBJECTS RELATING TO MINING CLAIMS

176. Sales, Agreements to Sell and Leases of Mining Claims.—It is not the purpose of this book to give complete instructions concerning the drawing of deeds, options or leases of mining claims. What is here said must necessarily be very elementary and incomplete. A mine claimant having an important deal pending had better not try to act as his own lawyer. He should hire a good lawyer, the best obtainable, and depend upon him to have the agreements carefully drawn and accurately expressed.

177. Deeds.—A mining claim is real estate, and cannot be conveyed by word of mouth. Any sale or agreement to sell must be evidenced by a written instrument to be valid. A mining claim may be conveyed by any form of deed appropriate for the conveyance of real estate.

178. Kinds of Deeds.—Deeds are of three general kinds, warranty, implied warranty and quit claim.

179. Warranty Deeds.—A warranty deed is one in which covenants of warranty are expressed in the deed itself. The following clauses indicate the usual covenants and the manner in which they may be expressed:

1. Seizin: "The party of the first part covenants with the party of the second part that the former is now seized in fee simple of the property granted;"

2. Quiet Enjoyment: "that the latter shall enjoy the same without any lawful disturbance;"

3. Against Incumbrances: "that the same is free from all incumbrances;"

4. Further Assurance: "that the party of the first part, and all parties acquiring any interest in the same through or for him, will, on demand, execute and deliver to the party of the second part, at the expense of the latter, any further assurance of the same that may be reasonably required;"

5. General Warranty: "and that the party of the first part will warrant to the party of the second part all the said property against every person lawfully claiming the same."

No one can properly give a straight warranty deed to an unpatented mining claim. His title is subject to the paramount title of the United States, and is subject to forfeiture in so many ways that he cannot safely undertake to warrant it against infirmity or the attacks of adverse claimants.

180. Deed of Implied Warranty.—Many states have statutory provisions by which the use of certain granting words implies certain covenants. In California and Montana the word "grant" is the significant word, and its use in a deed implies the following covenants: (a) That previous to the time of the execution of the deed the grantor has not conveyed the same property, or any interest therein, to any other person than the grantee; (b) that at the time of the execution of the deed the property is free from incumbrances done, made or suffered by the grantor, or any person claiming under him.

It will be seen that such a "grant" deed warrants the title during the period of the tenure of the property by the grantor. If he has mortgaged it, the mortgage constitutes an incumbrance "made" by him, and he must pay the mortgage, even after the conveyance is complete. If he has permitted taxes to remain unpaid, they constitute an incumbrance "suffered" by him, and he must discharge the taxes.

In some states the significant words in a deed of implied warranty are the words "bargain and sell," from which the deed has acquired the popular name of "bargain and sale deed."

A deed of implied warranty is a safe and proper conveyance to use in transferring a mining claim.

181. Form of Deed of Implied Warranty.—The following is a form of deed of implied warranty:

THIS INDENTURE, Made the 20th day of March, A. D. 1908, between James Davenport, an unmarried man, of Silver Bow county, Montana, party of the first part, and Thomas North, of the same place, party of the second part, WITNESSETH, That the said party of the first part, in consideration of the sum of five hundred dollars, lawful money of the United States to him in hand paid, the receipt whereof is hereby acknowledged, has granted, sold and conveyed, and by these presents does grant, sell and convey unto the said party of the second part, and to his heirs and assigns forever, all of the following described property, situated in Silver Bow county, State of Montana, to-wit: The Bob Evans Lode Mining Claim, location certificate of which is recorded in Book 15 of Lode Locations, page 71, records of said Silver Bow county.

*

Together with all and singular the tenements, hereditaments and appurtenances thereunto belonging, or in anywise appertaining, and the reversions, remainders, rents. issues and profits thereof.

To have and to hold, all and singular, the said premises, together with the appurtenaces, unto the said party of the second part, and to his heirs and assigns forever.
**

---

* Any exception or reservation from the property conveyed should be expressed here.
** Any express covenants of warranty should be inserted here. If any such covenants are expressed, the deed ceases to be one of implied warranty. The law presumes that the covenants expressed are intended to take the place of the implied covenants.

IN WITNESS WHEREOF, The said party of the first part has hereunto set his hand the day and year above written.

JAMES DAVENPORT.

Executed and delivered in the presence of
JOHN MILRAY.

STATE OF MONTANA,
County of Silver Bow, } ss.

On this 20th day of March, in the year 1908, before me, Samuel Williams, a Notary Public in and for said county and state, personally appeared James Davenport, known to me to be the person whose name is subscribed to the within instrument, and acknowledged to me that he executed the same.

IN WITNESS WHEREOF, I have hereunto set my hand and affixed my Notarial Seal the day and year in this certificate above written.
[Notarial Seal.]   SAMUEL WILLIAMS,
Notary Public in and for Silver Bow County, State of Montana.

182. Quit Claim Deeds.—A quit claim deed conveys merely the interest of the grantor, whatever it may be. If he has no interest, the deed is harmless, since the deed contains no covenants whatever. Yet a quit claim deed may convey as full and complete a title to property as a warranty deed containing all the usual covenants. It throws upon the purchaser the duty of ascertaining the state of the title.

183. Form of Quit Claim Deed.—The following is a form of quit claim deed:

THIS INDENTURE, Made the 1st day of April, in the year 1908, between John Smith and Sarah Smith, his wife, of Butte, Montana, parties of the first part, and Richard Roe of Helena, Montana, party of the second part, WITNESSETH: That the said parties of the first part, for and in consideration of the sum of one dollar, to them in hand paid by the said party of the second part, the receipt whereof is hereby acknowledged, do by these presents remise, release and forever quit claim unto the said party of the second part, and to his heirs and assigns forever, all that certain lot, piece or parcel of land, situate in the county of Silver Bow, state of Montana, and bounded and particularly described as follows, to-wit: The Phoenix Placer Claim, location certificate of which is recorded in Book 20 of Placer Locations, page 500, records of said Silver Bow county.

TOGETHER with all and singular, the tenements, hereditaments and appurtenances thereunto belonging or in anywise appertaining, and the reversion and reversions, remainder and remainders, rents, issues and profits thereof.

To have and to hold, all and singular, the said premises, together with the appurtenances unto the said party of the second part, and to his heirs and assigns forever.

IN WITNESS WHEREOF, the said parties of the first part have hereunto set their hands and seals the day and year first above written.

JOHN SMITH,   [Seal]
SARAH SMITH.   [Seal]

Signed, sealed and delivered in presence of
J. T. JONES

STATE OF MONTANA,   } ss.
  County of Silver Bow.

On this 1st day of April, in the year 1908, before me, J. T. Jones, a Notary Public in and for the county of Silver Bow, state of Montana, personally appeared John Smith and Sarah Smith, his wife, known to me to be the persons whose names are subscribed to the within instrument, and who severally acknowledged to me that they executed the same.

IN TESTIMONY WHEREOF, I have hereunto set my hand, and affixed my Notarial Seal on this 1st day of April, 1908.

J. T. JONES.
Notary Public in and for Silver Bow County, Montana.

184. Mining Rights—How Conveyed.—The right to follow a vein on its dip beyond the vertical plane of the side line is a right appurtenant to a lode claim. A deed conveying a mining claim with its "appurtenances" would doubtless convey all extralateral rights belonging to the property.

Where the entire claim is to be conveyed, it is safer to convey such mining rights under the general term "appurtenances" than to attempt to define them. When defined, it should be made clear that only such ore bodies are conveyed as have their apex withtin the tract conveyed.

Where a portion only of the claim is to be conveyed, care must be exercised to see that the mining rights granted with the tract conveyed do not deprive the ground retained of rights properly belonging to it. In important transactions of this kind, a wise man will not try to act as his own lawyer. In the celebrated "Drumlummon" case, after many years of litigation, the controversy finally turned in the supreme court of the United States upon the interpretation of a deed containing the following clauses:

"Together with all the mineral therein contained; together with all the dips, spurs and angles, and also all the metals, ores, gold and silver bearing quartz, rock and earth therein; and all the rights, privileges and franchises thereto incident, appendant and appurtenant, or therewith usually had and enjoyed; and, also all and singular the tenements, hereditaments and appurtenances thereto belonging or in anywise appertaining, and the rents, issues and profits thereof; and also all and every right, title, interest, property, possession, claim and demand whatsoever, as well in law as in equity, of the said party of the first part, of, in and to said premises, and every part and parcel thereof, with the appurtenances."

The tract in question was a small fractional part of the claim of the St. Louis Company, which had been originally conveyed in settlement of an adverse suit. The ore which later came into controversy underlaid this tract, but it apexed in the portion of the claim retained by the St. Louis Company. After many years of litigation, the supreme court of the United States held that the mineral conveyed by the deed was not limited to the mineral apexing in the tract conveyed, but included all mineral within the vertical boundaries of the tract, wherever it might apex. If the deed had been intended otherwise, it should have contained some words of exception or limitation (72). The case furnishes a warning to the grantor who conveys mining property adjacent to other mining property which he retains. In such case the mining rights of the property conveyed should be defined with care. Otherwise he may find the mining rights of the property conveyed conflict with those of the property retained.

185. Options to Purchase.—An option to purchase a mining claim, properly drawn, is also an agreement to convey. It should be in writing and signed by the party to be bound. It need be in no particular form, just so it expresses a consideration, and describes the property and the terms of sale with certainty. The following is a convenient and concise form for use:

MINE OPTION.

Received of..the sum of.................... Dollars, as part payment for the following described mining property, situated in.............................Mining District,................ ....County, State of Montana, to-wit:.....................

The entire price to be paid for the said above described mining property is the sum of...Dollars, to be paid as follows, viz:

...........................Dollars on or before.........................190......;
...........................Dollars on or before.........................190......;
...........................Dollars on or before.........................190......;
...........................Dollars on or before.........................190.......

If the said payments are made when due, then the undersigned...agree...... to execute and deliver to the said...a good and sufficient grant deed to the said premises.

(72) Montana Mining Co. vs. St. Louis Mining Co., 204 U. S. 204; for a similar case see Riley vs. North Star Mg. Co. (Cal.), 93 Pac. 194.

But if default shall be made in said payments, or any of them, when due, then the said..may, at............................option, consider this agreement void, and all payments theretofore made shall be forfeited to the said ....and held by........................as liquidated damages, TIME BEING OF THE ESSENCE OF THIS AGREEMENT TO CONVEY.

Signed at..., Montana this.................... day of..190.......

....
....
....

In the presence of

....

....

STATE OF MONTANA, }
  County of........................, } ss.

On this.............................day of............................., in the year 190......, before me, ..., a Notary Public in and for the county and state aforesaid, personally appeared ...., known to me to be the person...... whose name........................subscribed to the within instrument, and acknowledged to me that........he........executed the same.

IN WITNESS WHEREOF, I have hereunto set my hand and affixed my notarial seal the day and year first above written.

....
Notary Public in and for......................County, Mont.

186. Use of Acknowledgement.—The option is equally binding without being acknowledged. The only use of the acknowledgement is that it entitles the instrument to record. But on this very account many owners refuse to acknowledge a lease or option because they do not want the record title of the property encumbered by the recording of such instruments. They greatly encumber any abstract of title that may be made of the property ,and ordinarily the record does not show, nor can it be made to show, how if at all the rights of the lessee or holder of the option have terminated. For these reasons it is better from the owner's point of view to keep the instrument off the record by not acknowledging it. On the other hand, where the instrument is recorded, it furnishes constructive notice to all the world of its contents, thus precluding any evasion of its provisions through a sale or transfer of the claim to an innocent purchaser. However, where a lessee or grantee named in the option has actual possession of the property his possession furnishes notice to the world of his rights.

187. Leases and Options to Purchase Combined.—These are really two instruments in one. It is better that they should be combined than that they should be made in two instruments, since in the latter case the lease might become forfeited and the property still remain tied up under the option, or vice versa.

188. Form of Lease and Option.—In the following form the various parts of such an instrument are indicated, and the manner in which these parts may be properly expressed:

LEASE AND OPTION TO PURCHASE.

Parties named. This indenture, made the 20th day of March, 1908, between Samuel McCall and James Sievers, of Madison county, Montana, parties of the first part, and Timothy Harris, of the same place, party of the second part,

Consideration expressed. Witnesseth: That the parties of the first part, in consideration of the sum of one dollar, now paid, as well as in consideration of the due performance by the party of the second part of the covenants and conditions hereinafter set forth, has leased, demised and let, and by these presents does lease, demise and let unto the party of the second part, for the period of two years

Term of lease. from date hereof, and up to and including the 20th day of March, 1910, all the following described mining property, situated in Alder Gulch Mining District, Madison County, Montana, to-wit:

Description. The Midas Lode Claim, Survey No. 782.

Tenendum. Together with all and singular the tenements, hereditaments and appurtenances thereunto belonging or in any way appertaining.

Conditions. Upon condition, however:

That the party of the second part shall, on or before the 1st day of May, 1908, begin and thereafter continue mining work upon said premises with a force of not less than four men, each working not less than twenty days during each calendar month during the continuance of this lease;

That he shall sink the present working shaft upon said property to the depth of 300 feet on or before the 1st day of October, 1908;

That he shall do all of said work in a good and miner-like manner, securely timbering and lagging all shafts, drifts, crosscuts, and other workings wherever necessary, and shall keep all timbering in said property in good repair;

That he shall keep all passageways in said mine clear of waste and other debris;

That he shall render to the parties of the first part as royalty 25 per cent of the net proceeds of all ores smelted or milled during the continuance of this lease, and by net proceeds shall be understood the gross smelter or mill returns with only the costs of hauling, shipping and smelting or milling deducted;

That he shall deliver to the first parties a copy of the mill or smelter returns on all such shipments of ore, and shall pay the royalty above described to the first parties promptly upon the receipt of the returns from such mill or smelter;

That he will at all reasonable times permit the parties of the first part and their agents to inspect said premises and every part thereof, using for that purpose without compensation all hoists, ladder-ways, cages, cars, and other means of ingress and egress owned or used by the party of the second part thereon;

That at the termination of this lease, whether by forfeiture or the expiration of the term herein expressed, he will surrender peaceable possession of said premises and the whole thereof to the parties of the first part.

Forfeiture of Lease. If the party of the second part shall fail to perform the conditions in this instrument contained, or any of them, then the parties of the first part may, at their option, terminate this lease and declare all the rights of the second parties under this instrument forfeited, and will thereupon be entitled to demand and take possession of the leased premises, peaceably or by force, and to eject all persons found thereon, but in case of such forfeiture the party of the second **Removal of Machinery.** part shall have the right to remove at any time within thirty days any machinery which he shall have placed upon said premises.

Option. In consideration of the foregoing lease, the parties of the first part agree to sell and by a good and sufficient deed convey, at any time during the continuance of said lease, the above described premises for the sum of twenty-five thousand dollars, payable as follows, to-wit: Five thousand dollars on or before six months from date; ten thousand dollars on or before one year from date, and ten thousand dollars or or before two years from date.

Forfeiture of Agreement to Convey.

Time is of the essence of this agreement, and if said payments or any of them be not made when due, then the parties of the first part reserve the right to declare this lease and agreement to convey forfeited, and thereupon to take possession of the said premises in the same manner as in other cases of forfeiture. In case of such forfeiture, any payments upon said purchase price theretofore made shall be deemed liquidated damages to be retained by the parties of the first part because of the failure of the second party to complete said purchase.

Notice of Forfeiture,— How given.

Notice of forfeiture may be given by mailing a copy of such notice addressed to the second party at the post office of Virginia City, Montana.

Royalties credited on purchase price in case of purchase.

In case of the ultimate purchase of said property under the option hereby given, payments of royalty theretofore made shall be considered as payments upon the final payment of said purchase price, and shall be credited thereon.

Payments into Bank.

Payments of royalty or upon said purchase price may be made by depositing the same to the credit of the parties of the first part in the Madison State Bank.

Deed in Escrow.

Pursuant to the terms of this agreement, the parties of the first part have executed a deed to said property to the party of the second part, and deposited the same in said Madison State Bank with instructions to the cashier of said bank to deliver the same to the party of the second part if the said second party shall make the payments above described and otherwise comply with the conditions of this agreement.

Provision against permanent waiver of conditions.

The conditions of this agreement shall be deemed continuing ones so that any waiver by the parties of the first part of their right to enforce a forfeiture on the occasion of any breach thereof shall not be construed as a waiver of their right to enforce a forfeiture on the occasion of any subsequent breach.

Agreement binds heirs, administrators and assigns. The terms of this agreement shall extend to and be binding upon the heirs, administrators and assigns of the parties hereto, and shall be interpreted in the same manner and with like effect as between the parties themselves.

In witness whereof, the parties of the first part have hereunto set their hands the day and year first above written.

SAMUEL M'CALL,
JAMES SIEVERS.

If a lease and option is non-transferable it should be so stated. Otherwise, in the silence of the instrument on the subject it may be assigned.

189. Mining Corporations and Partnerships.—It is not within the purpose of this book to give directions as to the formation of corporations. Any association of persons desiring to form a corporation should employ a lawyer to advise and act for them.

190. Partnerships.—Two or more persons acting as an unincorporated company constitute in law a partnership. Each partner is liable for all the partnership debts. For this reason wealthy partners associated with impecunious ones are at a disadvantage. The latter can incur indebtedness and throw the entire burden of paying it on their wealthy associates. Furthermore there is no such thing as the rule of the majority in a partnership. The minority cannot be coerced by greater numbers. Hence, where the persons interested in a mining venture are numerous or greatly unequal in financial mans, they cannot act efficiently as a partnership.

191. Corporations.—In the eyes of the law, a corporation is an artificial person. As such, it has a definite name and term of existence. It holds property, and buys and sells in much the same manner as a natural person. It can sue and be sued, and can be forced into bankruptcy when it becomes insolvent. If its property is not sufficient to pay its debts, its creditors cannot as a rule collect the residue of their claims from the stockholders.

An exception to this rule is where the stock has not been fully paid. Stockholders are liable to creditors of a corporation to the amount of the unpaid stock held by them. This liability attaches to the unpaid stock, and may be enforced against the holder even though he may not have been the original subscriber to the stock.

Corporations are managed by their board of directors. After stockholders have elected directors their participation in the management of the company as a rule ceases. A majority of the directors constitutes a quorum for the transaction of business, and the majority vote of those present and acting binds the corporation, and the thing so done is the act of the corporation.

192. Liability of Directors for Corporate Debts.—Directors, as such, have no more liability for the debts of the corporation than stockholders. The statutes of many states, however, require each domestic corporation to file an annual report. This is a duty imposed upon the directors, and in case of their failure to do so, the law inflicts the penalty of making them personally liable for all the existing debts of the corporation. Where such statutes exist the law should be carefully observed by the directors.

193. Tenants in Common of Mining Claim.—Where a mining claim is owned by two or more persons, they sustain the relation to each other of tenants in common, or co-owners. Co-owners are not partners unless they join in operating the mining property.

Before patent, a co-owner, delinquent in performing his part of the annual labor for any calendar year, or in paying for it when performed by other co-owners, may be made to forfeit his interest in the claim to the co-owners who have performed the work. (See paragraph 107.) But this process of forfeiture, or "advertising out," as it is often termed, must be done before patent issues, otherwise it cannot be done.

As a rule, each tenant in common has an equal right to occupy and use the common property. One cannot exclude the other without becoming liable to the latter for damages, and on the other hand one tenant in common, not desirous of operating the property, cannot prevent his co-tenant from doing so, provided the property is operated in a proper manner and without waste. The extraction of ore is not necessarily waste.

In Montana, however, prior to 1899, there was the following statute in force:

"If any person shall assume exclusive ownership over, or take away, destroy, lessen in value, or otherwise injure or abuse any property held in joint tenancy, or tenancy in common, the party aggrieved shall have his action for the injury in the same manner as he would have if such joint tenancy or tenancy in common did not exist" (73).

Under this section it was held by the supreme court of Montana that one tenant in common might enjoin another from extracting ore from a mine held in common. In 1899, the legislature of Montana amended the section by adding the following proviso:

"Provided: That nothing herein contained shall prevent one co-tenant or joint tenant, or any number of co-tenants or joint tenants acting together less than all, from entering on the common property at any points or points not then in the actual occupancy of the non-joining co-tenants or joint tenants and enjoying all rights of occupancy of the property, without waste; and in the case of mining property, from mining the same in a miner-like manner, and extracting,

(73) Code Civ. Pro., Sec. 592.

milling and disposing of the ore from the common property, paying its or their own expenses, and subject to accounting to the non-joining co-tenant or joint tenant for the net profits of such mining operations, if any made; and all liens for labor and materials incurred in such mining shall attach only to the undivided interest or interests of the working co-tenants or joint tenants, but nothing herein shall prevent or preclude the co-tenant or joint tenant, not joining in the operation of such mining property from receiving his, its, or their proportionate share of all ore or ores on the dump upon payment or tendering payment of the actual cost of mining the same" (74).

The supreme court of Montana has held that the amended law applies only to tenancies in common created after the enactment of the amendment (75).

193. Grub-Stake Agreements.—A grub-stake agreement is the term commonly applied to the contract between the prospector for mines and the person who furnishes him his outfit. A stake is the money or other thing hazarded in a game of chance, and a grub-stake is the food or other equipment hazarded in a prospecting venture. Usually the prospector and the person furnishing the grub-stake share in a proportion agreed upon in the ownership of each claim located as the result of the venture. Such an agreement does not constitute a partnership unless it extends beyond the mere furnishing of supplies in consideration of a participation in the discoveries (76).

Grub-stake agreements are universally upheld by the courts. They are not required to be in writing unless a statute of the state in which they are made requires it. Such statutes exist in Nevada and Oregon. In Nevada the agreement must be recorded with the recorder of the county where the agreement is made, and in Oregon with the recorder of the county where claims are located. Where it is necessary to record such an instrument, it should be acknowledged before a notary public or other officer authorized to take acknowledgements. But where no record is necessary, the acknowledgement is unnecessary.

The prospector cannot subsequently ignore the rights of the outfitter in such an agreement. They are tenants in common of all claims located during the period of the agreement. If the prospector locates in his own name alone, he holds in trust for the outfitter the share in the property belonging to the latter, and can be made to convey it by an appropriate action (77).

194. Form of Grub-Stake Agreement.—As with other agreements, the important thing is that a grub-stake agree-

(74) Laws 1899, p. 124.
(75) Butte and Boston Con. M. Co. vs. Montana O. P. Co., 24 Mont. 125.
(76) Costello vs. Scott, 93 Pac. 1.
(77) Meylette vs. Brennan, 20 Colo. 242; 38 Pac. 75.

ment should express fully and accurately the contract between the parties. The form of the instrument is immaterial. Two letters, one making a definite proposition and the other accepting it, constitute a binding contract. In important ventures of this kind, however, the help of a good lawyer should be secured.

A grub-stake agreement should be dated; it should name with certainty the parties, the prospector on the one part and the outfitter on the other; it should express a consideration, which is usually the furnishing of the outfit, of whatever it may consist. This may be an outfit complete at the time of the agreement, or it may be an outfit to be furnished from time to time, as needed, during a fixed period.

The prospector should be bound to use diligence in the search for mines and to employ whatever part of his entire time for that purpose that may have been agreed upon. The period during which the agreement shall remain in force should be expressed, and if the parties have agreed upon a certain territory or mining district where the prospecting is to be done, it should be named in the agreement.

195. Inspection of Adjoining Mine.—A court of equity has authority to grant a mine owner the privilege of inspecting the underground workings of an adjoining mine when he has reason to believe that his own mining rights are being infringed upon by the adjoining claimant. Statutes permitting such inspection exist in Colorado (78), and Montana (79). But courts of equity have such authority independent of statutory provisions (80).

Such an order for survey should designate the portion of the adjoining mine which is to be inspected, name with certainty the person or persons who shall be permitted to enter the mine under the order, and provide that the petitioner for the order shall pay all expense incurred by the defendant in giving the surveying party access to such mine (81).

(78) Mills' An. Stats., Sec. 3164.
(79) Code Civ. Pro., Sec. 1317.
(80) The Montana Co. vs. St. Louis Mg. Co., 152 U. S. 160; Lindley on Mines, Sec. 873.
(81) State ex rel. Heinze vs. District Court, 29 Mont. 105.

STATE AND TERRITORIAL MINING LAWS

ALASKA.

(Enacted by Congress.)

An act providing a civil government for Alaska.

Be it enacted by the Senate and House of Representatives of the United States of America in Congress assembled:

Sec. 8. That the said district of Alaska is hereby created a land district, and a United States land office for said district is hereby located at Sitka. The commissioner provided for by this act to reside at Sitka shall be ex-officio register of said land office, and the clerk provided for by this act shall be ex-officio receiver of public moneys, and the marshal provided for by this act shall be ex-officio surveyor general of said district and the laws of the United States relating to mining claims, and the rights incident thereto, shall, from and after the passage of this act, be in full force and effect in said district, under the administration thereof herein provided for, subject to such regulations as may be be made by the secretary of the interior, approved by the president: Provided, That the Indians or other persons in said district shall not be disturbed in the possession of any lands actually in their use or occupation or now claimed by them, but the terms under which such persons may acquire title to such lands is reserved for future legislation by congress: And provided further, That parties who have located mines or mineral privileges therein under the laws of the United States applicable to the public domain, or who have occupied and improved or exercised acts of ownership over such claims, shall not be disturbed therein, but shall be allowed to perfect their title to such claims by payment as aforesaid: And provided also, That the land not exceeding six hundred and forty acres at any station now occupied as missionary stations among the Indian tribes in said section, with the improvements thereon erected by or for such societies, shall be continued in the occupancy of the several religious societies to which said missionary stations respectively belong until action by congress. But nothing contained in this act shall be construed to put in force in said district the general land laws of the United States.—Act of May 17, 1884.

An act extending the homestead laws and providing for right of way for railroads in the District of Alaska, and for other purposes:

Sec. 13. That native-born citizens of the Dominion of Canada shall be accorded in said District of Alaska the same mining rights and privileges accorded to citizens of the

United States in British Columbia and the Northwest Territory by the laws of the Dominion of Canada or the local laws, rules, and regulations; but no greater rights shall be thus accorded than citizens of the United States or persons who have declared their intention to become such may enjoy in said District of Alaska; and the secretary of the interior shall from time to time promulgate and enforce rules and regulations to carry this provision into effect.—Act of May 14, 1898.

An act making further provisions for a civil government for Alaska, and for other purposes:

*   *   *   *   *   *   *   *

Sec. 15. The respective recorders shall, upon the payment of the fees for the same prescribed by the attorney general, record separately, in large and well-bound separate books, in fair hand:

First. Deeds, grants, transfers, contracts to sell or convey real estate and mortgages of real estate, releases of mortgages, powers of attorney, leases which have been acknowledged or proved, mortgages upon personal property;

*   *   *   *   *   *   *   *

Ninth. Affidavits of annual work done on mining claims;

Tenth. Notices of mining location and declaratory statements;

Eleventh. Such other writings as are required or permitted by law to be recorded, including the liens of mechanics, laborers, and others: Provided, Notices of location of mining claims shall be filed for record within ninety days from the date of the discovery of the claim described in the notice, and all instruments shall be recorded in the recording district in which the property or subject-matter affected by the instrument is situated, and where the property or subject-matter is not situated in any established recording district the instrument affecting the same shall be recorded in the office of the clerk of the division of the court having supervision over the recording division in which such property or subject-matter is situated.

*   *   *   *   *   *   *   *

*   *   *   Provided, Miners in any organized mining district may make rules and regulations governing the recording of notices of location of mining claims, water rights, flumes and ditches, mill sites and affidavits of labor, not in conflict with this act or the general laws of the United States; and nothing in this act shall be construed so as to prevent the miners in any regularly organized mining district not within any recording district established by the court from electing their own mining recorder to act as such until a recorder therefor is appointed by the court: Provided further, All records heretofore regularly made by the United States commissioner at Dyea, Skagway, and the recorder at Douglas City, not in conflict with any records regularly made with the United States commissioner at Juneau, are hereby legalized.

And all records heretofore made in good faith in any regularly organized mining district are hereby made public records, and the same shall be delivered to the recorder for the recording district including such mining district within six months from the passage of this act.

Sec. 26. The laws of the United States relating to mining claims, mineral locations, and rights incident thereto are hereby extended to the district of Alaska: Provided, That subject only to such general limitations as may be necessary to exempt navigation from artificial obstructions all land and shoal water between low and mean high tide on the shores, bays, and inlets of Bering Sea, within the jurisdiction of the United States, shall be subject to exploration and mining for gold and other precious metals by citizens of the United States, or persons who have legally declared their intentions to become such, under such reasonable rules and regulations as the miners in organized mining districts may have heretofore made or may hereafter make governing the temporary possession thereof for exploration and mining purposes until otherwise provided by law: Provided further, That the rules and regulations established by the miners shall not be in conflict with the mining laws of the United States; and no exclusive permits shall be granted by the secretary of war authorizing any person or persons, corporation, or company to excavate or mine under any of said waters below low tide, and if such exclusive permit has been granted it is hereby revoked and declared null and void; but citizens of the United States or persons who have legally declared their intention to become such shall have the right to dredge and mine for gold or other precious metals in said waters, below low tide, subject to such general rules and regulations as the secretary of war may prescribe for the preservation of order and the protection of the interests of commerce; such rules and regulations shall not, however, deprive miners on the beach of the right hereby given to dump tailings into or pump from the sea opposite their claims, except where such dumping would actually obstruct navigation; and the reservation of a roadway sixty feet wide, under the tenth section of the act of May fourteenth, eighteen hundred and ninety-eight, entitled "An act extending the homestead laws and providing for right of way for railroads in the district of Alaska, and for other purposes," shall not apply to mineral lands or town sites.—Act of June 6, 1900.

ARIZONA.

Sec. 3231 (Revised Statutes). Location—By Whom Made. —On the discovery of mineral in place on the public domain of the United States, the same may be located as a mining claim by the discoverer for himself, or for himself and others or for others.

Sec. 3232. Location—Contents of Location Notice.—Such location shall be made by erecting at or contiguous to the point of discovery a conspicuous monument of stones not less than three feet in height, or an upright post, securely fixed, projecting at least four feet above the ground, in which monument of stones or on which post there shall be posted a location notice, which shall be signed by the name or names of the locator or locators. The location notice must contain:

1. The name of the claim located.
2. The name or names of the locators.
3. The date of the location.
4. The length and width of the claim in feet, and the distance in feet from the point of discovery to each end of the claim.
5. The general course of the claim.
6. The locality of the claim with reference to some natural object or permanent monument whereby the claim can be identified.

Sec. 3233. Right Acquired—When.—Until each and all of the above specified things shall have been done, no right thereto shall have been acquired.

Sec. 3234. Ninety Days.—From the time of the location of a mining claim, as above specified, the locator shall be allowed ninety days within which to do or cause to be done the following things:

1. To cause to be recorded in the office of the county recorder of the county in which the claim is situated a copy of the location notice.
2. To sink a discovery shaft in the claim to a depth of at least ten feet from the lowest part of the rim of the shaft at the surface, and deeper, if necessary, until there is disclosed in said shaft mineral in place.
3. To monument the claim on the ground so that its boundaries can be readily traced.

Sec. 3235. Abandonment.—The failure to do all things enumerated in this section in the time and place specified shall be construed into an abandonment of the claim, and all right and claim thereto of the discoverer and locator shall be forfeited.

Sec. 3236. Boundaries—How Marked. — Such surface

boundaries shall be marked by six substantial posts projecting at least four feet above the surface of the ground, or by substantial stone monuments at least three feet high, to-wit: One at each corner of said claim and one at the center of each end line thereof.

Sec. 3237. Discovery Work.—Any open cut, adit or tunnel which shall be made as above provided for, as a part of the location of a lode mining claim, and which shall be equal in amount of work to a shaft ten feet deep and four feet wide by six feet long, and which shall cut a lode or mineral in place at a depth of ten feet from the surface, shall be equivalent, as a discovery work, to a shaft sunk from the surface.

Sec. 3238. Amendments.—Location notices may be amended at any time and the monuments changed to correspond with the amended location: Provided, That no change shall be made that will interfere with the rights of others.

Sec. 3239. Annual Work.—The amount of assessment or representation work or improvements to be done or made during each year, after the completion of the location, as heretofore provided, and the time for doing the same, shall be as provided by the laws of the United States.

Sec. 3240. Affidavit of Annual Labor.—Within three months after the expiration of the period of time fixed for the performance of annual labor or the making of improvements upon any mining claim, the person on whose behalf such work or improvement was made, or some person for him knowing the facts, may make and record in the office of the county recorder of the county wherein such claim is situated an affidavit in substance as follows:

TERRITORY OF ARIZONA,
    County of..............................., } ss.

...., being duly sworn, deposes and says that he is a citizen of the United States and more than twenty-one years of age, resides at..............................., in ....County, Arizona Territory, and is personally acquainted with the mining claim known as.......................mining claim, situated in...........................mining district, Arizona Territory, the location notice of which is recorded in the office of the county recorder of said county, in book.............of records of mines at page.................; that between the.................... day of...................., A. D...................., and the....................day of....................A. D...................., at least....................dollars' worth of work and improvements were done and performed upon said claim, not including the location work of said claim. Such work and improvements were made by and at the expense of..., owners of said claim, for the purpose of complying with the laws of the United States pertaining to assessments of annual work, and (here name the miners or men who worked upon the claim in doing the work) were the men employed by said owner, and who labored upon said claim, did said work and improvements, the same being as follows, to-wit:

(Here describe the work done.)

    (Signature)..

Subscribed and sworn to before me this.........................day of........................A. D................

My commission as Notary Public expires on the.................. day of.........................A. D................

(Notarial Seal.) ....Notary Public.

Sec. 3241. Proof of Annual Labor—Relocation.—Such affidavit, when so recorded, shall be prima facie evidence of the performance of such labor or the making of such improvements, and said original affidavit, after it has been recorded, or a certified copy thereof, or the record thereof, shall be received as evidence accordingly by the courts of this Territory. The location of an abandoned claim shall be made in accordance with the provisions of Paragraph 3232 (Sec. 2) of Title 47, Chapter XLVII of the Revised Statutes of Arizona, 1901, except that the relocator may, if he so elect, perform his location work by sinking the original location shaft ten feet deeper than it was originally, or in case the original location work consisted of a tunnel or open cut, he may perform his location work by extending said tunnel or open cut by removing therefrom 240 cubic feet of rock or vein material.

Sec. 3242. Placer Claims.—The locator of a placer mining claim shall locate his claim in the following manner: By posting a location notice thereon containing the name of the claim, the name of the locator or locators, the date of the location and the number of acres claimed, a description of the claim with reference to some natural object or permanent monument that will identify the claim by marking the boundaries of his claim with a post or monument of stones at each angle of the claim located. When a post is used it must be at least four inches by four feet six inches in length, set one foot in the ground and surrounded by a mound of stone or earth.

Sec. 3243. Witness Posts.—Where it is practically impossible on account of a bed of rock or precipitous ground to sink such posts, they may be placed in a pile of stones. And if for any reason it is impossible to erect and maintain a post or monument of stone at any angle of such claim, a witness post or monument may be used, said witness monument to be placed as near the true corner as the nature of the ground will permit. When a mound of stone is used it must be at least three feet in height and four feet in diameter at the base.

Sec. 3244. Recording Location Notice.—The locator of

any placer claim shall, within sixty days after the date of location of such claim, have a copy of the location notice claim recorded in the office of the county recorder of the county in which said claim may be situated. Any record of the location of a placer mining claim which shall not contain all the requirements of this section shall be void.

Sec. 3245. . Delinquent Co-Owners.—Whenever a co-owner or co-owners shall give to a delinquent co-owner or co-owners the notice in writing or notice by publication provided for in section twenty-three hundred and twenty-four (2324) of the Revised Statutes of the United States, an affidavit of the person giving such notice, stating the time, place, manner of service, and by whom and upon whom such service was made, shall be attached to a true copy of such notice, and such notice and affidavit must be recorded in the office of the county recorder of the county in which the mining claim is situate within ninety (90) days after giving the notice, or if such notice is given by publication in a newspaper there shall be attached to a printed copy of such notice an affidavit of the editor, publisher or foreman of such paper, stating the date of the first, last and each insertion of such notice therein, and when and where the newspaper was published during that time and the name of such newspaper. Such affidavit and notice shall be recorded as aforesaid within one hundred and eighty days after the first publication thereof.

Sec. 3246. Record of Forfeiture as Evidence.—The original of such notice and affidavits, or the records thereof, shall be evidence that the delinquent mentioned in section 2324 has failed or refused to contribute his proportion of the expenditure required by that section, and of the services or publication of said notice: Provided, The writing or affidavit hereinafter provided for is not of record.

Sec. 3247. Contribution by Delinquent.—If such delinquent shall, within the ninety days required by section 2324 aforesaid, contribute to his co-owner or co-owners his proportion of such expenditures, such co-owner or co-owners shall sign and deliver to the delinquent or delinquents, a writing, stating that the delinquent or delinquents, by name, has, within the time required by section 2324 of the Revised Statutes of the United States, contributed his share for the year ....upon the....................mine, and further stating therein the districts, county and Territory wherein the same is situate, and the book and page where the location notice is recorded. Such writing shall be recorded in the office of the county recorder of said county.

Sec. 3248. Penalty for Failure to Acknowledge Contribution.—If such co-owner or co-owners shall fail to sign and deliver such writing to the delinquent or delinquents within twenty days after such contribution, the co-owner or co-owners, so failing as aforesaid, shall be liable to a penalty of one hundred dollars, to be recovered by any person for the use of the delinquent or delinquents in any court of competent jurisdiction. If such co-owner or co-owners fail to deliver such writing within twenty days, then the delinquent, with two disinterested persons having personal knowledge of said contribution, may make an affidavit, setting forth in what manner, the amount of, to whom and upon what mine such contribution was made. Such affidavit, or a record thereof, in the office of the county recorder of the county in which said mine is situate, shall be prima facie evidence of such contribution.

Sec. 3249. Description of Claim.—In all actions, judgments, grants or conveyances it shall be a sufficient description of a mining claim if it can be intelligently learned therefrom the name of the claim, the district, county and territory where it is situate, and the book tnd page where the location notice thereof is recorded.

Sec. 3250. County Records.—The county recorders of the several counties are authorized and required to procure suitable books in which the records of all mines and mineral deposits shall be kept, which said books shall be paid for out of the county treasury.

Sec. 3251. Prior Locations.—Nothing in this act shall be so construed as to affect the claims to mines and mineral deposits heretofore located and duly recorded.

Sec. 3252. Drainage.—Whenever adjacent or contiguous mines occupied and worked upon the same or upon separate lodes have a common ingress of water, or by reason of subterranean communication of water have a common drainage, it shall be the duty of the owners, lessees or occupants of said mines so related to provide for their proportionate share of such drainage, or to prevent the water in such mine from flowing in or upon neighboring mines, thereby imposing upon them an unjust burden.

Sec. 3253. Failure to Drain.—If any owners, lessees or occupants of any such mine shall fail or neglect to provide for the drainage thereof, and by reason of such failure or neglect, the owners, lessees or occupants of any adjacent or contiguous mine are compelled to pump or drain or otherwise provide for the water flowing in from such first mentioned mine, then, and in such event the owners, lessees or occupants of the mine so in default, shall pay, respectively, to those performing the work of drainage their proportion of the actual and necessary cost and expense of pumping, draining or otherwise providing for said water, and if they fail or refuse to make such payment, the same may be recovered by an action in any court of competent jurisdiction

Sec. 3254. Common Interest in Draining.—It shall be lawful for all mining corporations or companies and all individuals engaged in mining having thus a common interest in draining such mines to unite for the purpose of effecting the same under such common name and upon such terms and conditions as may be agreed upon; and every such association having filed a certificate of incorporation, as provided by law, shall be deemed a corporation, with all the rights, incidents and liabilities of a body corporate as far as the same may be applicable.

3255. Failure of Mutual Agreement.—Failing mutually to agree as indicated in the preceding section for drainage jointly, one or more of said parties may undertake the work of drainage after giving reasonable notice to the other parties interested as aforesaid, and should the remaining parties then fail, neglect or refuse to unite in equitable arrangements for doing or sharing the expense thereof, they shall be subject to an action therefor as already specified, to be enforced in any court of competent jurisdiction.

3256. Inspection of Mines Drained.—When an action is commenced, as provided herein, to recover the costs and expenses for draining a lode or mine, it shall be lawful for the plaintiff to apply to court or to the judge thereof in vacation, for an order to inspect and examine the lodes or mines claimed to have been drained by the plaintiff, and upon affidavit that such inspection or examination is necessary for a proper preparation of the case for trial, the court or judge shall grant an order for the underground inspection and examination of the lode or mine described in the petition. Such order shall designate the number of persons, not exceeding three, besides the plaintiff or his representative, who may examine and inspect such lode and mines, and take measurements for the purpose of showing the amount of water taken from the lode or mine, or the number of fathoms of ground mined and worked out of the lode or mines claimed to have been drained, the cost of such examination and inspection to be borne by the party applying therefor. The court or judge shall have power to cause the removal of any rock, debris or any other obstacle in any lode or vein when such removal is shown to be necessary to a just determination of the question involved: Provided, that no such order for inspection and examination shall be made except upon notice of at least three days, nor unless it appears that the plaintiff has been refused the privilege of making the examination by the defendant his or their agent.

3257. Undeveloped Mines.—The provisions hereof shall not apply to unopened or undeveloped mines, but shall apply to all open and developed mines which derive a benefit from being drained.

3258. Charge for Assays.—The Regents of the University

of Arizona shall charge for assaying ores taken from deposits and mines within the Territory of Arizona no higher rate than one dollar for each assay producing gold and silver, and two dollars for assays producing gold, silver and copper, and two dollars and fifty cents for assaying ores showing more than three metals; that the maximum rate for an assay shall be two dollars and fifty cents and the minimum rate for an assay shall be one dollar.

3259. Fee of County Recorder.—There shall be a uniform fee of one dollar charged by each county recorder in the Territory of Arizona for recording each notice of location of a mining claim, including certificate of work done to comply with the law regarding locations, the said one dollar to be in full for filing, recording and indexing said notice and certificate and certifying to the same under seal.

From the Revised Statutes of 1901.

CALIFORNIA.

Sec. 1. Affidavit of Expenditure.—Whenever any mine owner, company, or corporation shall have performed the labor and made the improvements required by law for the location and ownership of mining claims or lodes, such owner, company or corporation shall file, or cause to be filed, within thirty days after the time limited for performing such labor or making such improvements, with the county recorder of deeds of the county in which the mine or claim is situated, particularly describing the labor performed and improvements made, and the value thereof, which affidavit shall be prima facie evidence of the facts therein stated. Upon the failure of any claimant or mine owner to comply with the conditions of this act, in the performance of labor, or making of improvements upon any claim, mine or mining ground, the claim or mine upon which such failure occurred shall be opened to relocation in the same manner as if no location of the same had ever been made. But if, previous to relocation, the original locators, their heirs, assigns, or legal representatives, resume work upon such claim, and continue the same with reasonable diligence until the required amount of labor has been performed or improvements made, and the required statement of accounts and affidavit filed with the county recorder, then the claim shall not be subject to relocation because of previous failure to file accounts. Upon the failure of any one of the several co-owners to contribute his portion of the expenditures required hereby, the co-owners who have performed the labor or made the improvements may, at the expiration of the year, give such delinquent co-owners personal notice, in writing, or by publication in the newspaper published nearest the claim, for at least once a week for ninety days; and if, at the expiration of ninety days after such notice in writing or publication, such delinquent shall fail or refuse to contribute his portion of the expenditures required by this section, his interest in the claim shall become the property of his co-owners who made the required expenditures. A copy of such notice, together with an affidavit showing personal service or publication, as the case may be, of such notice, when filed or recorded with the recorder of deeds of the county in which such mining claim is situated, shall be evidence of the acquisition of title of such co-owners. Where a person or company has or may run a tunnel or cut for the purpose and in good faith for the purpose of developing a lode, lodes, or claims owned by said person, or company, or corporation, the money so expended in running said tunnel shall be taken and considered as expended on said lodes or claims; provided further, that said lode, claim or claims shall be distinctly marked on the surface as provided by law.

Sec. 2. Right of Way.—All mining locations and mining

claims shall be subject to a reservation of the right of way through or over any mining claims, ditches, roads, canals, cuts, tunnels, and other easements, for the purpose of working other mines; provided, that any damage occasioned thereby shall be assessed and paid for in the manner provided by law for land taken for public use under the right of eminent domain.—Act of March 31, 1891.

1159, Civil Code. Judgments affecting the title to or possession of real property, authenticated by the certificate of the clerk of the court in which such judgments were rendered (and notices of location of mining claims), may be recorded without acknowledgment, certificate of acknowledgment, or further proof. The record of all notices of location of mining claims heretofore made in the proper office without acknowledgment or certificate of acknowledgment, or other proof, shall have the same force and effect for all purposes as if the same had been duly acknowledged, or proved and certified as required by law. Affidavits showing work or posting of notices upon mining claims may also be recorded in the recorder's office of the county where such mining claims are situated.

Approved March 9, 1897. Session Laws 1897, p. 97.

COLORADO.

3139 (Mills' Annotated Statutes). Conditions Under Which a Person May Mine Under Buildings.—No person shall have the right to mine under any building or other improvement unless he shall first secure the parties owning the same against all damages except by priority of right.

3140. Tunnel Claim Must Be Recorded—What Specified. —If any person or persons shall locate a tunnel claim for the purpose of discovery, he shall record the same, specifying the place of commencement and termination thereof, with the names of the parties interested therein.

3141. Tunnel—Two Hundred and Fifty Feet on Each Side; Proviso; Claims; Right of Way.—Any person or persons engaged in working a tunnel, within the provisions of this chapter, shall be entitled to two hundred and fifty feet each way from said tunnel, on each lode so discovered: Provided, They do not interfere with any vested rights. If it shall appear that claims have been staked off and recorded prior to the record of said tunnel, on the line thereof, so that the required number of feet cannot be taken near said tunnel, they may be taken upon any part thereof where the same may be found vacant; and persons working said tunnel shall have the right of way through all lodes which may lie in its course.

3142. Lodes Crossing; Uniting; Rights of Parties.—When it shall appear that one lode crosses, runs into or united with any other lode, the priority of record shall determine the rights of claimants: Provided, That in no case where it appears that two lodes have crossed one another, shall the priority of record give any person the privilege of turning off from the crevice or lode which continues in the same direction of the main lode upon which he or they may have recorded their claim or claims, but such person or persons shall, at all times, follow the crevice running nearest in the general direction of the main lode upon which he or they may have recorded their claim or claims.

3143. Two Lodes Found to Be the Same—Priority.—Where two crevices are discovered at a distance from each other, and known by different names, and it shall appear that the two are one and the same lode, the persons having recorded on the first discovered lode shall be the legal owners.

3144. Flooding; Washing Down Tailings; Liability.—In no case shall any person or persons be allowed to flood the property of another person with water, or wash down the tailings of his or their sluice upon the claim or property of other persons, but it shall be the duty of every miner to take care of his own tailings, upon his own property, or become responsible for all damages that may arise therefrom.

3145. Right of Way for Hauling Quartz.—Every miner shall have the right of way across any and all claims for the purpose of hauling quartz from his claim.

3146. Claims of Enlisted Men; Limitation; Forfeit.—All claims taken up and recorded by persons who have since the recording of the same enlisted in the army of the United States, or the volunteer force of this state, shall be deemed and held as real estate for the period of two years from the expiration of their term of enlistment or discharge from service; after which time, if not represented by the said soldier or soldiers, all such claims shall be forfeited to any person who may take up the same.

3147. Records.—A copy of all the records, laws and proceedings of each mining district, so far (as) they relate to lode claims, shall be filed in the office of the county clerk of the county in which the district is situated, within the boundaries of the district attached to the same, which shall be taken as evidence in any court having jurisdiction in the matters concerned in such record or proceeding; and all such records of deeds and conveyances, laws and proceedings of any mining district heretofore filed in the clerk's office of the proper county, and transcripts thereof duly certified, whether such records relate to gulch claims, lode claims, building lots, or other real estate, shall have the like effect as evidence.

3148. Length.—The length of any lode claim hereafter located may equal but not exceed fifteen hundred feet along the vein.

3149. Width.—The width of lode claims hereafter located in Gilpin, Clear Creek, Boulder, and Summit counties shall be seventy-five feet on each side of the center of the vein or crevice; and in all other counties the width of the same shall be one hundred and fifty feet on each side of the center of the vein or crevice: Provided, That hereafter any county may, at any general election, determine upon a greater width, not exceeding three hundred feet on each side of the center of the vein or lode, by a majority of the legal votes cast at said election, and any county, by such vote at such election, may determine upon a less width than above specified.

3150. Location Certificate.—The discoverer of a lode shall, within three months from the date of discovery, record his within three months from the date of discovery, record his claim in the office of the recorder of the county in which such lode is situated, by a location certificate, which shall contain: 1st, the name of the lode; 2d, the name of the locator; 3d, the date of location; 4th, the number of feet in length claimed on each side of the center of the discovery shaft; 5th, the general course of the lode as near as may be.

3151. Any location certificate of a lode claim which shall not contain the name of the lode, the name of the locator, the date of location, the number of lineal feet claimed on each side of the discovery shaft, the general course of the lode, and such description as shall identify the claim with reasonable certainty, shall be void.

3152. Discovery Shaft and Staking.—Before filing such location certificate, the discoverer shall locate his claim by first sinking a discovery shaft upon the lode, to the depth of at least ten feet from the lowest part of the rim of such shaft at the surface, or deeper, if necessary, to show a well defined crevice; second, by posting at the point of discovery on the surface a plain sign or notice containing the name of the lode, the name of the locator and the date of discovery; third, by marking the surface boundaries of the claim.

3153. Such surface boundaries shall be marked by six substantial posts, hewed or marked on the side or sides which are in toward the claim, and sunk in the ground, to-wit: One at each corner and one at the center of each side line. Where it is practically impossible on account of bedrock or precipitous ground to sink such posts, they may be placed in a pile of stones.

3154. Equivalent to a Discovery Shaft.—Any open cut, crosscut, or tunnel, which shall cut a lode at the depth of ten feet below the surface, shall hold such lode the same as if a discovery shaft were sunk thereon, or an adit of at least ten feet in along the lode, from the point where the lode may be in any manner discovered, shall be equivalent to a discovery shaft.

3155. Sixty Days.—The discoverer shall have sixty days from the time of uncovering or disclosing a lode to sink a discovery shaft thereon.

3156. Claim Defined by the Surface Lines.—The location, or location certificate, of any lode claim shall be construed to include all surface ground within the surface lines thereof, and all lodes and ledges throughout their entire depth, the top or apex of which lies inside of such lines extended downward, vertically, with such parts of all lodes or ledges as continue to dip beyond the side lines of the claim, but shall not include any portion of such lodes or ledges beyond the end lines of the claim or the end lines continued, whether by dip or otherwise, or beyond the side lines in any other manner than by the dip of the lode.

3157. Vein May Not Be Followed on Strike.—If the top or apex of a lode in its longitudinal course extends beyond the exterior lines of the claim at any point on the surface, or as extended vertically downward, such lode may not be followed in its longitudinal course beyond the point where it is intersected by the exterior lines.

3158. Right of Way and Right of Surface.—All mining claims now located, or which may be hereafter located, shall be subject to the right of way of any ditch or flume for mining purposes, or of any tramway or pack trail, whether now in use, or which may be hereafter laid out across any such location: Provided, always, That such right of way shall not be exercised against any location duly made and recorded, and not abandoned prior to the establishment of the ditch, flume, tramway, or pack trail, without consent of the owner, except by condemnation, as in case of land taken for public highways. Parol consent to the location of any such easement, accompanied by the completion of the same over the claim, shall be sufficient without writings: And provided further, That such ditch or flume shall be so constructed that the water from such ditch or flume shall not injure vested rights by flooding or otherwise.

3159. Security to Owner of Surface.—When the right to mine is in any case separate from the ownership or right of occupancy to the surface, the owner or rightful occupant of the surface may demand satisfactory security from the miner, and if it be refused, may enjoin such miner from working until such security is given. The order for injunction shall fix the amount of bond.

3160. Relocation by the Owner.—If at any time the locator of any mining claim heretofore or hereafter located, or his assigns, shall apprehend that his original certificate was defective, erroneous, or that the requirements of the law had not been complied with before filing; or shall be desirous of changing his surface boundaries, or of taking in any part of an overlapping claim which has been abandoned; or in case the original certificate was made prior to the passage of this law, and he shall be desirous of securing the benefits of this act, such locator or his assigns may file an additional certificate, subject to the provisions of this act: Provided, That such relocation does not interfere with the existing rights of others at the time of such relocation, and no such relocation or the record thereof shall preclude the claimant or claimants from proving any such titles as he or they may have held under previous location.

3161. Affidavit of Improvement; Form; Prima Facie Evidence.—Within six months after any set time or annual period allowed for the performance of labor or making improvements upon any lode claim or placer claim, the person on whose behalf such outlay was made, or some person for him, may make and record in the office of the recorder of the county wherein such claim is situate, an affidavit in substance as follows:

STATE OF COLORADO, } ss.
...........................County,

Before me, the subscriber, personally appeared...................

............................, who, being duly sworn, saith that at least
..................................dollars' worth of work or improvements
were performed or made upon (here describe claim or part
of claim), situate in............................mining district, County
of........................., State of Colorado, between the.....................
day of.........................A. D. ...., and the....................day
of........................A. D. .... Such expenditure was
made by or at the expense of...,
owners of said claim, for the purpose of complying with the
law, and holding said claim.

Jurat: (Signature)..

And such affidavit when so recorded shall be prima facie
evidence of the performance of such labor or the making of
such improvements: Provided, That all affidavits of labor
or improvements upon placer claims heretofore filed and recorded within the period prescribed in this section, or within
the period prescribed in section twenty-four hundred and ten
of the general statutes, which shall contain in substance the
requirements of the affidavit prescribed by this section or said
section twenty-four hundred and ten, shall be prima facie
evidence of the performance of such labor or the making of
such improvements; and the original thereof, or a certified
copy of the record of the same, shall be received as evidence
accordingly by the courts of this state, and this class of evidence shall be receivable, where relevant or material, in all
cases, whether now pending or hereafter brought.

3162. Relocation of Abandoned Claims.—The relocation
of abandoned lode claims shall be by sinking a new discovery
shaft and fixing new boundaries in the same manner as if it
were the location of a new claim; or the relocator may sink
the original discovery shaft ten feet deeper than it was at the
time of abandonment, and erect new, or adopt the old boundaries, renewing the posts, if removed or destroyed. In either
case a new location stake shall be erected. In any case,
whether the whole or part of an abandoned claim is taken,
the location certificate may state that the whole or any part
of the new location is located as abandoned property.

3163. One Record for Each Claim.—No location certificate
shall claim more than one location, whether the location be
made by one or several locators. And if it purport to claim
more than one location, it shall be absolutely void, except as
to the first location therein described. And if they are described together, or so that it cannot be told which location
is first described, the certificate shall be void as to all.

3164. Right of Survey and Inspection.—In all actions pending in any district court of this Territory, wherein the title
or right of possession to any mining claim shall be in dispute,
the said court, or the judge thereof, may, upon the application
of any of the parties to such suit, enter an order for the under-

ground as well as surface survey of such part of the property in dispute as may be necessary to a just determination of the question involved. Such order shall designate some competent surveyor, not related to any of the parties to such suit, nor in anywise interested in the result of the same; and upon the application of the party adverse to such application, the court may also appoint some competent surveyor, to be selected by such adverse applicant, whose duty it shall be to attend upon such survey, and observe the method of making the same; said second survey to be at the cost of the party asking therefor. It shall also be lawful in such order to specify the names of witnesses named by either party, not exceeding three on each side, to examine such property, who shall hereupon be allowed to enter into such property and examine the same; said court, or the judge thereof, may also cause the removal of any rock, debris, or other obstacle in any of the drifts or shafts of said property, when such removal is shown to be necessary to a just determination of the questions involved: Provided, however, that no such order shall be made for survey and inspection, except in open court or in chambers, upon notice of application for such order of at least six days, and not then except by agreement of parties, or upon the affidavit of two or more persons that such survey and inspection is necessary to the just determination of the suit, which affidavits shall state the facts in such case, and wherein the necessity for survey exists; nor shall such order be made unless it appears that the party asking therefor had been refused the privilege of survey and inspection by the adverse party.

3165. **Unlawful Entry.**—In all cases where 'two or more persons shall associate themselves together for the purpose of obtaining the possession of any lode, gulch, or placer claim, then in the actual possession of another, by force and violence, or threats of violence, or by stealth, and shall proceed to carry out such purpose by making threats against the party or parties in possession, or who shall enter upon such lode or mining claim for the purpose aforesaid, or who shall enter upon or into any lode, gulch, placer claim, quartz mill, or other mining property, or not being upon such property, but within hearing of the same, shall make any threats, or make use of any language, signs, or gestures, calculated to intimidate any person or persons at work on said property from continuing to work thereon or therein, or to intimidate others from engaging to work thereon or therein, every such person so offending, shall, on conviction thereof, be fined in a sum not to exceed two hundred and fifty dollars, and be imprisoned in the county jail not less than thirty days nor more than six months; such fine to be discharged either by payment or by confinement in said jail until such fine is discharged at the rate of two dollars and fifty cents ($2.50) per day. On trials under this section, proof of a common purpose of two or more persons to obtain possession of property as aforesaid, or to intimidate laborers as above set forth, accmpanied or followed by any of the acts above specified by any of them, shall be sufficient evidence to convict any one committing such acts, although the parties may not be associated together at the time of committing thesame.

3166. Guilty of Murder.—If any person or persons shall associate and agree to enter or attempt to enter by force of numbers and the terror such numbers are calculated to inspire; or by force and violence, or by threats of violence against any person or persons in the actual possession of any lode, gulch, or placer claim; and upon such entry or attempted entry, any person or persons shall be killed, said persons, and all and each of them so entering or attempting to enter, shall be deemed guilty of murder in the first degree, and punished accordingly. Upon the trials of such cases, any person or parties cognizant of such entry, or attempted entry, who shall be present, aiding, assisting, or in anywise encouraging such entry, or attempted entry, shall be deemed a principal in the commission of said offense.

3172. Proportionate Share.—Whenever contiguous and adjacent mines upon the same or upon separate lodes have a common ingress of water, or from subterranean communication of the water have a common drainage, it shall be the duty of the owners, lessees, or occupants of each mine so related to provide for their proportionate share of the drainage thereof.

3173. Failure to Drain.—Any parties so related, failing to provide, as aforesaid, for the drainage of the mines owned or occupied by them, thereby imposing an unjust burden upon neighboring mines whether owned or occupied by them, shall pay respectively to those performing the work of drainage, their proportion of the actual and necessary cost and expense of doing such drainage, to be recovered by an action in any court of competent jurisdiction.

3174. Draining Corporation.—It shall be lawful for all mining corporations or companies, and all individuals engaged in mining, having thus a common interest in draining such mines, to unite for the purpose of effecting the same, under such common name and upon such terms and conditions as may be agreed upon; and every such association, having filed a certificate of incorporation, as provided by law, shall be deemed a corporation, with all the rights, incidents, and liabilities of a body corporate, so far as the same may be applicable.

3175. Failure to Mutually Agree.—Failing to mutually agree, as indicated in the preceding section, for drainage jointly, one or more of the said parties may undertake the work of drainage,after giving reasonable notice; and should the remaining parties then fail, neglect or refuse to unite in equitable arrangements for doing the work, or sharing the expense thereof, they shall be subject to an action therefor as already specified, to be enforced in any court of competent jurisdiction.

3176. Court Proceedings.—When action is commenced to recover the cost and expenses for draining a lode or mine, it shall be lawful for the plaintiff to apply to the court, if in session, or to the judge thereof in vacation, for an order to inspect or examine the lodes or mines claimed to have been drained by the plaintiff; or some one for him, shall make affidavit that such inspection or examination is necessary for a proper preparation of the case for trial. The court or judge shall grant an order for the underground inspection and examination of the lode or mines described in the petition. Such order shall designate the number of persons, not exceeding three besides the plaintiff or his representative, to examine and inspect such lode and mines, and take the measurement thereof, relating the amount of water drained from the lode or mine, or the number of fathoms of ground mined and worked out of the lode or mines claimed to have been drained, the cost of such examination and inspection to be borne by the party applying therefor. The court or judge shall have power to cause the removal of any rock, debris, or other obstacles in any lode or vein, when such removal is shown to be necessary to a just determination of the question involved: Provided, that no such order for inspection and examination shall be made except in open court, or at chambers, upon notice of application for such order of at least three days, and not then except by agreement of parties, nor unless it appears that the plaintiff has been refused the privilege of making the inspection and examination by the defendant, his or their agent.

3177. Water Beyond Control.—That hereafter, when any person or persons, or corporation, shall be engaged in mining or milling, and in the prosecution of such business shall hoist or raise water from the mines or natural channels, and the same shall flow away from the premises of such persons, or corporations, to any natural channel or gulch, the same shall be considered beyond the control of the party so hoisting or raising the same, and may be taken and used by other parties the same as that of natural water courses.

3178. Liable for Injury.—After any such water shall have been so raised, and the same shall have flown into any such natural channel, gulch, or draw, the party so hoisting or raising the same shall only be liable for injury caused thereby, in the same manner as riparian owners along natural water courses.

3179. Undeveloped Mines.—The provisions of this act

shall not be construed to apply to incipient or undeveloped mines, but to those which shall have been opened, and shall clearly derive a benefit from being drained.

3180. **Admissible Evidence.**—In trial of cases arising under this act, the court shall admit evidence of the normal stand, or position of the water while at rest in an idle mine, also the observed prevalence of a common water level, or a standing water line in the same, or separate lodes; also, the effect (if any) the elevating or depressing the water by natural or mechanical means in any given lode, has upon elevating or depressing the water in the same, contiguous, or separate lodes or mines; also, the effect which draining or ceasing to drain any given lode or mine had upon the water in the same or contiguous or separate lodes or mines, and all other evidence which tends to prove the common ingress or subterraneous communication of water into the same lode or mine, or contiguous or separate lodes or mines.

IDAHO.

Locating Claims.—Sec. 1.   That section 3100 of the Revised .
Statutes of Idaho be amended to read as follows:

Sec. 3100.   Mining claims hereafter located upon veins or
lodes of quartz, or other rock in place bearing any of the
metals or other valuable deposits mentioned in section 2320
of the Revised Statutes of the United States, may extend to
three hundred feet on each side of the middle of the vein or
lode: Provided, That when the locators have set stakes,
posts or monuments described in section 2 hereof, to indicate
the line of the vein, ledge or lode, such stakes, posts or monuments must be taken for the purpose of such location, to
mark correctly the line thereof, and such line must not afterwards be changed so as to affect rights acquired or interfere
with any locations made subsequent thereto.

Sec. 2.   Section 3101 of the Revised Statutes of Idaho be
amended to read as follows:

Sec. 3101.   The locator, at the time of making the discovery
of such vein or lode, must erect a monument at such place of
discovery, upon which he must place his name, the name of
the claim, the date of discovery and distance claimed along
the vein each way from such monument.   Within ten days
from the date of discovery, he must mark the boundaries of
his claim by establishing at each corner thereof, and at any
angle in the side lines, a monument, marked with the name
of the claim and the corner or angle it represents;   also at
the time of so marking his boundaries, he must post at his
discovery monument his notice of location in which must be
stated:

First.   The name of the locator.

Second.   The name of the claim.

Third.   The date of discovery.

Fourth.   The direction and distance claimed along the
ledge from the discovery.

Fifth.   The distance claimed on each side of the middle
of the ledge.

Sixth.   The distance and direction from the discovery monument, to such natural object or permanent monument, if
any such there be, as will fix and describe in the notice itself,
the location of the claim;   and

Seventh.   The name of the mining district, county and
state.

When from any cause a monument cannot be safely planted
at the true corner or angle, it may be placed as near thereto
as practicable, and so marked as to indicate the place of such
corner or angle.

Monuments may be made of any such material or form as
will readily give notice, and when of posts or trees, they must
be hewn and marked upon the side facing toward the discov-

ery, and must be at least four inches square or in diameter. Monuments must be at least four feet high above the ground, and trees must be so hewn as to readily attract attention. At the time the locator so marks the boundaries of his claim, he may do so in any direction that will not interfere with rights or claims which existed prior to his discovery.

Sec. 3. Within sixty days after such location, the locator or his assigns must sink a shaft upon the lode to the depth of at least ten feet from the lowest part of the rim of such shaft at the surface. And of not less than sixteen square feet area. Any excavation which shall cut such vein ten feet from the lowest part of the rim of such shaft and which shall measure one hundred and sixty cubic feet in extent shall be considered a compliance with this provision. Any located claim upon which work has been done in compliance with the above requirements is not, unless abandoned, subject to relocation for a period of ninety days from and after the date of location.

Sec. 4. Within ninety days after the location of the claim the locator or his assigns must file for record in the office of the county recorder of the county or of the deputy recorder of the mining district in which the claim is situated, a substantial copy of his notice of location.

Sec. 5. If at any time the locator of any mining claim heretofore or hereafter located, or his assigns, shall apprehend that his original certificate was defective, erroneous, or that the requirements of the law had not been complied with before filing, or shall be desirous of changing the surface boundaries, or of taking any part of an overlapping claim which has been abandoned, or in case the original certificate was made prior to the passage of this law, and he shall be desirous of securing the benefits of this act, such locator or his assigns may file an additional certificate subject to the conditions of this act and to contain all that this act required an original certificate to contain: Provided, That such amended location does not interfere with the existing rights of others at the time when such amendment is made.

Sec. 6. Within sixty days after any time set or period allowed for the performance of labor, or making improvements upon any lode, or placer claim, the person in whose behalf such work or improvement is performed, or some person for him must make and record an affidavit in substance as follows:

County of.........................., State of Idaho—ss.

Before me the subscribed personally appeared........................, who being first duly sworn says that at least........................dollars' worth of work for improvements were performed or made upon........................claim, situate in........................mining district, county of........................, State of Idaho: That such expenditure was made by, for, or at the expense of ...., owner of said claim, for the purpose of holding said claim, and all stakes, monuments or trees marking boundaries of said claims are in proper place and positions.

....

Subscribed and sworn to before me this..........................day of.., 190.........

The fee for administering the oath and recording the foregoing affidavit, when taken before the county recorder or deputy mining recorder, shall be fifty cents; the fee for recording the same when the oath is taken before any other officer authorized to administer oaths shall be fifty cents. Such affidavit, or a certified copy thereof in case the original is lost, shall be prima facie evidence of the performance of such labor. The failure to file such affidavit shall be considered prima facie evidence that such labor has not been done.

Sec. 7. The location of abandoned claims shall be done in the same manner as if the location were of a new claim; but the locator may, instead of sinking a new discovery shaft, sink the original discovery shaft ten feet deeper than it was at the time of his location, or he may drive the open cut, or tunnel ten feet further along the course of the lead, lode or vein, and must erect new posts or monuments.

Sec. 8. No location notice shall claim more than one location, whether the location is made by one or several locators, and if it purport to claim more than one location it is absolutely void.

Sec. 9. That section 3103 of the Revised Statutes of Idaho is hereby amended to read as follows:

Sec. 3103. For the convenience of prospectors and locators, the county recorder of the several counties must appoint a deputy at any place where he may deem it necessary, and at all places more than twenty miles distant from an existing office whenever ten or more mining locators interested petition for the appointment of a deputy. Upon failure of any recorder to appoint a deputy for ten days after the petition in writing has been presented to him, the resident miners in such district may appoint temporarily one of their number to act as the recorder for the district, whose record shall be as valid as if made by the deputy, and must be entered by the recorder as hereinafter required: Provided, That whenever at any time afterwards the recorder has appointed a deputy for such district or place, the authority of the person elected by the resident miners ceases.

Sec. 10. When the right to mine is in any case separate from the ownership or right of occupancy of the surface ground, the owners or rightful occupants of the surface ground may demand satisfactory security from the miners, and if it be refused or not given, may enjoin such miners from working such ground until such security is given. The court granting the writ of injunction shall fix the amount and nature of the security.

Sec. 11. Placer claims, as mentioned in section 2329 of the Revised Statutes of the United States may be located for the purpose of mining deposits and precious stones after the discovery of such deposits.

Sec. 12. The locator of any placer mining claim located for the purpose of mining placer deposits or precious stones must at the time of making the location place a substantial post or monument as is required in the location of quartz claims at each corner of the location, and must also post on one of the same a notice of location containing the date of the location, the name of the locator, the name and dimensions of the claim, the mining district (if any) and county in which the same is situated; and must also give the distance and direction from said post or monument to such natural object or permanent monument, if any such there be, as will fix and describe in the notice itself, the location of the claim. Within fifteen days after making the location, the locator must make an excavation upon the claim of not less than one hundred cubic feet, for the purpose of prospecting the same. Within thirty days after the location, the locator must file for record in the office of the county recorder of the county, or of the deputy recorder of the mining district in which the claim is situated, a substantial copy of his copy of notice of location, to which must be attached an affidavit such as is required in the case of quartz claims.

Sec. 13. That section 3104 of the Revised Statutes of Idaho be amended to read as follows:

Sec. 3104. At or before the time of presenting a location notice for record, whether it be for a quartz or placer claim, one of the locators named in the same must make and subscribe an affidavit in writing, on or attached to the notice, substantially in the following form, to-wit:

State of Idaho, County of..................................—ss.

I, ..., do solemnly swear that I am a citizen of the United States of America (or have declared my intentions to become such), and that I am acquainted with the mining ground described in this notice of location, and herewith called the..................................ledge, lode or claim; that the ground and claim therein described or any part thereof has not, to the best of my knowledge and belief, been located according to the laws of the United States and of this state, or if so located, that the same has been abandoned or forfeited by the reason of the failure of such former locators to comply in respect thereto with the requirements of said laws, and (in case of quartz claims) that I have opened new ground to the extent or depth of ten feet, as required by the laws of Idaho.

(Signature)..

Subscribed and sworn to before me this.........................day of...................A. D. 189.......

(Signature)..

Sec. 14. That section 3105 of the Revised Statutes of Idaho is amended so as to read as follows, to-wit:

Sec. 3105. The location notice herein required to be recorded must be recorded by the deputy appointed for the district, or the person appointed for that purpose as above provided (when the legal fee therefor is tendered) in a book to be kept for that purpose. Said book must be indexed, with the names of all the locators arranged in alphabetical order, according to the family or surname of each. The fee to be tendered for making such record, administering the oath to the locator and certifying the same, for indexing the names appearing on the notice, and to include recording the notice by the recorder as hereinafter required, and the indexing by said recorder, is two dollars, which fee must be equally divided between the recorder and the deputy or the person acting under an election as hereinbefore provided, and no other additional sum of money must be demanded or received by either of them for any services connected with the recording of any location notice made pursuant to the requirements of this chapter.

Mining Tunnels.—Sec. 1.   Any person or company who has or may hereafter have a tunnel or crosscut, the mouth of which is located upon his own ground or upon ground in his lawful occupation, shall have the right to drive and continue the same through and across any located or patented claim in front of the mouth of such tunnel, but not to follow or drive upon any vein belonging to the owner of such claim.

Sec. 2.   Each tunnel or crosscut may be driven and worked for the purpose of drainage and for the purpose of reaching and working mining ground of the tunnel owner beyond the intersected claim.   The owner or owners of any vein or any claim or claims so intersected, or his duly authorized agent, shall have the right to enter such tunnel upon application to the owner or owners or person in charge of said tunnel, without resorting to any process of law for the purpose of making a survey and inspecting such vein or veins as may be crossed within the boundary lines of such intersected claim, and if the owner or owners of such tunnel shall, by bulkheading, damming back or in any manner prevent the inspection or survey herein provided for, or if such owner or owners shall in any manner prevent the natural drainage of water from such intersected claim without the consent of the owner or owners thereof, it shall work a forfeiture of all rights granted under section one of this act.

Sec. 3.   If any ore, the property of the owner of the claim intersected or crossed, be extracted in driving such tunnel, it shall be the property of the owner of the vein from which it was taken, and the owner of the tunnel shall be liable for all actual damages or injury done to the owner of the claim crossed by his tunnel.

Sec. 4.   In all actions between the tunnel owner or others involving the right to any vein discovered in such tunnel, the burden of proving that the vein so discovered is not the property of the adverse claimant in such action shall be on the tunnel owner.

Approved March 15, 1899.

Recording Mining Contracts.—Sec. 1. Written contracts relating to prospecting or mining, or to the formation of co-partnership for that purpose, when signed by the parties thereto and indorsed by at least one witness, may be recorded in the office of the county recorder of the county wherein it is proposed to prosecute the business of said co-partnership, or where the property affected by such contract is situated.

Sec. 2. Such record shall be constructive notice to all persons of the matters contained in such contract or co-partnership agreement.

Approved March 7, 1899.

Regarding Aliens.—Sec. 1. That any person, whether citizen or alien (except as hereinafter provided), natural or artificial, may take, hold and dispose of mining claims and mining property, real or personal, tunnel rights, mill sites, quartz mills and reduction works used or necessary or proper for the reduction of ores, and water rights used for mining or milling purposes, and any other lands or property necessary for the working of mines or the reduction of the products thereof: Provided, That Chinese, or persons of Mongolian descent not born in the United States, are not permitted to acquire title to land or any real property under the provisions of this act.

Sec. 2. An emergency exists, and this act shall take effect from and after its passage.

Approved March 2, 1891.

Recording Location Notices.—Sec. 1. It shall be the duty of the county recorder of the several counties of this state, within fourteen days after receiving them, to transmit to the deputy mining recorder of the district wherein the claims located are situated, all location notices, both quartz and placer, which shall not have been already recorded in the office of the deputy mining recorder.

It shall be the duty of such deputy mining recorder to record in his records all such notices received by him, and he shall receive as compensation therefor from the clerk, sending them one-half the fee authorized by law to be charged for the recording of mining claims. After recording such notices the deputy mining recorder shall return the same to the county recorder.

Approved March 11th, 1903.

MONTANA.

Sec. 1. Method of Locating Claim.—Any person who discovers, upon the public domain of the United States, within the state of Montana, a vein, lode or ledge of rock in place, bearing gold, silver, cinnabor, lead, tin, copper, or other valuable deposits, or a placer deposit of gold, or other deposit of minerals having a commercial value which is subject to entry and patent under the mining laws of the United States, may, if qualified by the laws of the United States, locate a mining claim upon such vein, lode, ledge or deposit, in the following manner, viz:

I. He shall post, conspicuously, at the point of discovery a written or printed notice of location, containing the name of the claim, the name of the locator (or locators, if there be more than one), the date of the location, which shall be the date of posting such notice, and the approximate dimensions of area of the claim intended to be appropriated.

II. Within thirty days after posting the notice of location, he shall distinctly mark the location on the ground so that its boundaries can be readily traced. It shall be prima facie evidence that the location is properly marked if the boundaries are defined by a monument at each corner or angle of the claim, consisting of any one of the following kinds: (1) A tree at least eight inches in diameter, and blazed on four sides. (2) A post at least four inches square by four feet six inches in length, set one foot in the ground, unless solid rock should occur at a less depth, in which case the post should be set upon such rock, and surrounded in all cases by a mound of earth or stone at least four feet in diameter by two feet in height. A squared stump, for equivalent of a post and mound. (3) A stone at least six inches square by eighteen inches in length, set two-thirds of its length in the ground, with a mound of earth or stone along side at least four feet in diameter by two feet in height, or (4) a boulder at least three feet above the natural surface of the ground on the upper side.

Where other monuments, or monuments of lesser dimensions than those above described, are used, it shall be a question for the jury, or for the court where the action is tried without a jury, as to whether the location has been marked upon the ground so that its boundaries can be readily traced. Whatever monument is used, it must be marked with the name of the claim and the designation of the corner, either by number or cardinal point.

III. Within sixty days after posting such notice, he shall sink a shaft upon the vein, lode or deposit, at or near the point of discovery, to be known as the discovery shaft. Such shaft shall be sunk to the depth of at least ten feet, vertically, below the lowest part of the rim of such shaft at the surface, or deeper if necessary to disclose the vein or deposit located, and the cubical contents of such shaft shall be not less than one hundred and fifty cubic feet; provided, that any cut or tunnel which discloses the vein, lode or deposit located at a vertical depth of at least ten feet below the natural surface of the ground and which constitutes at least one hundred and fifty cubic feet of excavation, shall be deemed the equivalent of such shaft, and, provided also, that, where the vein, lode or deposit located is disclosed at a less vertical depth than ten feet, any deficiency in the depth of the discovery shaft, cut or tunnel may be compensated for by any horizontal extension of such working, or by any excavation done, elsewhere upon the claim, equalling, in cubical contents, the cubical extent of such deficiency; but in every case at least 75 cubic feet of excavation shall be made at the point of discovery.

Sec. 2. Record of Location.—Within sixty days after posting the notice of location and for the purpose of constituting constructive notice of the location, the locator shall record his location in the office of the county clerk of the county in which such mining claim is situated. Such record shall consist of a certificate of location containing:

I. The name of the lode or claim.

II. The name of the locator or locators, if there be more than one.

III. The date of location, and such a description of said claim, with reference to some natural object or permanent monument, as will identify the claim.

IV. In the case of a lode claim, the direction and distance claimed along the course of the vein each way from the discovery shaft, cut or tunnel, with the width claimed on each side of the center of the vein.

V. In the case of a placer claim, the dimensions or area of the claim, and the location thereon of the discovery shaft, cut or tunnel.

VI. The locator and claimant, at his option, may also set forth, in such certificate of location, a description of the discovery work, the corner monuments and the markings thereon, and any other facts showing a compliance with the provisions of this law.

Such certificate of location must be verified, before some officer authorized to administer oaths, by the locator, or one of the locators, if there be more than one, or by authorized agent. In the case of a corporation, the verification may be made by any officer thereof, or by an authorized agent. When the verification is made by an agent, the fact of the agency shall be stated in the affidavit.

A certificate of location so verified, or a certified copy thereof, is prima facie evidence of all facts properly recited therein.

Sec. 3. Mill Sites.—Mill site claims may be located and

recorded in the same manner as other claims, except that no discovery or discovery work is required. Where a mill site claim is appurtenant to a mining claim, the certificate of location of such mill site claim shall describe, by appropriate reference, the mining claim to which it is appurtenant.

Sec. 4. Location of Abandoned Claims.—The relocator of an abandoned or forfeited mining claim may adopt as his discovery any shaft or other working, existing upon such claim at the date of the relocation, in which the vein, lode or deposit is disclosed, but, in such shaft or other working, he shall perform the same discovery work as is required in the case of an original location.

Sec. 5. Rights of Locator Date From Posting Notice.— The rights of a relocator of any abandoned or forfeited mining claim, hereafter relocated, shall date from the posting of his notice of location thereon, and, while he is duly performing the acts required by law to perfect his location, his rights shall not be affected by any re-entry or resumption of work by the former locator or claimant.

Sec. 6. Amendments.—A locator or claimant may, at any time, amend his location and make any change in the boundaries which does not involve a change in the point of discovery as shown by the discovery shaft by marking the location as amended upon the ground, and filing an amended certificate of location conforming to the requirements of an original certificate of location. A defect in a recorded certificate of location may be cured by filing an amended certificate.

Sec. 7. Relocation by Owner.—A locator or claimant may, at any time, relocate his own claim for any purpose, except to avoid the performance of annual labor thereof, and, by such relocation, may change the boundaries of his claim, or the point of discovery, or both, but such relocation must comply in all respects with the requirements of this law as to an original location.

Sec. 8. Rights Under Former Location.—Where a locator or claimant amends or relocates his own claim, such amendment or relocation shall not be construed as a waiver of any right or title acquired by hi mby virtue of the previous location or record thereof, except as to such portions of the previous location as may be omitted from the boundaries of the claim as amended or relocated.

As to the portion of ground included both in the original location and the location as amended or relocated, he may rely either upon the original location or the location as amended or relocated, or upon both. Provided, that nothing herein contained shall be construed as permitting the locator or claimant to hold a tract which does not include a valid discovery.

Sec. 9. Intervening Rights Reserved.—No amendment of

relocation of a mining claim by the locator or claimant thereof shall interfere with the right of any third person existing at the time of such amendment or relocation.

Sec. 10. Former Locations Cured.—All mining locations, made and recorded under the laws of this state, heretofore in force, that in any respect have failed to conform to the requirements of such laws, shall, nevertheless, in the absence of the rights of third persons accruing prior to the passage of this act, be valid if the making and recording of such locations conform to the requirements of this act.

Sec. 11. Periods Prescribed Not Mandatory.—The period of time, prescribed by this law for the performance of any act, shall not be deemed mandatory where the act is performed before the rights of third persons have intervened, and no defect in the posted notice or recorded certificate shall be deemed material, except as against one who has located the same ground, or some portion thereof, in good faith and without notice.

Notice to an agent, who makes a location in behalf of another, shall be deemed notice to his principal, and notice to one of several co-claimants shall be deemed notice to all.

Sec. 12. Conclusiveness of Patent.—The issuance of a United States patent for a mining claim shall be deemed conclusive that the requirements of the laws of this state relative to the location and record of such mining claim, have been duly complied with; provided, however, that where questions of priority are involved the date of the location shall be an issuable fact where it is claimed to have been prior to the date of the record of the location.

Approved February 18, 1907.

Sec. 3614, Political Code. Affidavit of Representation.—The owner of a lode or placer claim who performs or causes to be performed the annual work or makes the improvements required by the laws of the United States in order to prevent the forfeiture of the claim, may, within twenty days after the annual work, file in the office of the county clerk of the county in which such claim is situated an affidavit of his own, or an affidavit of the person who performed such work or made the improvements, showing:

1. The name of the mining claim and where situated.

2. The number of days' work done, and the character and value of the improvements placed thereon.

3. The dates of performing such work and of making the improvements.

4. At whose instance the work was done or the improvements made.

5. The actual amount paid for work and improvements, by whom paid, when the same was not done by the owner.

Such affidavits, or a certified copy thereof are prima facie evidence of the facts therein stated .

Sec. 3616. Surveyed Location.—Where a locator or owner of a mining claim has the boundaries and corners of his claim established by a United States deputy mineral surveyor, and his claim connected with a corner of the public or minor surveys, or an established initial point, and incorporates into the declaratory statement the field notes of such survey, and attaches to and files with such declaratory statement, a certificate by the surveyor setting forth:

1.   That such survey was actually made by him, giving the date thereof.

2.   The names of the claim surveyed and the locators thereof.

3.   That the description incorporated in the declaratory statement is sufficient to identify the claim.

Such survey and certificate becomes a part of the declaratory statement and such declaratory statement is prima facie evidence of the facts therein contained.

Sec. 1062, Penal Code.....Every person who intentionally:

1.   Defaces, obliterates, tears down or destroys any copy or transcript or extract from or of any law of the United States or of this state, or any proclamation, advertisement or notification set up at any place in this state by authority of any law of the United States or of this state, or by order of any court, before the expiration of the time for which the same was to remain set up; or,

2.   Defaces, obliterates, tears or destroys any notice placed or posted on a mining claim or removes or destroys any stake or monument placed thereon to identify it, is punishable by imprisonment in the county jail not exceeding three months or by a fine not exceeding one hundred dollars, or both.

Sec. 942, Penal Code. Use of False Pretenses in Selling Mines.—Every person who, with intent to cheat, wrong, or defraud places in or upon any mine or mining claim any ores or specimens of ores not extracted therefrom, or exhibits any ore, or certificate of assay of ore not extracted therefrom, for the purpose of selling any mine or mining claim, or interest therein, or who obtains any money or property by any such false pretenses or artifices, is guilty of a felony.

Sec. 1317, Code of Civil Procedure. Inspection of Adjoining Mines.—Whenever any person shall have any right to or interest in any lead, lode, or mining claim which is in the possession of another person, and it shall be necessary for the ascertainment, enforcement, or protection of such right or interest that an inspection, examination, or survey of such lead, mine, lode or mining claim should be had or made; or whenever any inspection, examination, or survey of any such lode or mining claim shall be necessary to protect, ascertain, or enforce the right or interest of any person in another mine, lode or mining claim, and the person in possession of the same shall refuse, for a period of three days after demand therefor in writing, to allow such inspection, examination or survey to be had or made, the party so desiring the same may present to the district court, or a judge thereof, of the county wherein the mine, lead, lode, or mining claim is situated, a petition, under oath, setting out his interest in the premises, describing the same, that the premises are in the possession of a party, naming him, the reason why such examination, inspection, or survey is necessary, the demand made on the person in possession so to permit such examination, inspection, or survey, and his refusal so to do. The court or judge shall thereupon appoint a time and place for hearing such petition, and shall order notice thereof to be served upon the adverse party, which notice shall be served at least one day before the day of hearing. On the hearing either party may read affidavits or produce oral testimony, and if the court or judge is satisfied that the facts stated in the petition are true, he shall make an order for an inspection, examination, or survey of the lode or mining claim in question in such manner, at such time, and by such persons as are mentioned in the order. Such person shall thereupon have free access to such mine, lead, lode, or mining claim for the purpose of making such inspection, examination, or survey, and any interference with such person while acting under such order shall be contempt of court. If the order of the court is made while an action is pending between the parties to the order, the costs of obtaining the order shall abide the result of the action, but all costs of making such examination or survey shall be paid by the petitioner.

NEW MEXICO.

Sec. 2286, Compiled Laws. Requirements of a Location.— Any person or persons desiring to locate a mining claim upon a vein or lode of quartz or other rock in place bearing gold, silver, cinnabar, lead, tin, copper or other valuable deposit, must distinctly mark the location on the ground so that its boundaries may be readily traced, and post in some conspicuous place on such location a notice in writing stating thereon the name or names of the locator or locators, his or their intention to locate the mining claim, giving a description thereof by reference to some natural object or permanent monument as will identify the claims; and also within three months after posting such notice, cause to be recorded a copy thereof in the office of the recorder of the county in which the notice is posted: And provided, no other record of such notice shall be necessary.

Sec. 2287. Recording Location Certificates.— In order to carry out the intent of the preceding section, it is hereby made the duty of the probate clerk of the several counties of this territory, and they are hereby required to provide at the expense of their respective counties such book or books as may be necessary and suitable in which to enter the record hereinbefore provided for. The fees for recording such notices shall be ten cents for every one hundred words.

Sec. 2289. Ejectment.— An action of ejectment will lie for the recovery of the possession of the mining claim, as well also of any real estate, where the party suing has been wrongfully ousted from the possession thereof, and the possession wrongfully detained.

Sec. 2290. Suit by Contestant.— That when an application is made for a patent to a mine or mining claim under the laws of the United States by any person, persons, company or corporation claiming to own or have an interest therein, and such application is contested by any other person, persons, company or corporation in the land office of the United States, such person, persons, company or corporation so contesting may bring suit of ejectment in the district court of the county in which the mine or mining claim is situated for the recovery of the same, whether in or out of possession of such mine or claim, and the question as to who was in the possession of the mine or claim at the time when the application was made for patent, or when the suit was begun, shall not be considered by the court, except as it may be necessary in determining the interests of the respective claimants, and their right to the possession of said mine or claim.

Sec. 2291. Special Verdict—Trespass.— The court, in an action for the recovery of a mine or mining claim where a patent is applied for, and the contest is pending in the land office of the United States, may, upon motion of either party to the suit, require the jury to return a special verdict, if tried by a jury; if not, then the judge trying the same shall make a special finding as to the particular interest each party owns in the mine or claim in dispute, under and by virtue of the mining laws of the United States, which special verdict or finding shall be entered into the judgment and upon the record of the court trying the same: Provided, however, There shall be no special verdict by the court or jury, except where the evidence shows both parties to the suit to have a bona fide interest in the mine or claim sued for: And provided further, That no third person who may have entered upon such mining claim or any part thereof, for the purpose of locating or claiming the same before or during such litigation in the district court growing out of any contest in any United States land office in this territory, shall acquire any interest either at law or in equity in the claim or any part thereof in dispute, and shall be deemed and declared a trespasser or trespassers, unless he or they have been, or may, during the pendency of such litigation in the district court resulting from such contest in the United States land office, by a proper application to the court, be made party or parties to such suit adverse to either of such litigants, or both, or shall have taken such legal steps to assert his or their claim in a court of competent jurisdiction within six months after the commencement of such contest in the United States land office.

Sec. 2292. Work During Pendency of Suit.—That nothing herein shall prohibt the working and developing of a mine or mining claim by either party in interest who may be in possession of the mine or claim during the pendency of the suit, nor shall this act prohibit any one from bringing an action for damages or a suit in equity to prevent waste. This act shall apply to any and all suits for the recovery of a mine or mining claim which are now or are hereafter commenced.

Sec. 2293. Measuring or Surveying During Suit.—In all actions at law, or suits in equity, now pending in any of the district courts of this territory, or hereafter commenced in such courts, wherein the title or right of possession to any mining claim, or ores and minerals is in dispute, or any party to such action or suit shall have the right to go upon or enter the workings of said mining claim for the purpose of measuring or surveying the same, either upon the surface or in the workings thereof, peaceably, and without molestation; the costs and expenses of such measurement or survey to be paid by the party for whose use and benefit the same was done.

Sec. 2294. Who Shall Survey.—The right to go upon and enter said mining claim shall be extended to the party applying therefor, as well as a surveyor and two chain carriers.

Sec. 95. Notice of Survey.—Before any person may enter

upon or go into the workings of such mine without the consent of the person or corporation in possession, he shall give not less than five days' notice in writing to such person in possession, or to his agent or manager, and if the possession is held by a corporation, said notice shall be served upon the president, agent or manager of such corporation, or upon the foreman in charge of the mine, that at a certain date, specified in said notice, he desires to enter upon or go into the workings of said mine, as the case may be, for the purpose of surveying and taking a measurement of the same, in order that he may be able to present the facts on the trial.

Sec. 2296. Court Proceeding on Refusal of Survey.—If such person or corporation shall not permit any party in interest in such suit or action to go upon or enter said mine, as contemplated in the preceding sections, after having been notified in the manner designated, the court may, upon proper showing, verified by affidavit or otherwise, exclude all evidence offered on the trial by the party so refusing, to (and) render judgment or decree in favor of the party giving such notice: Provided, That the court may, in its discretion, make an order directing the sheriff to go upon the ground with the party applying for the measurement and survey of such mine, and place the person so applying in possession, for the purpose of measuring and surveying the same, in which case the court may direct the payment of costs as may be just and proper.

Sec. 2297. Survey as Evidence.—The competency, relevancy and effect of such survey and measurement, as evidence, shall be governed by the ordinary rules of evidence in civil cases.

Sec. 2298. Discovery Shaft or Equivalent.—The locator or locators of any mining claim, located after this act shall take effect, shall, within ninety days from the date of taking possession of the same, sink a discovery shaft upon such claim, to a depth of at least ten feet from the lowest part of the rim of such shaft at the surface, exposing mineral in place, or shall drive a tunnel, adit, or open cut upon such claim, to at least ten feet below the surface, exposing mineral in place.

Sec. 2299. Boundaries—How Marked.—The surface boundaries of mining claims hereafter located shall be marked by four substantial posts or monuments, one at each corner of such claim, on the ground, so that its boundaries can be readily traced, and shall otherwise conform to section 2286.

Sec. 2300. Relocation—How Made.—The relocation of any mining ground, which is subject to relocation, shall be made in the same way as an original location is required by law to be made, except the relocator may either sink a new shaft upon the ground relocated to the depth of at least ten feet from the lowest part of the rim of such shaft at the surface, exposing mineral in place, or drive a new tunnel, adit, or open cut upon such ground, at least ten feet below the surface, exposing mineral in place, or the relocator may sink the original discovery shaft ten feet deeper. than it is at the time of relocation, or drive the original tunnel, adit, or open cut upon such claim ten feet further.

Sec. 2301. Amended or Additional Location.—If at any time the owner of any mining claim heretofore or hereafter located, or his assigns, shall apprehend that the original notice of location is defective, erroneous or the requirement of law has not been complied with before filing; or shall be desirous of changing his surface boundaries or to take in any part of an overlapping claim which has been abandoned, or in case the original notice of location was made prior to the passage of this act and the owner shall be desirous of obtaining the benefits of this act, such owner may file in the office where notices of location are by law required to be filed, an amended or additional notice of location, subject to the provisions of this act: Provided, That such additional or amended notice of location does not interfere with the existing right of others at the time of filing such notice; and no such amended or additional location, or record thereof, shall preclude the claimant or his assigns from proving any such title as he or they may have held under the previous location.

Sec. 2302. Destroying Location Notices.—Any person who shall take down, remove, alter or destroy any stake, post, monument or notice of location upon any mining claim without the consent of the owner or owners thereof, shall be deemed guilty of a misdemeanor, and on conviction, shall be punished by a fine not exceeding one hundred dollars or by imprisonment in the county jail not exceeding six months, or by both such fine and imprisonment.

Sec. 2303. Abandonment; How Evidenced—Liens Protected.—In addition to the provision of law now in force in respect to the abandonment of mining claims, they may be abandoned in the following manner: The owner or owners of any mining claim, wishing to abandon the same, may sign and acknowledge in the same manner provided by law for the acknowledgment of deeds, and file for record in the office of the county recorder, a certificate describing the same, stating when and by whom located, the name of the claim, the book and page where the notice of location of such claim is recorded; that he or they give up and abandon such claim, and that the same is open and subject to relocation. Upon the filing of such certificate, the mining claim therein described shall be considered abandoned and open to relocation as if the same had never been located, and the owner or owners thereof forever estopped from claiming any right or interest therein under the location mentioned in said certificate: Provided, That this provision for abandonment shall not apply to any claim or location upon which any mortgage, lien or other incumbrance exists.

Sec. 2304. Liens—How Protected.—When the owner or owners of any mining claim or claims now located or which may hereafter be located, upon which there shall exist any mortgage, miner's or mechanic's lien, or other incumbrance of any kind which may be hereafter made or incurred, shall refuse, neglect, or fail, up to the first day of December of any year, to perform thereon the annual labor or make thereon the annual expenditure required by law to be made in order to prevent the same from becoming open to relocation, in such case the holder or owner of such mortgage lien or encumbrance, may, upon the first day of December of such year or any time thereafter, before any such mining claim or claims shall have been relocated, enter with his or their workmen and employes upon the same and perform, or cause to be performed, the one hundred dollars' worth of labor or make the one hundred dollars' worth of improvements upon such claim or claims as by law required to be done or made each year in order to prevent such claim or claims from becoming open to relocation; that such work shall be done and improvements made in a workmanlike manner; that for the purpose of performing or causing to be performed such labor and improvements, the holder or holders of such mortgage, miner's or mechanic's lien, or other encumbrance, shall be considered the agent or the agents of the owner or owners of such mining claim or claims; that the owner or owners of such mining claim or claims, or any person or persons, shall not in any manner prevent, obstruct, hinder, or delay the performance of any labor or the making of such improvements, and may be restrained from so doing by an injunction; that upon the completion of the one hundred dollars' worth of labor or improvements by the holder or holders of any mortgage, miner's or mechanic's lien or other encumbrance as aforesaid, upon any mining claim, as herein provided, all sum or sums of money expended by him or them shall be and become a lien upon the said mining claim or claims, and from the date of the completion of the same, draw the same rate of interest as the principal sum of such mortgage, miner's or mechanic's lien, or other encumbrance, and may be foreclosed according to law.

Sec. 2305. Punishment for Obstructing Certain Work.—Any person or persons who shall prevent, obstruct, hinder or delay the performance of the labor or the making of the improvements mentioned in the last preceding section of this act, shall be deemed guilty of a misdemeanor, and upon conviction, shall be punished by a fine of not less than one hundred dollars, or over five hundred dollars, or by imprisonment in the county jail for a period not less than six months, nor more than one year, or by both fine and imprisonment.

Sec. 2306. Rights of Stockholders.—Any person owning stock in any corporation or company owning or operating mines in this territory, shall at any time during the business hours of the day have the right to enter in and upon any and all mines of such corporation or company, and all underground workings connected therewith for the purpose of examining the same.

Sec. 2307. Punishment for Refusal to Stockholder.—Every corporation or company or officer or agent of such corporation or company who shall refuse to allow upon demand any person owning in such corporation or company, to enter such mines, as provided in section two thousand three hundred and six, shall be guilty of a misdemeanor, and the corporation or company shall forfeit and pay to the party injured a penalty of one hundred dollars for every such refusal, and all damages resulting therefrom.

Sec. 2308. Definition of Stockholder.—Whenever the words Any person owning stock occur in the above section, they shall be taken and considered to mean stockholders whose names appear on the stock book of the company as owners of stock, and none others.

Sec. 2311. Punishment for Defacing Location Notice.—Any person or persons, or the manager, officer, agent or employe of any person, firm, corporation or association, who shall in any manner alter, deface or change the location notice of any mining claim in this teritory, located under the laws of the United States and of this territory, or any local regulations in force in the district wherein such claim is situated thereby in any manner affecting the rights of any person, firm or corporation, to such claim or location, or the land covered thereby, shall be deemed guilty of a misdemeanor, and upon conviction thereof before any court of competent jurisdiction, shall be fined in a sum not less than one hundred dollars, nor more than five hundred dollars, or imprisoned in the county jail for not less than sixty days, nor more than one year, or by both such fine and imprisonment in the discretion of the court trying the case. Nothing herein contained shall affect the rights of such locator or locators, and his or their assigns, to correct errors in such notice and file amended location notices as provided in section two thousand three hundred and one, and the laws of the United States: Provided, Such change shall not affect or change the date of such location notice, or affect the rights of any other person.

Sec. 2312. Punishment of Certain Persons for Fraudulent Relocation.—Any person or persons, or the manager, officer, agent or employe of any person, firm or corporation, who shall, either by himself or acting in collusion with others, relocate or attempt to relocate, or procure, or become interested, directly or indirectly in, and the relocation of, or in any manner attempt to hold possession of any forfeited mining claim, contrary to the provisions of this act, or who shall locate, or in any manner become interested in the location of any other claim which shall include the whole, or any portion of the ground covered by such forfeited claim, contrary to this act, shall be deemed guilty of a misdemeanor, and upon conviction thereof before any court of competent jurisdiction shall be subject to the same penalty and punishment as provided in section two thousand three hundred and eleven.

Sec. 2313. Trespass—Court Proceedings.—When any person, firm or corporation shall be lawfully and peaceably in possession of any mining claim in this territory, and shall have complied with all the requirements of law and regulations in force in the district in which said mining claim is situated, such persons, firm or corporation shall be deemed to be the rightful possessor of such mining claim and of the land included therein; and any person or the officer, agent or employe of any corporation who shall by force, intimidation, fraud, or stealth, or in the temporary absence of the rightful possessor, enter upon such mining claim with intent to hold the same, or any part thereof, against the rightful possessor, shall be considered a trespasser, and the judge of the district court for the district in which such claim is situated shall, upon the proper showing of such facts made by affidavit or by oral testimony upon a hearing ordered for that purpose, and upon the filing with the clerk of said district court of a good and sufficient bond, grant an order to show cause why a writ of injunction should not issue, enjoining and restraining such trespasser, his servants, agents and employes, and any person associated with him, from in any manner interfering with the rightful possessor in the possession of such claim until the final disposition of said cause.

Sec. 2314. Miners' Rules.—The owner or owners of lands within this territory, the title to which has been vested by letters patent from the United States government, may make and file in the office of the county clerk of the county in which such lands are situated, such rules and regulations, not inconsistent with the laws of the United States and of this territory, as they may see fit, governing the location and acquisition of mining claims thereon, which rules and regulations when so filed shall be binding upon all parties, and a copy thereof duly certified by the county recorder shall be received and admitted as evidence in any suit or proceedings relating to such mining claims; such rules and regulations may be changed and supplemented from time to time by other rules and regulations filed in like manner, providing that such change shall not affect rights acquired prior thereto.

Sec. 2315. Affidavit of Work Done.—The owner or owners of any unpatented mining claim in this territory, located under the laws of the United States and of this territory, shall, within sixty days from and after the time within which the assessment work required by law to be done upon such claim should have been done and performed, cause to be filed with the recorder of the county in which such mining claim is situated an affidavit setting forth the time when such work was done, and the amount, character and actual cost thereof, together with the name or names of the person or persons who performed such work; and such affidavit, when made and filed as herein provided, shall be prima facie evidence of the facts therein stated. The failure to make and file such affidavit as herein provided shall, in any contest, suit or proceedings touching the title to such claim throw the burden of proof upon the owner or owners of such claim to show that such work has been done according to law.

Sec. 1. Failure to Do Annual Work.—Whenever the locator or locators of any mining claim in this territory, located under the laws of the United States and of this territory, shall fail or neglect to do and to perform, or cause to be done and performed, upon such mining claim, the amount and character of work necessary to be done and performed thereon as required by section 1 of chapter XXV of the acts of the 28th session of the legislative assembly of the Territory of New Mexico, within the ninety days from the date of such location as provided in said section, such locator, or locators, and his or her assigns, shall forfeit all right to such mining claim, and shall henceforth for a period of ninety days from and after the expiration of such ninety days, be debarred and prohibited from relocating or procuring, or becoming interested, directly or indirectly, except as a bona fide purchaser for value in the relocation of such claim, or the location of any other claim which will include any portion of the ground which was included in such forfeited claim.

Sec. 2. Forfeited Claims.—Whenever the locator or locators, or his or their assigns, of any lode or placer mining claim in this territory, located under the laws of the United States and of this territory, shall fail to do or cause to be done, the amount of the assessment work required by law to be done thereon, within the time prescribed by law, such claim shall be considered forfeited and abandoned, and such locator or locators, and his or their assigns, shall thenceforth for the period of ninety days from and after the expiration of the time within which such work should have been done, be debarred and prohibited from relocating such claim, or becoming interested directly or indirectly, except as a bona fide purchaser for value, in the location or relocation of any claim which shall include the land covered by such forfeited claim, or any part thereof. And the subsequent locator of such claim, or of any claim including the whole or any part of the land covered by such forfeited claim, shall not be entitled to credit for any work that may have been done thereon before the time of such forfeiture, nor shall the former owner of any such forfeited claim have any right to compensation therefor.

Sec. 3. Altering or Defacing Mining Notices.—Any person or persons, or the manager, officer, agent or employe of any person, firm, corporation or association, who shall in any manner alter, deface or change the location notice of any mining claim in this territory located under the laws of the United States and of this territory, or any local regulations in force in the district wherein such claim is situated, thereby in any manner affecting the rights of any person, firm or corporation, to such claim or location, or the land covered thereby, shall be deemed guilty of a misdemeanor, and upon conviction thereof before any court of competent jurisdiction, shall be fined in a sum not less than one hundred dollars, nor more than five hundred dollars, or imprisoned in the county jail for not less than sixty days, nor more than one year, or by both such fine and imprisonment, in the discretion of the court trying the case.

Nothing herein contained shall affect the rights of such locator or locators, and his or their assigns, to correct errors in such notice and file amended location notices as provided in section 4 of said chapter XXV of the session laws of 1889, and the laws of the United States; Provided, Such change shall not affect or change the date of such location notice, or affect the rights of any other person.

Sec. 4. Illegal Relocations.—Any person or persons, or the manager, officer, agent or employe of any person, firm or corporation, who shall, either by himself, or acting in collusion with others, relocate or attempt to relocate, or procure, or become interested, directly or indirectly in, and the relocation of, or in any manner attempt to hold possession of, any forfeited mining claim, contrary to the provisions of this act, or who shall locate or in any manner become interested in the location of any other claim which shall include the whole, or any portion, of the ground covered by such forfeited claim, contrary to this act, shall be deemed guilty of a misdemeanor, and upon conviction thereof before any court of competent jurisdiction shall be subject to the same penalty and punishment as provided in section 3 of this act.

Sec. 5. Possession—Trespass.—When any person, firm or corporation shall be lawfully and peaceably in possession of any mining claim in this territory, and shall have complied with all the requirements of law and regulations in force in the district in which said mining claim is situated, such persons, firm, or corporation, shall be deemed to be the rightful possessor of such mining claim and of the land included therein; and any person or the officer, agent or employe of any corporation who shall by force, intimidation, fraud or stealth, or in the temporary absence of the rightful possessor enter upon such mining claim with intent to hold the same, or any part thereof against the rightful possessor, shall be considered a trespasser; and the judge of the district court for the district in which such claim is situated shall, upon the proper showing of such facts made by affidavit or by oral testimony upon a hearing ordered for that purpose, and upon the filing with the clerk of said district court of a good and sufficient bond, grant an order to show cause why a writ of injunction should not issue, enjoining and restraining such trespasser, his servants, agents, and employes, and any persons associated with him, from in any manner interfering with the rightful possessor in the possession of such claim until the final disposition of said cause.

Sec. 6. Boundaries; How Marked.—That section 2 of chapter XXV of the acts of the 28th session of the legislative assembly of the Territory of New Mexico be, and the same is hereby, amended to read as follows:

"Within one hundred and twenty days from the date of locating any mining claim within this territory, the locator or locators thereof shall cause the surface boundaries of such claim to be plainly marked by eight substantial posts or stone monuments, each projecting at least three feet above the surface of the ground, to-wit: One at each corner of said claim, and one at the center of each end and side line thereof, each of which posts or monuments shall be plainly marked so as to show the name of such claim and the direction thereof from each post or monument."

NORTH DAKOTA.

1426, Rev. Code 1899. Length of Lode Claims.—The length of any lode claim hereafter located within this state may equal but shall not exceed fifteen hundred feet along the vein or lode.

1427. Lode Claims, Width.—The width of lode claims shall be one hundred and fifty feet on each side of center of the vein or crevice; provided, that any county may at any general election determine upon a greater width, not exceeding three hundred feet on each side of the center of the vein or lode, by a majority of the legal votes cast at such election, and any county by such vote at such election may determine upon a less width than specified; provided, that not less than twenty-five feet on each side of the vein or lode shall be prohibited.

1428. Location Certificate; Contents and Record.—The discoverer of a lode shall within sixty days from the date of discovery record his claim in the office of the registrar of deeds of the county in which such lode is situated by a location certificate, which shall contain:

1.   The name of the lode;
2.   The name of the locator;
3.   The date of the location;
4.   The number of feet in length claimed on each side of the discovery shaft;
5.   The number of feet in width claimed on each side of the vein or lode;
6.   The general course of the lode, as near as may be.

1429. Location Certificate Void; When.—Any location certificate of a lode claim which shall not contain the name of the lode, the name of the locator, the date of location, the number of lineal feet claimed on each side of the discovery shaft, the number of feet in width claimed, the general course of the lode, and such description as shall identify the claim with reasonable certainty, shall be void.

1430. Discovery Shaft; Posting Notice; Manner of Locating Claim.—Before filing such location certificate the discoverer shall:

1.   Locate his claim by first sinking a discovery shaft thereon sufficient to show a well-defined mineral vein or lode;

2.   By posting at the point of discovery on the surface, a plain sign or notice containing the name of the lode, the name of the locator and the date of discovery, the number of feet claimed in length on either side of the discovery and the number of feet in width claimed on each side of the lode;

3.   By marking the surface boundaries of the same.

1431. Marking Boundaries.—Such boundaries shall be marked by eight substantial posts, hewed or blazed on the side facing the claim and plainly marked with the name of the lode and the corner, end, or side of the claim that they respectively represent, and sunk in the ground as follows: One at the corner and one at the center of each side line and one at each end of the lode. When it is impracticable on account of rock or precipitous ground to sink such posts, they may be placed in a monument of stone.

1432. Equivalent of Discovery Shaft.—Any open cut, cross-cut or tunnel at a depth sufficient to disclose the mineral vein or lode, or an adit of at least ten feet in along the lode from the point where the lode may be in any manner discovered, shall be equivalent to a discovery shaft.

1433. Time Within Which Discovery Shaft Must Be Completed.—The discoverer shall have sixty days from the time of uncovering or disclosing a lode in which to sink a discovery shaft thereon.

1434. Intralimital and Extralateral Rights.—The location or location certificate of any lode claim shall be so construed as to include all surface ground within the surface lines thereof, and all lodes and ledges throughout their entire depth, the top or apex of which lies inside of such lines extended vertically, with such parts of all lodes or ledges as continue by dip beyond the side lines of the claim, but shall not include any portion of such lodes or ledges beyond the end lines of the claim or the end lines continued, whether by dip or otherwise, or beyond the side lines in any other manner than by the dip of the lode.

1435. Lode Not to Be Pursued on Strike Beyond End Line.—If the top or apex of the lode in its longitudinal course extends beyond the exterior lines of the claim at any point on the surface, or as extended vertically downward, such lode may not be followed in its longitudinal course beyond the point where it is intersected by the exterior.

1436. Amended Location Certificate; Change of Boundaries.—If at any time the locator of any mining claim heretofore or hereafter located, or his assigns, shall apprehend that his original certificate was defective, erroneous, or that the requirements of the law had not been complied with before filing, or shall be desirous of changing his surface boundaries, or of taking in any part of an overlapping claim which has been abandoned, or in case the original certificate was made prior to the passage of this law, and he shall be desirous of securing the benefit of this chapter, such locator or his assigns may file an additional certificate subject to the provisions of this chapter; provided, that such relocation does not interfere with the existing rights of others at the time of such relocation; and no such relocation nor the record thereof shall preclude the claimant from proving any such title as he may have held under previous locations.

1439. Relocation of Abandoned Lode Claims.—The relocation of abandoned lode claims shall be made by sinking a new discovery shaft and fixing new boundaries in the same manner as if it were the location of a new claim, or the locator may sink the original shaft, cut, or adit to a sufficient depth to comply with sections 1430 and 1434, and erect new or adopt the old boundaries, renewing the posts, if removed or destroyed. In either case a new location stake shall be erected. In any case whether the whole or part of an abandoned claim is taken, the location certificate must state that the whole or any part of the new location is located as abandoned property.

1438. Amount of Annual Work.—The amount of annual work to be done or improvements made during each year to hold possession of a mining claim shall be that prescribed by the laws of the United States; provided, that the period within which the work required to be done annually on all unpatented claims so located shall commence on the first day of January succeeding the date of the location of such claim.

1440. Location Certificate Must Cover But Single Claim.—No location certificate shall contain more than one location, whether the location is made by one or several locators; and if it purports to claim more than one location it shall be absolutely void, except as to the first location therein described; and if they are described together, or so that it cannot be told which location is first described, the certificate shall be void as to all.

5918. Local Customs and Regulations.—In actions respecting mining claims proof must be admitted of the customs, usages, or regulations established and in force at the bar or diggings embracing such claim; and such customs, usages, or regulations, when not in conflict with the laws of this state and the United States, must govern the decision of the action.

NEVADA.

Sec. 1. How to Locate—What Notice Must Contain.—
Any person, a citizen of the United States or one who has declared his intention to ecome such, who discovers a vein or lode, may locate a claim upon such vein or lode by defining the boundaries of the claim in the manner hereinafter described, and by posting a notice of such location at the time and point of discovery, which notice must be posted upon one of the several monuments prescribed in Sec. 2 of this act, and such notice must contain:

First—The name of the lode or claim;

Second—The name of the locator or locators;

Third—The date of the location;

Fourth—The number of linear feet claimed in length along the course of the vein, each way from the point of discovery, with the width on each side of the center of the vein, and the general course of the vein or lode as near as may be.

Sec. 2. What Constitutes Location Work—Boundaries.—
The locator of the lode mining claim must sink a discovery shaft upon the claim located four feet by six feet to the depth of at least ten feet from the lowest part of the rim of such shaft at the surface, or deeper, if necessary to show by such work a lode deposit of mineral in place; a cut or crosscut or tunnel which cuts the lode at a depth of ten feet or an open cut along the said ledge or lode, equivalent in size to a shaft four feet by six feet by ten feet deep, is equivalent to a discovery shaft. The locator must define the boundaries of his claim by removing the top of a tree (having a diameter of not less than four inches) not less than three feet above the ground, and blazing and marking the same, or by a rock in place, capping such rock with smaller stones, such rock and stones to have a height of not less than three feet, or by setting a post or stone one at each corner and one at the center of each side line. When a post is used, it must be at least four inches in diameter by four and one-half feet in length set one foot in the ground. When it is practically impossible, on account of bedrock or precipitous ground, to sink such posts, they may be placed in a mound of earth or stones, or where the proper placing of such posts or other monuments is impracticable or dangerous to life or limb, it shall be lawful to place such posts or monuments at the nearest point properly marked to designate its right place. When a stone is used (not a rock in place) it must be not less than six inches in diameter and eighteen inches in length set two-thirds of its length in the top of a mound of earth or stone, four feet in diameter and two and one-half feet in height. All trees, posts or rocks used as monuments, when not four feet in diameter at the base, shall be surrounded by a mound of

earth or stone four feet in diameter by two feet in height, which trees, posts, stones or rock monuments must be so marked as to designate the corners of the claim located; provided, however, that the locator of a mining claim shall within twenty days from the date of posting the notice of location define the boundaries of said claim by placing at each corner and at the center of each side line one of the hereinbefore described monuments, and shall within ninety days of the date of posting said location notice perform the location work hereinbefore prescribed.

Sec. 3. Location Notice to Be Recorded—What Notice Must Contain.—Any locator or locators of a mining claim, after having established the boundaries of said claims, and after having complied with the provisions of this act with reference to the establishment of such boundaries, may file with the district mining recorder a notice of location, setting forth the name given to the lode or vein, the number of linear feet claimed in length along the course of the vein, the date of location, the date on which the boundaries of the claim were completed, and the name of the locator or locators. Should any claim be located in any section or territory where no district has been as yet formed, or where there is no district recorder, the locator or locators of such claims may file with the county recorder notice of location as set forth above, and said notice of location will be prima facie evidence in all courts of justice of the first location of said lode or vein. Wtihin ninety days of the date of posting the location notice upon the claim the locator shall record his claim with the mining district recorder and the county recorder of the mining district or county in which such claim is situated by location certificate which must contain:

First—The name of the lode or vein;

Second—The name of the locator or locators;

Third—The date of the location and such description of the location of said claim, with reference to some natural object or permanent monument as will identify the claim;

Fourth—The number of linear feet claimed in length along the course of the vein each way from the point of discovery, with the width on each side of the center of the vein, and the general course of the lode or vein as near as may be;

Fifth—The dimensions and location of the discovery shaft or its equivalent, sunk upon the claim;

Sixth—The location and description of each corner, with the markings thereon.

Any record of the location of a lode mining claim which shall not contain all the requirements named in this section shall be void. All records of lode or placer mining claims, mill sites or tunnel rights heretofore made by any recorder of any mining district or any county recorder are hereby declared to be valid and to have the same force and effect as records made in pursuance of the provisions of this act.

And any such record, or a copy thereof duly verified by a mining recorder or duly certified by a county recorder shall be prima facie evidence of the facts therein stated.—Laws of 1907, p. 418.

Sec. 4. Superseded by act of 1907.

Sec. 5. What Location Includes.—The location or record of any vein or lode claim shall be construed to include all surface ground within the surface lines thereof, and all lodes and ledges throughout their entire depth, the top or apex of which lies inside of such lines extended downward, vertically with all parts of such lodes or veins as continue to dip beyond the side lines of the claim, but shall not include any portion of such lodes, veins or ledges beyond the end lines of the claim, or the end lines continued, whether by dip or otherwise, or beyond the side lines in any other manner than by the dip of the lode.

Sec. 6. End Lines.—If the top or apex of the lode in its longitudinal course extends beyond the exterior lines of the claim at any point on the surface, or as extended vertically downward, such lode may not be followed in its longitudinal course where it is intersected by the exterior lines.

Sec. 7. Relocation in Case of Defective Certificate.—If at any time the locator of any mining claim heretofore or hereafter located, or his assigns, shall apprehend that his original certificate was defective, erroneous, or that the requirements of the law had not been complied with before filing; or shall be desirous of changing his surface boundaries or of taking in any part of an overlapping claim which has been abandoned; or in case the original certificate was made prior to the passage of this law, and he shall be desirous of securing the benefits of this act, such locator or his assigns may file an additional certificate, subject to the provisions of this act; provided, that such relocation does not interfere with the existing rights of others at the time of such relocation, and no such relocation or the record thereof shall preclude the claimant or claimants fiom proving any such titles as he or they may have held under previous location.

Sec. 8. Work to Be Done on Relocation.—The relocation of abandoned lode claims shall be by sinking a new discovery shaft and fixing new boundaries, in the same manner as if it were the location of a new claim; or the relocator may sink the original discovery shaft ten feet deeper than it was at the time of abandonment, in which case the record must give the depth and dimensions of the original discovery shaft at the date of such relocation, and erect new or adopt the old boundaries, renewing the posts or monuments if removed or destroyed. In either case a new location stake shall be erected. In any case, whether the whole or part of an abandoned claim is taken, the record may state that the whole or any part of the new location is located as abandoned property. If it is not known to the relocator that his location is on an abandoned claim, then the provisions of this section do not apply.

Sec. 9. Survey and Certificate of Surveyor Become Part of Record.—Where a locator, or his assigns, has the boundaries and corners of his claim established by a United States deputy mineral surveyor, or a licensed surveyor of this state, and his claim connected with the corner of the public or minor surveys of an established initial point, and incorporates into the record of the claim the field notes of such survey, and attaches to and files with such location certificate a certificate of the surveyor, setting forth: First, that said survey was actually made by him, giving the date thereof; second, the name of the claim surveyed and the location thereof; third, that the description incorporated in the declaratory statement is sufficient to identify. Such survey and certificate becomes a part of the record, and such record is prima facie evidence of the facts therein contained.—Laws 1897, p. 103.

Sec. 1. Falsely Dating Location Notices.—On and after the first day of April, 1907, it shall be unlawful for any person to antedate or to put any false date, or date other than the one on which the location is made, upon any notice of location of any mining claim in the State of Nevada.

Sec. 2. Any person violating the provisions of this act shall be deemed guilty of a felony and, upon conviction therefor, shall be imprisoned in the state prison for not less than three nor more than ten years.—Laws 1907, p. 373.

Sec. 1. Location of Placer Claim.—The location of a placer claim shall be made in the following manner: By posting thereon, upon a tree, rock in place, stone, post, or monument, a notice of location, containing the name of the claim, name of locator or locators, date of location, and number of feet or acres, claimed, and by marking the boundaries and the location point in the same manner and by the same means as required by the laws of this state for marking the boundaries of lode claim locations: Provided, that where the United States survey has been extended over the land embraced in the location, the claim may be taken by legal subdivisions, and, except the marking of the location point as hereinbefore prescribed, no other markings than those of said survey shall be required.

Sec. 2. Relating to Location.—Within ninety days after the posting of the notice of location of a placer claim, the locator shall perform not less than twenty dollars' worth of labor upon the claim for the development thereof, and shall have recorded by the mining district recorder and the county recorder of the district and county in which the claim is situated a certificate which shall state the name of the claim, designating it as a placer claim, name of locator or locators, date of location, number of feet or acres claimed, a description of the claim with regard to some natural object or permanent monument, so as to identify the claim, and the kind and amount of work done by him as herein required, and the place on the claim where said work was done. This certificate, or the record thereof, or a duly certified copy of said record, shall be prima facie evidence of the recitals therein. But if such certificate do not state all the facts herein required to be stated, it shall be void.—Laws 1899, p. 94.

Sec. 1. Contents Location Notice Tunnel Right.—The locator of a tunnel right or location shall locate his tunnel right or location by posting a notice of location at the face or point of commencement of the tunnel, which must contain: First—The name of the locator or locators. Second—The date of the location. Third—The proposed course or direction of the tunnel. Fourth—The height and width thereof. Fifth—The position and character of the boundary monuments. Sixth—A description of the tunnel by such reference to a natural object or permanent monument as shall identify the claim or tunnel right.

Sec. 2. Boundary Lines.—The boundary lines of the tunnel shall be established by stakes or monuments placed along such lines at an interval of not more than three hundred feet from the face or point of commencement of the tunnel to the terminus of three thousand feet therefrom. The stakes or monuments shall be of the same size and character as those provided for lode or placer claims in this act.

Sec. 3. Locator Shall Record.—The locator of a tunnel right or location shall, within sixty days of the date of the location, record his location with the mining district recorder and the county recorder of the county or district in which such location is situated, which must be similar in all respects to the one posted on the location. Any record of a tunnel right or location which shall not contain all the requirements named in this section shall be void.

Sec. 4. Relating to Blind Lodes or Veins.—All blind lodes, or veins or lodes not previously known to exist, discovered in a tunnel run for the development of a vein or lode, or for the discovery of mines, and within three thousand feet from the face of such tunnel, shall be located upon the surface and held in like manner as other lode claims under the provisions of this act.

Sec. 5. Provisions of Act Applicable.—The provisions of this act shall be construed as equally applicable to all classes of locations except where the requirement as to any one class is manifestly inapplicable to any other class or classes.—Laws 1897, p. 108.

Sec. 1. Location of Saline Lands.—Any person may locate, claim and hold not exceeding one hundred and sixty acres of the public lands within this state containing salt or saline matter.

Sec. 2. Duty of Persons Locating Saline Lands.—It shall be the duty of any person or persons locating salt lands to have the same surveyed by the county surveyor of the county in which said lands are located, within thirty days from the date of location; and the surveyor shall, within thirty days from the completion of said survey, make and deliver to the party employing him to make the survey, a correct description and plat of the lands thus surveyed, and the same shall be recorded in the office of the county recorder of said county within thirty days from the delivery thereof by the surveyor.

Sec. 3. Prior Locations Ratified.—All locations made prior to the passage of this act upon saline lands are hereby ratified and confirmed to the locators thereof, their heirs and assigns: Provided, The parties now holding and occupying said lands shall, within sixty days from the passage of this act, have the same surveyed and recorded as provided in section two of this act.

Sec. 4. When Subject to Relocation.—All persons claiming and holding saline lands under the provisions of this act shall keep and hold actual possession of said lands by occupying the same, and whenever said lands are abandoned for a period longer than sixty days, the same shall be subject to relocation.

Sec. 1. Mill Site.—The proprietor of a vein or lode claim or mine, or the owner of a quartz mill or reduction works, may locate five acres of non-mineral land as a mill site.

Sec. 2. Notice to Contain.—The locator of a mill site location shall locate his claim by posting a notice of location thereon, which must contain: First—The name of the locator or locators. Second—The name of the vein, or lode claim, or mine, of which he is the proprietor, or the name of the quartz mill or reduction works of which he is the owner. Third—The date of the location. Fourth—The number of feet or acres claimed. Fifth—A description of the claim by such reference to a natural object or permanent monument as shall identify the claim or mill site. And by marking the boundaries of his claim in the same manner as provided in this act for the marking of the boundaries of a placer mining claim, so far as the same may be applicable thereto.

Sec. 3. Locator Shall Record.—The locator of a mill site or location shall, within thirty days from the date of his location, record his location with the mining district recorder and the county recorder of the district or county in which such location is situated, by a location certificate which must be similar in all respects to the one posted on the location.

Sec. 4. When Location Is Void.—Any record of a mill site location which shall not contain the name of the locator or locators, the name of the vein or lode claim or mine of which the locator is the proprietor, or the name of the quartz mill or reduction works of which the locator is the owner, the number of feet or acres claimed, and such description as shall identify the claim with reasonable certainty, shall be void.—Laws 1897, p. 107.

Sec. 1. Annual Labor.—The amount of work done or improvements made during each year to hold possession of a mining claim shall be that prescribed by the laws of the United States, to-wit: One hundred dollars annually. In estimating the worth of labor required to be performed upon any mining claim, to hold the same under the laws of the United States, the value of a day's labor is hereby fixed at the sum of four dollars: Provided, however, That in the sense of this statute eight hours of labor actually performed upon the mining claim shall constitute a day's labor.

Sec. 2. Affidavit of Work Performed.—Within sixty days after the performance of labor or making of improvements, required by law to be annually performed or made upon any mining claim, the person in whose behalf such labor was performed or improvements made, or someone in his behalf, shall make and have recorded by the mining district recorder or the county recorder, in books kept for that purpose, in the mining district or county in which such mining claim is situated, an affidavit setting forth the amount of money expended, or value of labor or improvements made, or both, the character of expenditures or labor or improvements, a description of the claim or part of the claim affected by such expenditures, or labor or improvements, for what year, and the name of the owner or claimant of said claim at whose expense the same was made or performed. Such affidavit, or a copy thereof, duly certified by the county recorder, shall be prima facie evidence of the performance of such labor or the making of such improvements, or both.

Secs. 1 and and 2, Statutes 1897, p. 105.

Sec. 3. Recorder's Fee.—For taking and recording the affidavit herein required the mining recorder shall receive a fee of one dollar.

Sec. 4. Records to Impart Notice.—The instruments and records mentioned in sections one and two shall be deemed to impart to subsequent purchasers and encumbrancers, and to all other persons whomsoever, notice of the contents thereof.

Secs. 3 and 4, Laws 1887, p. 137.

Sec. 5. Notice to a Delinquent Co-Owner.—Whenever a co-owner or co-owners shall give to a delinquent co-owner or co-owners the notice in writing or notice by publication provided for in section 2324 Revised Statutes of the United States, an affidavit of the person giving such notice, stating the time, place, manner of service and by whom and upon whom such service was made, shall be attached to a true copy of such notice, and such notice and affidavit must be recorded by the mining district recorder or the county recorder, in books kept for that purpose, in the mining district or county in which the claim is situated; within ninety days after the giving of such notice, or if such notice is given by publication in a newspaper, there shall be attached to a printed copy of such notice an affidavit of the printer or his foreman or principal clerk of such paper, stating the date of the first, last and each insertion of such notice therein, and when and where the newspaper was published during that time, and the name of such newspaper. Such affidavit and notice shall be recorded as aforesaid within one hundred and eighty days after the first publication thereof. The original of such notice and affidavits, or a duly certified copy of the record thereof, shall be evidence that the delinquent mentioned in section 2324 has failed or refused to contribute his proportion of the expenditure required by that section and of the service or publication of said notice: Provided, The writing or affidavit hereinafter provided for is not of record. If such delinquent shall, within the ninety days required by section 2324 aforesaid, contribute to his co-owner or co-owners his proportion of such expenditures, such co-owner or co-owners shall sign and deliver to the delinquent or delinquents a writing, stating that the delinquent or delinquents by name, has within the time required by section 2324 of the Revised Statutes of the United States contributed his share for the year.............., upon the........................mine, and further stating therein the district, county and state wherein the same is situate and the book and page where the location notice is recorded; such writing shall be recorded in the office of the county recorder of said county. If such co-owner or co-owners shall fail to sign and deliver such writing to the delinquent or delinquents within twenty days after such contribution, the co-owner or co-owners so failing as aforesaid shall be liable to a penalty of one hundred dollars, to be recovered by any person for the use of the delinquent or delinquents in any court of competent jurisdiction. If such co-owner or co-owners fail to deliver such writing within said twenty days, then the delinquent with two disinterested persons having personal knowledge of such contribution, may make affidavit setting forth in what manner ,the amount of, to whom and upon what mine such contribution was made. Such affidavit, or a record thereof in the office of the county recorder of the county in which said mine is situate, shall be prima facie evidence of such contribution.

Laws 1897, p. 106.

Sec. 1. Grubstake Contracts Must Be Recorded.—All grub-stake contracts and prospecting agreements hereafter entered into, and which may in any way affect the title of mining locations, or other locations under the mining laws of this state, shall be void and of no effect, except between the parties to said contract or agreement, unless the instrument shall first have been recorded in the office of the county recorder of the county in which said instrument is made. The instrument or instruments shall be duly acknowledged before a notary public or other person competent to take acknowledgments. Grubstake contracts and prospecting agreements, duly acknowledged and recorded as provided for in this act, shall be prima facie evidence in all courts of justice in this state in all cases wherein the title to mining locations and other locations under the mining laws of this state are in dispute.

Sec. 1. Duties of Mining Recorders—Duplicate Notices.— It shall be the duty of each and every mining recorder of the several mining districts of the state to require all persons locating and recording a mining claim to make a duplicate copy of each and every mining notice, which copy the said mining recorder shall carefully compare with the original, and mark "duplicate" on its face or margain, and he shall immediately deposit with or transmit the same to the county recorders of the respective counties in which said mining district may be located.

Sec. 2. Fee to Be Collected.—The said district mining recorders, at the time of comparing said duplicate notices with the original, shall collect from the locators of said mining claims the sum of one dollar for each and every notice compared, which sum he shall transmit, together with the said duplicate notices, to the county recorders of the respective counties in which said mining claims shall be located.

Sec. 3. Duplicates to Be Filed.—Whenever, owing to the distance of the mining district from the county seat, it becomes inconvenient for the district mining recorder to personally deposit the duplicate copy with the county recorder, then in that case he may forward the same by mail or express, or such other manner as will insure safe transit and delivery to the county recorder.

Sec. 4. Fees for Recording.—The county recorders of the several counties shall receive for their services for recording each of said duplicate notices mentioned in section two of this act, the sum of one dollar: Provided, That in case the location is made outside of any organized mining district, or in the absence of a mining recorder in any organized district, then the person or persons making such location shall, within ninety days after making such location, transmit a duplicate copy of such notice to the recorder of the county in which the location is made, and the recorder shall record the same for a fee of one dollar.

Sec. 5. Duplicate Notice to Have Force.—The record of any original or duplicate notice of the location of a mining claim in the office of the county recorder, as herein provided, shall be received in evidence, and have the same force and effect in the courts of the state as the original mining district records.

Secs. 4 and 5 as amended Statutes 1897, p. 77.

Sec. 6. Penalty.—Any person neglecting or refusing to comply with the provisions of this act, shall be deemed guilty of a misdemeanor, and, upon conviction thereof, shall be punished by a fine not exceeding five hundred dollars, or by imprisonment in the county jail not exceeding six months, or by both such fine and imprisonment.

Sec. 7. County Recorders to Be Ex-Officio District Mining Recorders.—In every mining district in this state, in which the seat of government of any county is situated, the county recorder of said county shall be ex-officio district mining recorder, subject in the discharge of his duties to such rules, regulations and compensations as may be now in force or hereafter prescribed by the mining laws of the mining districts respectively to which this act is applicable. He shall, as such ex-officio mining recorder, be responsible on his official bond for the faithful performance of the duties of his office and the correct and safe keeping of all the records thereof, and the correct and safe keeping of the copies of all the records mentioned and referred to in section two of this act.

Sec. 8. Records to Impart Notice.—All instruments of writing relating to mining claims now copied into books of mining or other records, now in the office of the county recorders of the several counties of this state, shall, after the passage of this act, be deemed to impart to subsequent purchasers and encumbrancers, and all other persons whomsoever, notice of the contents thereof: Provided, That nothing herein contained shall be construed to affect any rights heretofore acquired or vested.

Sec. 9. Copies May Be Read in Evidence.—Copies of the records of all such instruments mentioned in section one of this act, duly certified by the recorder in whose custody such records are, may be read in evidence under the same circumstances and rules as are now or may hereafter be provided by law, for using copies of instruments relating to mining claims or real estate, duly executed or acknowledged, or proved and recorded.

Sec. 1. Receipt of Records.—Whenever the locator of a mining claim shall file his certificate of location in accordance with the law and pay the prescribed fees therefor, it shall be the duty of the mining district recorder, and of the county recorder, with whom said certificate is filed, forthwith to give such locator, or his agent, a receipt therefor; said receipt shall contain name of the claim given in notice filed and date of location thereof, stating the day and hour such certificate of location was filed.

Sec. 2. Prima Facie Evidence.—The receipt called for in section one of this act shall be prima facie evidence that the certificate of location has been duly filed, and the date of filing.

Sec. 3. Seal of Mining Recorder.—Each district mining recorder shall provide a seal on which shall be engraved the name of the mining district, the county and state, with which said seal he shall authenticate all of his official acts, which seal, together with his official documents and books, shall not be liable to be seized on execution.

Sec. 4. Duties of County Recorders.—It shall be the duty of the several county recorders, within ten days after the passage of this act, to notify each of the several district mining recorders in their respective counties of the passage of this act, which shall take effect on and after the first day of April, 1907.

Sec. 5. Penalties.—Any mining district recorder or county recorder neglecting or refusing to comply with the provisions of this act shall be deemed guilty of a misdemeanor, and upon conviction thereof shall be punished by a fine not exceeding five hundred ($500) dollars, or by imprisonment in the county jail not exceeding six months, or by both such fine and imprisonment.

Sec. 1. Conveyances.—Conveyance of mining claims shall hereafter require the same formalities and be subject to the same rules of construction as the transfers and conveyances of other real estate.

Sec. 2. Former Conveyances Construed.—All conveyances of mining claims heretofore made by bills of sale or other instruments in writing with or without seals, recorded or unrecorded, shall be construed in accordance with the lawful local rules, regulations and customs of the miners in the several mining districts of this territory; and if heretofore regarded valid and binding in such districts, shall have the same force and effect between the parties thereto, as prima facie evidence of sale, as if such conveyance had been made by deed under seal.

Sec. 3. How Proved.—The location and transfers of mining claims heretofore made, shall be established and proved in contestation before courts, by the local rules, regulations or customs of the miners in the several mining districts of the territory in which such location and transfers were made.

Sec. 4. Lands Defined.—The term "lands," as used in this act, shall be construed as coextensive in meaning with lands, tenements, and hereditaments, and shall include in its meaning all possessory right to the soil for mining and other purposes, and the term "estate and interest in lands," shall be construed and embrace every estate and interest, present and future, vested and contingent, in lands as above defined.

Sec. 5. Mortgage to Be Recorded.—A mortgage for a good and valuable consideration upon possessory claims to public lands, all buildings and improvements upon such lands, all quartz and mining claims, and all such personal property as shall be fixed in its structure to the soil, acknowledged in manner and form as mortgages upon real estate are required by law to be acknowledged and recorded in the office of the recorder in the county in which the property is situated, shall have the same effect against third persons as mortgages upon real estate.

Sec. 6. Mining Rules.—This act shall not be so construed as to interfere or conflict with the lawful mining rules, regulations, or customs in regard to the locating, holding, or forfeiture of claims, but, in all cases of mortgages of mining interests under this act, the mortgagee shall have the right to perform the same acts that the mortgagor might have performed for the purpose of preventing a forfeiture of the same under the said rules, regulations, or customs of miners, and shall be allowed such compensation therefor as shall be deemed just and equitable by the court ordering the sale upon a foreclosure: Provided, That such compensation shall, in no case, exceed the amount realized from the claim by a foreclosure and sale.

Sec. 7. Deed of Minor Held Valid—Proviso—Suits Pending.—In all cases in this state, since the first day of July, A. D. eighteen hundred and sixty-seven, where minors over the age of eighteen years have sold interests acquired by them in mining claims or locations by virtue of their having located such claims, or having been located therein by others and have executed deeds purporting to convey such interests, such deeds, if otherwise sufficient in law, shall be held valid and sufficient to convey such interest fully and completely, notwithstanding the minority of the grantor, and without any power or right of subsequent revocation; Provided, That this section shall not apply to cases where any fraud was practiced upon such minor, or any undue or improper advantage was taken by his purchaser or any other person to induce such minor to execute such deed; And provided further, That this section shall not apply to or affect any suits which may now be pending in any courts of this state, in which the legality or validity of such deeds may be involved.

Sec. 8. Minors Empowered to Sell or Convey.—All minors in this state, over the age of eighteen years, are hereby authorized and empowered to sell and convey by deed such interests as they may have acquired, or may hereafter acquire, in mining claims or mining locations within this state, by virtue of locating the same, or being located therein, and such deed shall, if otherwise sufficient in law, be held valid and sufficient to convey such interest fully and completely, and without the right of subsequent revocation, notwithstanding the minority of the grantor, subject, however, to the same provisions and limitations contained in the first section of this act.

Sec. 1. Right of Possession.—In all actions brought to determine the right of possession of a mining claim, or metalliferous vein or lode, where an application has been made to the proper officers of the government of the United States by either of the parties to such action for a patent for said mining claim, vein, or lode, it shall only be necessary to confer jurisdiction on the court to try said action, and render a proper judgment therein, that it appear that an application for a patent for such mining claim, vein or lode has been made, and that the parties to said action are claiming such mining claim, vein, or lode, or some part thereof, or the right of possession thereof.

Sec. 2. Trial, When Postponed.—In actions involving the title to mining claims and quartz ledges, if it be made to appear to the satisfaction of the court that in order that justice may be done, and the action fairly tried on its real merits, it is necessary that further developments should be made, and that the party applying has been guilty of no laches and is acting in good faith, the court shall grant the postponement of the trial of the action, giving the party a reasonable time in which to prepare for trial. And in granting such postponement, the court may, in its discretion, annex as a condition thereto, an order that the party obtaining such postponement shall not, pending the trial of the action, remove from the premises in controversy any valuable quartz, rock, earth, or ores, and for any violation of an order so made, the court or the judge thereof may punish for contempt, as in the cases of violation of an order of injunction, **and may also vacate** the order of postponement.

OREGON.

3829 (Hill's An. Laws). Plurality of Claims—When Allowed.—Any person may hold one claim by location, as hereinafter provided, upon each lead or vein, and as many by purchase as the local laws of the miners in the district where such claims are located may allow; and the discoverer of any new lead or vein not previously located upon shall be allowed one additional claim for the discovery thereof; nothing in this section shall be so construed as to allow any person not the discoverer to locate more than one claim upon any one lead or vein.

Sec. 1. Vein Locations—How Made.—Any person, a citizen of the United States, or one who has declared his intention to be come such, who discovers a vein or lode of mineral bearing rock in place upon the unappropriated public domain of the United States within this state, may locate a claim upon such vein or lode so discovered, by posting thereon a notice of such discovery and location, which said notice shall contain: First, the name of the lode or claim; second, the name or names of the locator or locators; third, the date of the location; fourth, the number of linear feet claimed along the vein or lode each way from the point of discovery, with the width on each side of the said vein or lode; fifth, the general course or strike of the vein or lode as nearly as may be, with reference to some natural object or permanent monument in the vicinity thereof; and by defining the boundaries upon the surface of each claim, so that the same may be readily traced. Such boundaries shall be marked within thirty days after posting of such notice by six substantial posts, projecting not less than three feet above the surface of the ground, and not less than four inches square or in diameter, or by substantial mounds of stone, or earth and stone, at least two feet in height, to-wit: one such post or mound of rock at each corner and at the center ends of such claims.

Sec. 2. Record of Locations.—Such locator shall, within sixty days from and after the posting of the location notice by him upon the lode or claim, file for record with the recorder of conveyances, if there be one, who shall be the custodian of mining records and miners' liens, otherwise with the clerk of the county wherein the said claim is situated, a copy of the notice so posted by him upon the lode or claim, having attached thereto an affidavit showing that the work required to be done by section 3 of this act has been done and performed, and shall pay to the recorder or clerk a fee of one dollar for such record thereof, which said sum the recorder or clerk shall immediately pay over to the treasurer of such county, and shall take his receipt therefor, as in case of other county funds coming into the possession of such officer. Such recorder or clerk shall immediately record such location notice and the affidavit annexed thereto. No location notice shall be entitled to record, or recorded, until the work required by section 3 of this act has been done and the affidavit or proof thereof is attached to the notice to be recorded.

Sec. 3. Work on Discovery Shaft.—Before the expiration of sixty days from the date of the posting of the notice of discovery upon his claim as aforesaid, and before recording the notice of location as required by section 2 of this act, the locator must sink a discovery shaft upon his claim located to a depth of at least ten feet from the lowest part of the rim of such shaft at the surface, or deeper if necessary, to show by such work a lode or vein of mineral deposit in place. A cut or crosscut or tunnel which cuts the lode at a depth of ten feet, or an open cut at least six feet deep, four feet wide, and ten feet in length along the lode from the point where the same may be in any manner discovered, is equivalent to such discovery shaft. Such work shall be deemed a part of the assessment work required by the Revised Statutes of the United States. The locator or some one for him who did work upon and has knowledge of the facts relating to the sinking of the discovery shaft shall make and attach to the copy of the notice of location to be recorded an affidavit showing the compliance by the locator with the provisions of this section, which affidavit shall be recorded with such copy of the location notice.

Sec. 4. Abandoned Claims.—Abandoned claims shall be deemed unappropriated mineral lands, and titles thereto shall be obtained as in this act specified, without reference to any work previously done thereon.

Sec. 5. Real Estate.—Mining claims so located shall thereafter be deemed real estate, and the owner of the possessory right thereto shall have a legal estate therein, within the meaning of section 316 of Hill's Code.

Sec. 6. Exempt from Taxation.—Prior to the obtaining of patent from the general government of the United States to such claim, the same shall be exempt from taxation, except as to the improvements, machinery and buildings thereon.

Sec. 7. Proceedings to Divest Title.—All conveyances of mining claims, or of interests therein, either quartz or placer, shall be subject to the provisions governing transfers and mortgages of other realty as to execution, recordation, foreclosure, execution sale, and redemption thereunder, but such redemption by the judgment debtor must take place within sixty days from date of confirmation, or such right is lost.

Sec. 8. Proceedings in Redemption.—In case of redemption from sale under judgment or decree, the redemptioner shall pay such sum or sums as are now required by law for redemption under execution sale, and such additional sum as may have been expended upon the property so redeemed by the purchaser under execution, or his assigns, in order to keep alive the possessory right thereto after such execution sale, not exceeding the sum of one hundred dollars for each claim, with ten per centum interest thereon from date of such expenditure or expenditures.

Sec. 9. Ditches Are Real Estate.—Ditches and mining flumes, permanently affixed to the soil, are hereby declared to be real estate: Provided, That whenever any person, company, or corporation, being the owner of any such ditch, flume, and the water right appurtenant thereto, shall cease to operate or exercise ownership over said ditch, flume or water right, for a period of five years, and every person, company, or corporation who shall remove from this state with the intent or purpose to change his or its residence, and shall remain absent one year without using or exercising ownership over such ditch, flume or water right, shall be deemed to have lost all title, claim, and interest therein.

Sec. 10. Void Location.—Any and all locations or attempted locations of quartz mining claims within the state subsequent to the thirty-first day of December, 1898, that shall not comply and be in accordance with the provisions of this act shall be null and void.

Sec. 11. Grub-Staking.—That all contracts of mining co-partnership commonly known as grub-staking shall be in writing, and filed for record with the recorder of conveyances of the county wherein locations thereunder are made. Such contracts must contain, first, the names of the parties thereto, and, second, the duration thereof. Otherwise such contracts shall be null and void.

Sec. 1. Debris.—That any location of any mining claim made upon any natural stream, or contiguous or near to any placer mine, or upon or below the dump of any placer mine, shall be subject to the prior right of all mines in operation prior to the making of such location, to discharge debris, gravel, earth and slickens as the same was discharged, or may be discharged, at the time of making such subsequent location of mining claim or claims.

Approved Feb. 25, 1901. Session Laws 1901, p. 122.

Sec. 1. Misdemeanor—Punishment.—If any person or persons shall wilfully and maliciously deface, remove, pull down, injure, or destroy any location stake, side post, corner post, landmark or monument, or any other legal land boundary monument in this state, designating, or intending to designate, the location boundary or name of any mining claim, lode or vein of mineral, or the name of the discoverer, or date of discovery thereof, the person or persons so offending shall be guilty of a misdemeanor, and on conviction thereof, shall be punishable by a fine of not more than five hundred dollars ($500), or by imprisonment in the county jail for a period of not more than six months, or by both, such fine and imprisonment in the discretion of the court: Provided, That this act shall not apply to abandoned property.

Approved Feb. 27, 1901. Session Laws 1901, p. 175.

Sec. 1. If any person shall maliciously, wantonly, or wilfully cut, break down, injure, destroy, or remove any water ditch, canal, flume, trench, pipe or reservoir, or any other thing used for conveying, receiving or holding water used or designed for mining, irrigating, manufacturing, or domestic purposes; or any dam, reservoir, gate, flume, flashboard, or other appurtenance used or designed for any of said purposes, or any wheel, wheel gear, or machinery of any mill or manufactory or machinery used for pumping water for any of said purposes, or shall maliciously or without color of right obstruct, draw off or use any portion of the water flowing through or contained in such water ditch, canal, trench, pipe, dam, or reservoir, or any mill pond or other receptacle used for containing such water, said person upon conviction thereof, shall be punished by a fine of not less than ten dollars (10) nor more than five hundred dollars ($500).

Approved Feb. 21, 1905.

Sec. 1. Annual Labor; Forfeiture to Co-Owner, Etc.— When ever any quartz or placer mines shall be owned by one or more persons, companies, or corporations, or when any person, company, or corporation shall own any quartz, or placer mines, in common with any other person, company, or corporation, any such person, company, or corporation owning an interest in said mine or mines, whether said interest be legal or equitable, shall have the right to perform the annual assessment work required by the laws of the United States and of the state of Oregon to be performed upon such mine or mines; such work, when so performed, shall, when it complies with the laws of the United States and of the State of Oregon, protect such mine or mines from relocation. Upon the failure of any one of several co-owners of such mine or mines to contribute his proportion of the expenditures required in such assessment work, or to perform or pay for his or their proportion thereof, the co-owner or co-owners of such mine or mines who have performed or caused to be performed the said labor or assessment work, may, at the expiration of the year for which such assessment work was performed, give such delinquent co-owner or co-owners notice that the assessment work for said year has been performed, stating by whom performed, and the amount of work performed, and the dates between which the same was performed, together with a statement of the amount due from said delinquent co-owner or co-owners for his or their proportion of said assessment work, and requiring said delinquent co-owner or co-owners, within ninety days from the date of the service of said notice, to pay to the co-owner or co-owners who performed or caused to be performed such assessment work, his or their proportion thereof. Such notice shall further state that if such delinquent co-owner or co-owners shall fail or refuse to contribute his or their proportion due for the said assessment work, his or their interest in said mine or mines will become the property of such co-owner or co-owners who have performed or caused to be performed such assessment work. Such notice shall be in writing and signed by the co-owner or co-owners who performed or caused to be performed such assessment work, and shall be served upon said delinquent co-owner or co-owners, personally, by the sheriff of the county in which said mines are situate, if said delinquent co-owner or co-owners be within said county. If said delinquent co-owner or co-owners can be found in any other county within the state of Oregon, then such notice shall be served by the sheriff of such county in which said delinquent co-owner or co-owners then are. If said delinquent co-owner or co-owners cannot be found within the State of Oregon, or if said delinquent co-owner or co-owners be at the time of giving said notice without the State of Oregon, then the service of said notice shall be made by the publication thereof in the weekly newspaper published in said county nearest to where said mines are situate; if there be two or more papers published in said county at the same distance from said mines, then the co-owner or co-owners giving such notice may elect as to which paper said notice shall be published in. If there be no weekly newspaper published within said county, then service of said notice shall be made by publication in any other weekly newspaper within the State of Oregon, published nearest the said mines; said notice shall be published at least once a week for a period of ninety days from and after the first publication thereof. If said notice shall be served by any sheriff of this state, as herein provided, such sheriff shall make return thereof by filing such notice with his return showing such service with the county recorder for the county within which such mine or mines are situate, if there be a county recorder in said county; and, if not, he shall file the same with the county clerk in such county in which said mine or mines are situate. If personal service of such notice cannot be had, as herein provided, proof of such service shall be made by the filing with the county recorder of the county in which said mine or mines are situate, if there be a county recorder, and if there be no county recorder in said county, then by filing with the county clerk of said county said notice as published, attached to an affidavit, made by the printer, foreman, or publisher of such newspaper, to the effect that such newspaper is of general circulation throughout said county, is published weekly, and that such notice was published at least once a week in said newspaper for a period of not less than ninety days from and after the first publication thereof. That at the expiration of ninety days from the date of the personal service of said notice upon said delinquent co-owner or co-owners, or, if at the expiration of ninety days from the date of the last publication of said notice, said delinquent co-owner or co-owners shall not have paid to the co-owner or co-owners who performed or caused to be performed such assessment work, his or their proportion thereof, then the title to the interest of said delinquent co-owner or co-owners in said mine or mines shall be immediately vested in the co-owner or co-owners who performed or caused to be performed such assessment work; and the co-owner or co-owners who performed such assessment work shall be entitled to file with the county recorder of the county where said mines are situate, or, if there be no county recorder in said county, then with the county clerk of said county, his or their affidavit or affidavits, to the effect that said payment has not been made; and upon the filing of such affidavit or affidavits said county recorder or county clerk, as the case may be, shall record such notice, proof of service thereof, and affidavit or affidavits in a book kept by him for such purpose, and shall then and there issue to such co-owner or co-owners who shall have performed or caused to be performed such assessment work, a certificate to the effect that he has filed and recorded said notice, proof of service, and affidavit or affidavits of non-payment, and to the effect that such co-owner or co-owners who have performed or caused to be performed such assessment work, have become and are the owners of all of the right, title, and interest of said delinquent co-owner or co-owners of said property. Such certificate shall not be issued until such co-owner or co-owners entitled to the same shall have paid to the said county recorder or county clerk, as the case may be, a fee of $1 for such certificate. If, prior to the issuing of such certificate, there shall be filed with said county recorder or county clerk an affidavit or affidavits to the effect that such payment has not been made by such delinquent co-owner or co-owners, and there shall also within said time have been filed with said county recorder or county clerk an affidavit by the delinquent co-owner or co-owners that such payment has been made, then said county recorder or county clerk, as the case may be, shall not issue such certificate, but such parties shall be left to establish such fact by suit to quiet the title to said premises, and if, in such suit, it shall appear either that the assessment work was not performed by the co-owner or co-owners claiming to have performed the same, or that the delinquent co-owner or co-owners have performed or paid his or their proportion of said assessment work, then a decree shall be entered in said suit to that effect; but if, in said suit, it shall be established that said assessment has been performed by or has been caused to be performed by the co-owner or co-owners claiming to have performed, or caused the same to have been performed, and that the delinquent co-owner or co-owners have not performed their proportion thereof, or have not paid their proportion thereof, then a decree shall be entered therein decreeing the co-owner or co-owners who have performed said assessment work to be the owner or owners of all of the interest of said delinquent co-owner or co-owners in said premises, which decree shall be entitled to record in the miscellaneous records kept by the county recorder or county clerk in said county, and shall be indexed in the index with the record of deeds and mining conveyances for said county. Such certificate, when issued as herein provided, shall be equivalent to a deed from such delinquent co-owner or co-owners of all of their interests in and to all of said mines described in such notice, and shall convey the interest of the delinquent co-owner or co-owners in said premises to the co-owner or co-owners who performed or caused to be performed such assessment work; such certificate may be introduced in evidence in any cause where the ownership of said property may become material, and when so introduced shall have the same force and effect as would a duly executed and delivered deed from such delinquent co-owner or co-owners of said premises, a certified copy of such certificate, and the certified copy of such notice and return when made and certified to by such county recorder or county clerk, as the case may be, shall be admissible in evidence in any trial where it is material to establish the proof of service of such notice or the ownership of said property. Such certificate, when given by such recorder or county clerk, shall be entitled to record in the office of the officer issuing the same, upon the payment of the same fees as are required for the recording of said mining conveyances; such county clerk or county recorder, as the case may be, shall keep a record book, showing the record of such certificates as shall be recorded by him, and upon recording the same, shall index the said certificates in a book kept by him for that purpose, and shall likewise index the same in the deed records of mining conveyances kept by him. Such indexing and recording shall have the same force and effect as the indexing and recording of deeds to other real property, and shall give like constructive notice.

Sec. 2. All fees collected under this act shall be the property of the county in which the same are collected, and shall be accounted for by the officer collecting the same, the same as other recording fees are accounted for.

Approved February 26, 1903.

SOUTH DAKOTA.

Sec. 2656 (Grantham's An. Stats.). Length of Claim.—The length of any lode claim hereafter located within this state may equal but shall not exceed fifteen hundred feet along the vein or lode.

Sec. 2657. Width of Claim.—The width of lode claim shall be three hundred (300) feet on each side of the center of the vein or crevice, provided that any county may at any general election determine upon a less width than above specified: Provided, That not less than twenty-five (25) feet on each side of the vein or lode shall be prohibited.

Sec. 2658. Discoverer to Record Claim.—The discoverer of a lode shall within sixty days from the date of discovery record his claim in the office of the register of deeds of the county in which such lode is situated, by a location certificate, which shall contain: 1st, the name of lode; 2d, the name of the locator, or locators; 3d, the date of location; 4th, the number of feet in length claimed on each side of the discovery shaft; 5th, the number of feet in width claimed on each side of the vein or lode; 6th, the general course of the lode, as near as may be; 7th, that when the location certificate is filed for record in the office of the register of deeds, the register of deeds shall immediately furnish to the locator or locators a certificate giving the name of the location; the name of the locator or locators; the date of filing in the office of the register of deeds; and the book and page where recorded, for which certificate the register of deeds shall receive the sum of ten cents in addition to the amount now allowed by law for filing and recording location certificates, which certificate shall be delivered to the locator or locators, who shall post the same, or a copy thereof, on the said claim on the same post or tree where the original notice is posted and in a conspicuous place. And if said certificate from said register of deeds or a copy thereof is not so posted within ninety days from the date of the original notice the said claim shall be deemed abandoned ground and be subject to relocation by any qualified locator. The said register of deeds shall, at the time of issuing said certificate, make a notation on the margin of the recorded certificate giving the date of the delivery of said certificate, which notation shall be prima facie evidence of the delivery and posting of the same as herein provided.

Sec. 2659. Certificate; When Void.—Any location certificate of a lode claim which shall not contain the name of the lode, the name of the locator, the date of location, the number of lineal feet claimed on each side of the discovery shaft, the number of feet in width claimed, the general course of the lode, and such description as shall identify the claim with reasonable certainty, shall be void.

Sec. 2660. Manner of Locating.—Before filing such location certificate the discoverer shall locate his claim by first sinking a discovery shaft thereon sufficient to show a well-defined mineral vein or lode, and not less than ten (10) feet in depth on the lower side; second, by posting at the point of discovery, on the surface, a plain sign or notice containing the name of the lode, the name of the locator or locators and the date of discovery, the number of feet claimed in length on either side of the discovery, and the number of feet in width claimed on each side of the lode; third, by working (marking) the surface boundaries of the claim.

Sec. 2661. Marking Surface Boundaries.—Such surface boundaries shall be marked by eight substantial posts, hewed or blazed on the side or sides facing the claim and plainly marked with the name of the lode and the corner, end or side of the claim that they respectively represent, and sunk in the ground, to-wit: one at each corner and one at the center of each side line, and one at each end of the lode. When it is impracticable on account of rock or precipitous ground to sink such posts, they may be placed in a monument of stone.

Sec. 2662. Requisites of a Location.—Any open cut, at least ten-foot face, crosscut, or tunnel, at a depth sufficient to disclose the mineral vein or lode, or an adit of at least ten feet in along the lode from the point where the lode may be in any manner discovered shall be equivalent to a discovery shaft.

Sec. 2663. Time for Performing Labor.—The discoverer shall have sixty days from the time of uncovering or disclosing a lode to sink a discovery shaft thereon.

Sec. 2664. Certificate Construed.—The location or location certificate of any lode claim shall be so construed to include all surface ground within the surface lines thereof and all lodes and ledges throughout their entire depth, the top or apex of which lie inside of such lines extended vertically, with such parts of all lodes or ledges as continue by dip beyond the side lines of the claim, but shall not include any portion of such lodes or ledges beyond the end lines of the claim or the end lines continued, whether by dip or otherwise, or beyond the side lines in any other manner than by the dip of the lode.

Sec. 2665. Claim Not to Extend Beyond Boundary Line.—If the top or apex of the lode in its longitudinal course extends beyond the exterior lines of the claim at any point on the surface, or as extended vertically downward, such lode may not be followed in its longitudinal course beyond the point where it is intersected by the exterior.

Sec. 2666. Security From Miner.—When the right to mine is in any case separate from the ownership or right of occupancy to the surface, the owner or rightful occupant of the surface may demand satisfactory security from the miner, and if it be refused may enjoin such miner from working until such security is given. The order for injunction shall fix the amount of bond.

Sec. 2667. Amended Certificate Filed.—If at any time the locator of any mining claim heretofore or hereafter located, or his assigns, shall apprehend that his original certificate was defective, erroneous, or that the requirements of the law had not been complied with before filing, or shall be desirous of changing his surface boundaries, or of taking in any part of an overlapping claim which has been abandoned, or in case the original certificate was made prior to the passage of this law, and he shall be desirous of securing the benefits of this act, such locator or his assigns may file an additional certificate subject to the provisions of this act: Provided, That such relocation does not interfere with the existing rights of others at the time of such relocation; and no such relocation or the record thereof shall preclude the claimant or claimants from proving any such title or titles as he or they may have held under previous locations.

Sec. 2668. Amount of Annual Work.—The amount of work to be done or improvements made during each year to hold possession of a mining claim shall be that prescribed by the laws of the United States, to-wit, one hundred dollars annually: Provided, That the period within which the work to be done annually on all unpatented claims so located shall commence on the first day of January succeeding the date of location of such claim.

Sec. 2669. Relocating Abandoned Claim.—The relocation of abandoned lode claims shall be by sinking a new discovery shaft and fixing new boundaries in the same manner as if it were the location of a new claim, or the relocator may sink the original shaft, cut or adit to a sufficient depth to comply with sections twenty hundred and one and twenty hundred and three, and erect new or adopt the old boundaries, renewing the posts if removed or destroyed. In either case, a new location stake shall be erected. In any case, whether the whole or part of an abandoned claim is taken, the location certificate must state that the whole or any part of the new location is located as abandoned property.

Sec. 2670. Certificate Contains But One Location.—No location certificate shall claim more than one location, whether the location be made by one or several locators, and if it purport to claim more than one location it shall be absolutely void, except as to the first location therein described; and if they are described together, or so that it cannot be told which location is first described, the certificate shall be void as to all.

Sec. 2671. Recording Fee.—The register of deeds shall be entitled to receive the sum of one dollar for each location certificate recorded and certified by him, and shall furnish the locator or locators with a certified copy of such certificate when demanded, for which he shall be entitled to receive fifty cents.

UTAH.

Sec. 1. Extent—No Location to Be Made Until Discovery of Vein.—A mining claim, whether located by one or more persons, may equal, but shall not exceed, one thousand five hundred feet in length along the vein or lode; but no location of a mining claim shall be made until the discovery of the vein or lode within the limits of the claim located. Any lode mining claim may extend three hundred feet on each side of the middle of the vein at the surface, except where adverse rights render a lesser width necessary. The end lines of each claim must be parallel.

Sec. 2. Monument—Notice.—The locator, at the time of making the discovery of such vein or lode, must erect a monument at the place of discovery, and post thereon his notice of location, which notice shall contain: 1st, the name of the lode or claim; 2d, the name of the locator or locators; 3d, the date of the location; 4th, if a lode claim, the number of linear feet claimed in length along the course of the vein each way from the point of discovery, with the width on each side of the center of the vein, and the general course of the vein or lode, as near as may be, and such description of the claim, located by reference to some natural object or permanent monument as will identify the claim; 5th, if a placer or mill site claim, the number of acres or superficial feet claimed, and such a description of the claim or mill site located by reference to some natural object or permanent monument as will identify the claim or mill site.

Sec. 3. Boundaries Marked.—Mining claims and mill sites must be distinctly marked on the ground so that the boundaries thereof can be readily traced.

Sec. 4. Filing Copy of Notice—Fee.—Within thirty days from the date of posting the location notice upon the claim, the locator or locators, or his or their assigns, must file for record in the office of the county recorder of the county in which such claim is situated, if said claim be situated without and beyond an original mining district, a substantial copy of such notice of location. Such county recorder shall charge and collect a fee of seventy-five cents for filing and recording and indexing and abstracting such notice: Provided, That such notice of location shall not be abstracted unless a subsequent conveyance affecting the same property be filed for record, when said notice shall be abstracted.

Sec. 5. Notice of Assessment Work Being Done.—Every person or company owning a group of claims and doing the development or assessment work for said group at one point, shall post a notice upon each claim at the discovery monument, stating where such work is being done, and also post a notice at the entrance of the workings where said work is done, stating the name of the claims for which the work is done.

Sec. 6. Filing Affidavit of Work Done.—The owner of any quartz lode or placer mining claim who shall do or perform or cause to be done or performed the annual labor or improvements required by the laws of the United States, in order to prevent a forfeiture of the claim, must, within thirty days after the completion of such work or improvements, file in the office of the county recorder in which the greater part of the mining district in which such claim is located is situated, his affidavit or an affidavit or affidavits of the person or persons who performed or directed such labor, or made or directed such improvements, and shall file a duplicate thereof with the district mining recorder of the district in which said claim is situated, showing, 1st, the name of the claim and where situated; 2d, the number of days' work done and the character and value of the improvements placed thereon; 3d, the date or dates of performing said labor and making said improvements and number of cubic feet of earth or rock removed; 4th, at whose instance or request said work was done or improvements made; 5th, the actual amount paid for said labor and improvements, and by whom paid when the same was not done by the owner or owners of said claim. Such affidavits or duly certified copies thereof shall be prima facie evidence of the facts therein stated.

Sec. 7. Reorganization of Mining Districts.—Mining districts may be organized, and all existing districts may be reorganized and the rules and regulations of the said mining district shall govern the said district according to the laws of the United States, in cases where a district organization is desired: Provided, That the nearest boundary line of any mining district shall not be within ten miles from the county recorder's office of any county.

•Sec. 8. Copying Records—Expense.—Upon application of the district mining recorder of any mining district to the board of county commissioners of the county having in custody the records of the said mining district, the said board of county commissioners shall cause the records of such district to be copied by the county recorder and shall cause all records of documents pertaining to district mining records, recorded since June 4th, 1896, up to the time of delivery ,to be recorded in the original records of the mining district in which the property is situated, and the original records, when so amended, shall be delivered to such district mining recorder. The copy so made shall remain in the office of the county recorder, and shall be considered as the original record. One-half of the expense of copying such records shall be paid out of the county treasury and one-half shall be paid out of the state treasury.

Sec. 9. Duplicate Notice of Location—Fee—Penalty.—It shall be the duty of every district mining recorder to require every person depositing for record a notice of location to make a duplicate copy thereof, which copy said mining recorder shall carefully compare with the original and mark "duplicate," and endorse thereon his name, and the date and hour and fact of filing in his office of the original. He shall, at the time of filing the duplicate notice with the original, collect, in addition to his own fee, the sum of seventy-five cents, which shall be the fee for the county recorder for recording such duplicate. He shall immediately deposit the duplicate copy with the county recorder of the county in which the greater part of the said mining district is located for record, or forward the same to him by mail or express, or in such other manner as will insure safe transit and delivery. The fee of seventy-five cents shall accompany the duplicate. The county recorder shall record said duplicate with the endorsements thereon for the said fee. The record of said duplicate notice in the office of the county recorder shall be considered an original record. Every person neglecting or refusing to comply with any of the provisions of this section shall be deemed guilty of a misdemeanor, and, upon conviction thereof, shall be punished by a fine not exceeding five hundred dollars or by imprisonment in the county jail not exceeding six months, or by both such fine and imprisonment.

Sec. 10. Copies of Notices to Be Received as Evidence.—Copies of notices of mining claims, mill sites and tunnel sites, heretofore recorded in the records of the several mining districts, and copies of the mining rules and regulations in force in the several mining districts, in like manner recorded, heretofore duly certified by the mining recorder, shall be receivable in all tribunals and before all officers of this state as prima facie evidence.

Sec. 11. Where books, records and documents pertaining to the office of district mining recorder have been or shall hereafter be deposited in the office of any county recorder of this state, such county recorder is authorized to make and certify copies therefrom, and such certified copies shall be receivable in all tribunals and before all officers of this state in the same manner and to the same effect as if such records had been originally filed or made in the office of the county recorder.

Sec. 12. County Recorder to Record Rules—Certified Copies.—It shall be the duty of each county recorder to record the mining rules and regulations of the several mining districts in his county without fee, and certified copies of such records shall be received in all tribunals and before all officers of this state as prima facie evidence of such rules and regulations, and it shall be his duty to record, index and abstract, all mining location notices presented for record, for a fee not to exceed seventy-five cents for each notice, and to file and index all affidavits of labor presented for filing affecting one mining claim for a fee not to exceed twenty-five cents: Provided, That when an affidavit of labor contains the name of more than one mining claim, an additional fee of ten cents shall be charged for each additional claim named therein.

Sec. 13. Recorder of Mining District to Give Bond.—The recorder of each mining district shall take the oath of office and give bond with sureties in the penal sum of one thousand dollars. Such bond must be approved by the district judge and filed in the office of the county clerk of the county in which the greater part of the said mining district is located. Where the recorder of any mining district appoints a deputy, the recorder and his bondsmen shall be responsible for the official acts of such deputy.

Sec. 14. District Recorder to Make Copies.—It shall be the duty of the recorder of a mining district upon request and payment, or tender of the fees therefor, to make and deliver to any person requesting the same, duly certified copies of any records in his custody and for a failure so to do, or for receiving larger fees for any such service than those provided he shall be deemed guilty of a misdemeanor.

Sec. 15. Vacancy—County Recorder to Receive Records.—Whenever there is a vacancy in the office of the recorder of any mining district, or the person holding such office shall remove from the district, leaving therein no qualified successor in office; or whenever from any cause there is no person in such district authorized to retain the custody and give certified copies of the records, it shall be the duty of the person having custody of the records to deposit the same in the office of the county recorder of the county in which such mining district or the greater part thereof is situated, and the county recorder shall receive such records, and is hereby authorized to make and certify copies therefrom, and such certified copies shall be received in evidence in all courts and before all officers and tribunals. The production of a certified copy so made shall be, without other proof, evidence that such records were properly in the custody of the county recorder.

Sec. 16. Fees of Mining Recorder.—Every mining recorder shall be allowed the same fees for recording and making copies of any record in his custody as are allowed by law to county recorders for similar services: Provided, That fees for recording location notices may equal but shall not exceed one dollar for each notice.—Act of March 3, 1899.

WASHINGTON.

3151 (Ballinger's An. Stats.). Governed How.—All mining claims upon veins or lodes of quartz, or other rock in place, bearing gold, silver, or other valuable mineral deposits heretofore located, shall be governed as to length along the vein or lode by the customs, regulations, and laws in force at the date of such location.

3152. Extent—Restrictions.—A mining claim located upon any vein or lode of quartz, or other rock in place, bearing gold, silver, or other valuable mineral deposits, after the approval of this act by the governor, whether located by one or more persons, may equal but shall not exceed one thousand five hundred feet in length along the vein or lode; but no location of a mining claim shall be made until the discovery of the vein or lode within the limits of the claims located. No claims shall extend more than three hundred feet on each side of the middle of the vein at the surface, nor shall any claims be limited by any mining regulations to less than fifty feet of surface, on each side of the middle of such vein or lode at the surface, excepting where adverse rights, existing at the date of the approval of this act, shall make such limitation necessary. The end lines of each claim shall be parallel to each other.

3153. Exclusive Right to What.—The locators of all mining locations heretofore made, or hereafter made under the provisions of this article, on any mineral vein, lode or ledge on the public domain, and their heirs or assigns, so long as they comply with the laws of the United States, and the state and local laws relating thereto, shall have the exclusive right to the possession and enjoyment of all surface included within the lines of their location, and of all veins, lodes, and ledges throughout their entire depth, and the top or apex of which lies within the surface lines of such location, extending downward vertically, although such veins, lodes, or ledges may so far depart from the perpendicular in their course downward as to extend outside of the vertical side line of said surface location.

3154. Conditions for Holding.—In order to hold the possessory right to a location of a mine not less than one hundred dollars' worth of work must be performed or improvements made thereon annually: Provided, That the period within which the work required to be done annually on all unpatented claims so located shall commence on the first day of January succeeding the date of location of such claim.

3155. Recorder.—The miners of each mining district may elect a recorder of the said district. When so elected, such recorder shall provide books of record, in which it shall be his duty to record all notices of locations or transfers, bonds, conveyances or assignments of mining claims within his district, when the same shall be presented to him for record. Such records are hereby declared to be public records open to inspection, and shall have the same force and effect, so far as notice is concerned, as the records of deeds and mortgages in this state.

3156. Term; Oath; Fees.—When a recorder shall be elected as provided in the last preceding section of this article, he shall hold his office for a term of one year from the date of his election, and until his successor is elected and qualified. He shall, immediately after his election, file with the county auditor of the county in which his district is situated, an oath to the effect that he will faithfully discharge the duties of his office. He shall be a certifying officer, and certified copies of his records shall have the same force and effect as similar papers certified by other officers of this state. His fees shall be the same as those of the county auditor for similar work; and should the office of recorder in any mining district at any time become vacant, it shall be the duty of the person last holding said office, and of any person into whose possession the same may come, to forthwith transmit all the records, papers and files of the said office to the auditor of the county in which such district is located, and such auditor shall thereafter keep the same as part of the records and files of his office.

3157. Where Recorded.—Inasmuch as the last two preceding sections of this article leave the election of a recorder for a mining district optional with the miners thereof, all location notices, bonds, assignments and transfers of mining claims shall be recorded in the office of the county auditor of the county where the same is situated within thirty days after the execution thereof: Provided, That all records of mining claims and of assignments, deeds, bonds and transfers heretofore made by any recorder of any mining district, or by any county auditor, are hereby declared to be valid and to have the same force and effect as records made in pursuance of the provisions of this article.

7146a. Relating to Monuments and Notices on Mining Claims.—Any person who shall wilfully and maliciously deface, remove, injure or destroy any location stake, side post, corner post, landmark or monument, or any other land boundary monument, the same having been erected or implanted for the purpose of designating the location, boundary or name of any mining claim, lode or vein or mineral, or for posting the name of the discoverer, locator or owner or date of discovery thereon; or any person who shall so deface, obliterate, remove or destroy any notice having been placed or posted upon any mining claim for the purpose of marking or identifying the same, shall be deemed guilty of a misdemeanor, and upon conviction thereof shall be punished by a fine not less than one hundred dollars ($100) nor more than five hundred dollars ($500), or by imprisonment in the county jail not exceeding one year: Provided, however, That the provisions of this act shall not apply to abandoned mining claims.

Approved March 16, 1897.

Sec. 1. Alienation of Real Estate—To Permit Indians to Sell Property.—Any Indian who owns within this state any land or real estate allotted to him by the government of the United States, may, with the consent of congress, either special or general, sell and convey by deed made, executed and acknowledged before any officer authorized to take acknowledgments to deeds within this state, any stone, mineral, petroleum or timber contained on said land, or the fee thereof, and such conveyance shall have the same effect as a deed of any other person or persons within this state; it being the intention of this act to remove from Indians residing in this state all existing disabilities relating to alienation of their real estate.

Approved March 13, 1899. Session Laws 1899, p. 155.

Sec. 1. Location Record.—The discoverer of a lode shall within ninety (90) days from the date of discovery record in the office of the auditor of the county in which such lode is found a notice containing the name or names of the locators, the date of the location, the number of feet in length claimed on each side of the discovery, the general course of the lode, and such a description of the claim or claims located by reference to some natural object or permanent monument as will identify the claim.

Sec. 2. Location and Marking of Claims.—Before filing such notice for record the discoverer shall locate his claim by first sinking a discovery shaft upon the lode, to the depth of ten (10) feet from the lowest part of the rim of such shaft at the surface, and shall post at the discovery at the time of discovery a notice containing the name of the lode, the name of the locator or locators, and the date of discovery, and shall mark the surface boundaries of the claim by placing substantial posts or stone monuments bearing the name of the lode and date of location; one post or monument must appear at each corner of such claim; such posts or monuments must be not less than three (3) feet high; if posts are used, they shall be not less than four inches in diameter, and shall be set in the ground in a substantial manner. If any such claim be located on ground that is covered wholly or in part with brush or trees, such brush shall be cut and trees be marked or blazed along the lines of such claim to indicate the location of such lines.

Sec. 3. **Discovery.**—Any open cut or tunnel having a length of ten (10) feet, which shall cut a lode at the depth of ten (10) feet below the surface, shall hold such lode the same as if a discovery shaft were sunk thereon, and shall be equivalent thereto.

Sec. 4. **Definition.**—The term "lode" as used in this act shall be construed to mean ledge, vein or deposit.

Sec. 5. **Amendment.**—If at any time the locator of any quartz or lode mining claim heretofore or hereafter located, or his assigns, shall learn that his original certificate was defective, or that the requirements of the law had not been complied with before filing, or shall be desirous of changing his surface boundaries, or of taking in any additional ground which is subject to location, or in any case the original certificate was made prior to the passage of this law, and he shall be desirous of securing the benefits of this act, such locator or his assigns may file an amended certificate of location, subject to the provisions of this act, regarding the making of new locations.

Sec. 6. **Affidavit of Labor.**—Within thirty (30) days after the expiration of the period of time fixed for the performance of annual labor, or the making of improvements upon any quartz or lode mining claim or premises, the person in whose behalf such work or improvement was made, or some person for him knowing the facts, shall make and record in the office of the county auditor of the county wherein such claims are situate an affidavit or oath of labor performed on such claim. Such affidavit shall state the exact amount and kind of labor, including the number of feet of shaft, tunnel or open cut made on such claim, or any other kind of improvements allowed by law or by rules of mining districts made thereon.

Sec. 7. **Evidence.**—Such affidavit when so recorded shall be prima facie evidence of the performance of such labor or the making of such improvements, and such original affidavit after it has been recorded, or a certified copy of record of same, shall be received as evidence accordingly by all the courts of this state.

Sec. 8. **Relocation.**—The relocation of forfeited or abandoned quartz or lode claims shall only be made by sinking a new discovery shaft and fixing new boundaries in the same manner and to the same extent as is required in making a new location, or the relocator may sink the original discovery shaft ten feet deeper than it was at the date of commencement of such relocation, and shall erect new, or make the old monuments the same as originally required; in either case a new location monument shall be erected, and the location certificate shall state if the whole or any part of the new location is located as abandoned property.

Sec. 9. **Cascade Mountains.**—The provision herein relating to discovery shafts shall not apply to any mining location west of the summit of the Cascade Mountains.

Sec. 10. **Placers.**—The discoverer of placer or other forms of deposit subject to location and appropriation under mining laws applicable to placers shall locate his claim in the following manner:

First. He must immediately post in a conspicuous place at the point of discovery thereon a notice or certificate of location thereof, containing (a) the name of the claim; (b) the name of the locator or locators; (c) the date of the discovery and posting of the notice hereinbefore provided for, which shall be considered as the date of the location; (d) a description of the claim by reference to legal subdivisions of sections, if the location is made in conformity with the public surveys, otherwise a description with reference to some natural object or permanent monument as will identify the claim, and where such claim is located by legal subdivisions of the public surveys, such location shall, notwithstanding that fact, be marked by the locator upon the ground the same as the other locations.

Second. Within thirty (30) days from the date of such discovery, he must record such notice or certificate of location in the office of the auditor of the county in which such discovery is made, and so distinctly mark his location on the ground that its boundaries may be readily traced.

Third. Within sixty (60) days from the date of the discovery, the discoverer shall perform labor upon such location or claim in developing the same to an amount which shall be equivalent in the aggregate to at least ten (10) dollars' worth of such labor for each twenty acres, or fractional part thereof contained in such location or claim.

Fourth. Such locator shall, upon the performance of such labor, file with the auditor of the county an affidavit showing such performance, and generally the nature and kind of work so done.

Sec. 11. **Evidence.**—The affidavit provided for in the last section, and the aforesaid placer notice or certificate of location, when filed for record shall be prima facie evidence of the facts therein recited. A copy of such certificate, notice or affidavit certified by the county auditor shall be admitted in evidence in all actions or proceedings with the same effect as the original, and the provisions of sections six (6) and seven (7) of this act shall apply to placer claims as well as lode claims.

Sec. 12. **Future Locations.**—All locations of quartz or placer formations or deposits hereafter made shall conform to the requirements of this act in so far as the same are respectively applicable thereto.

Sec. 13. **Mining Districts.**—Any mining district organized in the State of Washington in accordance with the laws of the United States, shall have power to make rules and regulations for such mining district, providing such rules and regulations do not conflict with the laws of the State of Washington or of the United States.

Sec. 14. **Road Building.**—Any mining district shall have the power to make road building to mining claims within such district applicable as assessment work, or improvement upon such claims: Provided, That rules pertaining to such road buliding shall be made only at a public meeting of the miners of such district regularly called by the mining recorder of such district: Provided further, That such meeting shall be attended by at least twelve (12) property holders of such district, and that no such rule can be made without the assent of the majority of the property holders of such district, who are present at such meeting. Such meeting to designate where, when and how such road work shall be done, and shall designate some one of their number who shall superintend such road building or construction, and who shall receipt for such labor to the performer thereof such receipts to be filed with the county auditor of the county in which such work is performed by the holder or holders of such receipts, and shall be received as prima facie evidence of labor performed as annual assessment work upon such claim or claims, as may be designated by an affidavit or oath of labor as provided for in section six (6) of this act: Provided, That nothing in this act can be construed as being mandatory upon any owner or holder of mining property to perform labor upon any such road.

Approved March 8, 1899. Session Laws 1899, p. 69.

WYOMING.

Sec. 2533 (Rev. Stats.). Organization of Mining District.— In any mining district or in any mining field of discovery of veins, leads, lodes or ledges, or of gold placers, petroleum fields, soluble salt deposits, or of any mineral lands whatever, or of any lands that are, or may be hereafter, opened to location under the laws governing mineral deposits, the miners may meet and organize and elect a recorder and make regulations, not in conflict with the laws of the United States or with the laws of this state governing the location, manner of recording and amount of annual work necessary to hold possession of a mining claim within the district, subject to the following requirements:

1. That any five miners, having locations, or owning in part or in whole, claims within the proposed district, shall give notice by at least three written or printed or partially writtten and partially printed notices, posted in prominent places within the proposed district of a meeting called by them for organizing such district at a date at least ten days subsequent to the posting of such notices.

2. That the meeting thus called shall be attended by at least ten persons, all having locations, or owning, in part or in whole, claims within the proposed district.

3. That the recorder elected for such an organized district, shall hold his office until his successor is elected and qualified according to law. Such recorder is required to give bonds with at least two sureties, to the people of Wyoming, in the penal sum of not less than one thousand dollars, for the faithful performance of his duties, and for the turning over of all books, papers, records, etc., of his office, to his duly elected and qualified successor, which bond shall be approved by the judge of the district court and filed in the office of the county clerk and ex-officio register of deeds. The recorder of such a mining district may appoint a deputy, for whose official acts he shall be responsible.

4. That no district need be organized if the majority at the meeting as hereinbefore provided so desire, but when a district is once organized, it cannot be subdivided except in accordance with the local laws of the district, enacted at the regular or special meetings, or by action of the legislature of this state. In case of the abandonment of any district for any cause whatever, it shall be the duty of the district recorder, as soon as practicable thereafter, to deposit all records and other papers pertaining to his office, in the office of the county clerk and ex-officio register of deeds of the county in which such district is located.

5. Each mining district may regulate the fees to be charged by the local recorder for recording location certificates, affi-

davits of labor, and all other instruments to be filed in the said recorder's office.

Sec. 2534. Copy of Laws and Proceedings to Be Filed.—A copy of all laws and the proceedings of each mining district, shall be filed by the recorder of the district in the office of the county clerk and ex-officio register of deeds of the county in which the district is situated, which shall be taken as evidence in any court having jurisdiction in the matter concerned under such laws or proceedings; and all such laws and proceedings of any mining district heretofore filed in the county clerk's office of the proper county, and transcripts thereof, duly certified, shall have the like effect in evidence. Such copies of laws and proceedings shall be filed in the office of the said county clerk and ex-officio register of deeds by the recorder of each mining district within sixty days after the organization of each new mining district, or within sixty days after new laws were adopted or proceedings had.

Sec. 2535. Use of Water.—Whenever any person, persons or corporation, shall be engaged in mining or milling in this state, and in the prosecution of such business shall hoist or bring water from mines or natural water courses, such person, persons or corporation shall have the right to use such water in such manner, and direct it into such natural course or gulch as their business interests may require: Provided, That such diversion shall not infringe on vested rights. The provisions of this section shall not be construed to apply to new or undeveloped mines, but to those only which shall have been open and require drainage or other direction of water.

Sec. 2536. Mining Claims Subject to Right of Way.—All mining claims or property now located, or which may hereafter be located within this state, shall be subject to the right of way of any ditch or flume for mining purposes, or of any tramway, pack trail or wagon road, whether now in use, or which may hereafter be laid out across any such location, claim or property; Provided, always, That such right of way shall not be exercised against any mining location, claim or property duly made and recorded as herein required, and not abandoned prior to the establishment of any such ditch, flume, tramway, pack trail or wagon road, without the consent of the owner or owners, except in condemnation, as in the case of land taken for public highways. Consent to the location of the easements above enumerated over any mineral claim, location or property, shall be in writing; and Provided, further, That any such ditch or flume shall be so constructed that water therefrom shall not injure vested rights by flooding or otherwise.

Sec. 2537. Protection of Surface Properties.—Where a mining right exists in any case and is separated from the ownership or right of occupancy to the surface, such owner or rightful occupant of the said surface may demand satisfactory security from the miner or miners, and if such security is refused, such owner or occupant of the surface may enjoin the miner or miners from working such mine until such security is given. The order for such injunction shall fix the amount of the bond therefor.

Sec. 2538. Relocation Certificate.—Whenever it shall be apprehended by the locator, or his assigns, of any mining claims or property heretofore or hereafter located, that his or their original location certificate was defective, erroneous, or that the requirements of the law had not been complied with before the filing thereof, or shall be desirous of changing the surface boundaries of his or their original claim or location, or of taking in any part of an overlapping claim or location which has been abandoned, or in case the original certificate was made prior to March 6, 1888, and he or they shall be desirous of securing the benefit of this law, such locator or locators, or his or their assigns, may file an additional location certificate in compliance with and subject to the provisions of this chapter; Provided, however, That such relocation shall not infringe upon the rights of other existing at the time of such relocation, and that no such relocation, or other record thereof, shall preclude the claimant or claimants from proving any such title or titles as he or they may have held under any previous location.

Sec. 2539. Certificates Shall Describe But One Claim.—No location certificate shall contain more than one claim or location, whether the location be made by one or more locators, and any location certificate that contains upon its face more than one location claim shall be absolutely void, except as to the first location named and described therein, and in case more than one claim or location is described together so that the first one cannot be distinguished from the others, the certificate of location shall be void as an entirety.

Sec. 2540. Stealing Mining Claims—Penalty—Evidence.—In all cases when two or more persons shall, through collusion or other wise, associate themselves together for the purpose of obtaining possession of any lode, gulch or placer, or other mineral claim or mining property within this state, then in the actual possession of another or others, by force and violence, or threats of violence, or by stealth, and shall proceed to carry out such purpose by making threats to and against the party or parties in possession, or who shall enter upon such lode, gulch, placer or other mineral claim or mining property for the purposes aforesaid, or who shall enter upon or into mineral claim or mining property; or, not being on such mining claim or mineral property, but within hearing of the same, shall make any threats or any use of any language, signs, gestures, intended to intimidate any person or persons in possession or at work on the said claim or claims of mineral property of whatever kind or nature, from continuing such possession or work thereon or therein, or to intimidate others from engaging to be employed thereon or therein, every such person or persons so engaging shall be guilty of a misdemeanor, and upon conviction thereof, shall be fined in a penal sum not exceeding two hundred and fifty dollars, and be imprisoned in the county jail for not less than thirty days nor more than six months. On trial of any person or persons charged with any of the offenses enumerated in this section, the proof of a common purpose of two or more persons to unlawfully secure possession of any mining claim or mineral property within the state, or to intimidate any one in the possession of, or laborers at work on any mining claim or mineral property aforesaid, accompanied or followed by any acts or utterances of such person or persons as herein enumerated, shall be sufficient evidence to convict any one committing such acts, although such parties may not be associated or acting together at the time of the commission of such offenses.

Sec. 2541. Destroying Mining Property—Penalty.—Any person or persons who shall unlawfully cut down, break down, level, demolish, destroy, injure, remove or carry away any sign, notice, post, mark, monument or fence upon or around any shaft, pit, hole, incline or tunnel, or any building, structure, machinery, implements or other property on any mining claim or mineral property, ground or premises, shall be guilty of a misdemeanor, and upon conviction thereof, shall be fined a penal sum of money not less than fifty dollars nor more than one thousand dollars, or be imprisoned for not less than thirty days nor more than one year, or both, in the discretion of the court.

Sec. 2542. Mining Swindlers—Penalty.—Any person or persons who shall defraud, cheat, swindle or deceive any party or parties in relation to any mine or mining property by "salting" or by placing or causing to be placed in any lode, placer or other mine, any genuine metals or material representing genuine minerals, which are designed to cheat and deceive others, for the purpose of gain, whereby others shall be deceived and injured by such, shall be guilty of a felony, and upon conviction thereof shall be fined in a penal sum of not less than fifty dollars, and not more than five thousand dollars, or imprisoned in the penitentiary for not more than three years, or both, in the discretion of the court.

Sec. 2543. Protection of Live Stock From Shafts.—Every person, persons, company or corporation, who have already sunk mining shafts, pits, holes, inclines, upon any mining claim, or on any mineral property, ground or premises, or who may hereafter sink such openings aforesaid, shall forthwith secure such shafts and openings against the injury or destruction of live stock running at large upon the public domain, by securely covering such shafts and other openings, as aforesaid, in a manner to render them safe against the possibility of live stock falling into them, or in any manner becoming injured or destroyed thereby; or by forthwith making a strong, secure and ample fence around such shafts and other openings aforesaid. Any person, persons, corporation or company that shall fail or refuse to fully comply with the provisions of this section shall be guilty of a misdemeanor, and on conviction thereof, shall be liable for any damages sustained by injury or loss of live stock thereby.

Sec. 2544. Length of Lode Claim.—The length of any lode mining claim located within Wyoming, shall not exceed fifteen hundred feet measured horizontally, along such lode or vein. Nor can the regulations of any mining district limit a locator to less than this length.

Sec. 2545. Width of Lode Claim.—The width of any lode claim located within Wyoming shall not exceed three hundred feet on each side of the discovery shaft, the discovery shaft being always equally distant from the side lines of the claims. Nor can any mining district limit the locator to a width of less than one hundred and fifty feet on either side of the discovery shaft.

Sec. 2546. Recording Claims—Requisites of Certificate.—A discoverer of any mineral lead, lode, ledge or vein shall, within sixty days from the date of discovery, cause such claim to be recorded in the office of the county clerk and ex-officio register of deeds of the county within which such claim may exist, by a location certificate which shall contain the following facts:

1. The name of the lode claim.
2. The name or names of the locator or locators.
3. The date of location.
4. The length of the claim along the vein measured each way from the center of the discovery shaft, and the general course of the vein as far as it is known.
5. The amount of surface ground claimed on either side of the center of the discovery shaft or discovery workings.
6. A description of the claim by such designation of natural or fixed object, or if upon ground surveyed by the United States system of land survey, by reference to section or quarter section corners, as shall identify the claim beyond question.

Sec. 2547. Imperfect Certificates Void.—Any certificate of the location of a lode claim which shall not fully contain all the requirements named in the preceding section, together with such other description as shall identify the lode or claim with reasonable certainty, shall be void.

Sec. 2548. Prerequisites to Filing Certificate.—Before the filing of a location certificate in the office of the county clerk and ex-officio register of deeds, the discoverer of any lode, vein or fissure shall designate the location thereof as follows:

1. By sinking a shaft upon the discovery lode or fissure to the depth of ten feet from the lowest part of the rim of such shaft at the surface.

2. By posting at the point of discovery, on the surface, a plain sign or notice containing the name of the lode or claim, the name of the discoverer and locator, and the date of such discovery.

3. By marking the surface boundaries of the claim, which shall be marked by six substantial monuments of stone or posts, hewed or marked on the side or sides, which face is toward the claim, and sunk in the ground, one at each corner and one at the center of each side line, and when thus marking the boundaries of a claim, if any one or more of such posts or monuments of stone shall fall, by necessity, upon precipitous ground, when the proper placing of it is impracticable or dangerous to life or limb, it shall be lawful to place any such post or monument of stone at the nearest point properly marked to designate its right place; Provided, That no right to such lode or claim or its possession or enjoyment, shall be given to any person or persons, unless such person or persons shall discover in said claim mineral bearing rock in place.

Sec. 2549. What Open Cut Equivalent to Discovery Shaft. —Any open cut which shall cut the vein ten feet in length and with face ten feet in height, or any cross-cut tunnel, or tunnel on the vein ten feet in length which shall cut the vein ten feet below the surface, measured from the bottom of such tunnel, shall hold such lode the same as if a discovery shaft were sunk thereon.

Sec. 2550. Time Given Discoverer to Sink Shaft. —The discoverer of any mineral lode or vein in this state shall have the period of sixty days from the date of discovering such lode or vein in which to sink a discovery shaft thereon.

Sec. 2551. Mineral Boundaries Defined. —The locators of all mining locations heretofore made, or which shall hereafter be made, on any mineral vein, lode or ledge, situated on the public domain, their heirs and assigns, shall have the exclusive right of possession and enjoyment of all the surface included within the lines of their locations, and of all veins, lodes and ledges throughout their entire depth, the top or apex of which lies inside of surface lines extended downward vertically although such veins, lodes or ledges may so far depart from a perpendicular in their course downward as to extend outside the vertical side lines of such surface locations. But their right of possession to such outside parts of such veins or ledges shall be confined to such portions thereof as lie between vertical planes drawn downward as above described, through the end lines of their locations, so continued in their own direction that such planes will intersect such exterior parts of such veins or ledges. And nothing in this section shall authorize a locator or possessor of a vein or lode which extends in its downward course beyond the vertical lines of his claim to enter upon the surface of a claim owned or possessed by another.

Sec. 2552. Relocation of Abandoned Claims.—Any abandoned lode, vein or strata' claim may be relocated and such relocation shall be perfected by sinking a new discovery shaft and by fixing new boundaries in the same manner as provided for the location of a new claim; or the relocator may sink the original discovery shaft ten feet deeper than it was at the time of its abandonment, and erect new, or adopt the old boundaries, renewing the posts or monuments of stone if removed or destroyed. In either event, a new location stake shall be fixed. The location certificate of an abandoned claim may state that the whole or any part of the new location is located as an abandoned claim.

Sec. 2553. Location Certificates of Placer Claims.—Hereafter the discoverer of any placer claim shall, within ninety days after the date of discovery, cause such claim to be recorded in the office of the county clerk and ex-officio register of deeds of the county within which such claim may exist, by filing therein a location certificate, which shall contain the following:

1. The name of the claim, designating it as a placer claim.
2. The name or names of the locator or locators thereof.
3. The date of location.
4. The number of feet or acres thus claimed.
5. A description of the claim by such designation of natural or fixed objects as shall identify the claim beyond question. Before filing such location certificate, the discoverer shall locate his claim: First, by securely fixing upon such claim a notice in plain painted, printed or written letters, containing the name of the claim, the name of the locator or locators, the date of the discovery, and the number of feet or acres claimed; second, by designating the surface boundaries by substantial posts or stone monuments at each corner of the claim.

Sec. 2554. Assessment Work on Placer Claims.—For every placer claim, assessment work, as hereinafter provided, shall be done during each and every calendar year after the first day of January following the date of location. Such assessment work shall consist in manual labor, permanent improvements made on the claim in buildings, roads or ditches made for the benefit of working such claims, or after any manner, so long as the work done accrues to the improvement of the claim, or shows good faith and intention on the part of the owner or owners and their intention to hold possession of said claim.

Sec. 2555. Amount of Assessment Work.—On all placer claims heretofore or hereafter located in this state not less than one hundred dollars' worth of assessment work shall be performed during each calendar year from the first day of January after the date of location.

Sec. 2556. Assessment Work Upon Contiguous Claims.—When two or more placer mining claims lie contiguous and are owned by the same person, persons, company or corporation, the yearly expenditure of labor and improvements required on each of such claims may be made upon any one of such contiguous claims if the owner or owners shall thus prefer.

Sec. 2558. Effect of Failure to Do Assessment Work.—Upon failure of the owners to do or have done the assessment work required within the time above stated, such claim or claims upon which such work has not been completed, shall thereafter be open to relocation on or after the first day of January of any year after such labor or improvements should have been done, in the same manner and on the same terms as if no location thereof had ever been made; Provided, That the original locators, their heirs, assigns or legal representatives have not resumed work upon such claim or claims after failure, and before any subsequent location has been made.

Sec. 2559. Affidavit of Assessment Work Done.—Upon completion of the required assessment work for any mining claim, the owner or owners or agent of such owner or owners shall cause to be made by some person cognizant of the facts, an affidavit setting forth that the required amount of work was done, which affidavit shall within sixty days of the completion of the work, be filed for record, and shall thereafter be recorded in the office of the county clerk and ex-officio register of deeds of the county in which said claim is located.

Sec. 2560. Patents to Placer Claims.—When any person, persons or association, they and their grantors, have held and worked their placer claims in conformance with the laws of this state and the regulations of the mining district in which such claim exists, if such be organized, for five successive years after the first day of January succeeding the date of location, then such person, persons or association, they and their grantors, shall be entitled to proceed to obtain a patent for their claims from the United States without performing further work; but where such person, persons or association, they or their grantors, desire to obtain a United States patent before the expiration of five years from the date hereinbefore mentioned, they shall be required to expend at least five hundred dollars' worth of work upon a placer claim.

REGULATIONS OF THE GENERAL LAND OFFICE.

Nature and Extent of Mining Claims.

1. Mining claims are of two distinct classes: Lode claims and placers.

Lode Claims.

2. The status of lode claims located or patented previous to the 10th day of May, 1872, is not changed with regard to their extent along the lode or width of surface; but the claim is enlarged by sections 2322 and 2328, by investing the locator, his heirs or assigns, with the right to follow, upon the conditions stated therein, all veins, lodes, or ledges, the top or apex of which lies inside of the surface lines of his claim.

3. It is to be distinctly understood, however, that the law limits the possessory right to veins, lodes, or ledges, other than the one named in the original location, to such as were not adversely claimed on May 10, 1872, and that where such other vein or ledge was so adversely claimed at that date the right of the party so adversely claiming is in no way impaired by the provisions of the Revised Statutes.

4. From and after the 10th May, 1872, any person who is a citizen of the United States, or who has declared his intention to become a citizen, may locate, record, and hold a mining claim of fifteen hundred linear feet along the course of any mineral vein or lode subject to location; or an association of persons, severally qualified as above, may make joint location of such claim of fifteen hundred feet, but in no event can a location of a vein or lode made after the 10th day of May, 1872, exceed fifteen hundred feet along the course thereof, whatever may be the number of persons composing the association.

5. With regard to the extent of surface ground adjoining a vein or lode, and claimed for the convenient working thereof, the Revised Statutes provide that the lateral extent of locations of veins or lodes made after May 10, 1872, shall in no case exceed three hundred feet on each side of the middle of the vein at the surface, and that no such surface rights shall be limited by any mining regulations to less than twenty-five feet on each side of the middle of the vein at the surface, except where adverse rights existing on the 10th May, 1872, may render such limitation necessary; the end lines of such claims to be in all cases parallel to each other. Said lateral measurements can not extend beyond three hundred feet on either side of the middle of the vein at the surface, or such distance as is allowed by local laws. For example: 400

feet can not be taken on one side and 200 feet on the other. If, however, 300 feet on each side are allowed, and by reason of prior claims but 100 feet can be taken on one side, the locator will not be restricted to less than 300 feet on the other side; and when the locator does not determine by exploration where the middle of the vein at the surface is, his discovery shaft must be assumed to mark such point.

6. By the foregoing it will be perceived that no lode claim located after the 10th May, 1872, can exceed a parallelogram fifteen hundred feet in length by six hundred feet in width, but whether surface ground of that width can be taken depends upon the local regulations or state or territorial laws in force in the several mining districts; and that no such local regulations or state or territorial laws shall limit a vein or lode claim to less than fifteen hundred feet along the course thereof, whether the location is made by one or more persons, nor can surface rights be limited to less than fifty feet in width unless adverse claims existing on the 10th day of May, 1872, render such lateral limitation necessary.

7. Locators can not exercise too much care in defining their locations at the outset, inasmuch as the law requires that all records of mining locations made subsequent to May 10, 1872, shall contain the name or names of the locators, the date of the location, and such a description of the claim or claims located, by reference to some natural object or permanent monument, as will identify the claim.

8. No lode claim shall be located until after the discovery of a vein or lode within the limits of the claim, the object of which provision is evidently to prevent the appropriation of presumed mineral ground for speculative purposes, to the exclusion of bona fide prospectors, before sufficient work has been done to determine whether a vein or lode really exists.

9. The claimant should, therefore, prior to locating his claim, unless the vein can be traced upon the surface, sink a shaft or run a tunnel or drift to a sufficient depth therein to discover and develop a mineral-bearing vein, lode, or crevice; should determine, if possible, the general course of such vein in either direction from the point of discovery, by which direction he will be governed in marking the boundaries of his claim on the surface. His location notice should give the course and distance as nearly as practicable from the discovery shaft on the claim to some permanent, well-known points or objects, such, for instance, as stone monuments, blazed trees, the confluence of streams, point of intersection of well-known gulches, ravines, or roads, prominent buttes, hills, etc., which may be in the immediate vicinity, and which will serve to perpetuate and fix the locus of the claim and render it susceptible of identification from the description thereof given in the record of locations in the district, and should be duly recorded.

10. In addition to the foregoing data, the claimant should state the names of adjoining claims, or, if none adjoin, the

relative positions of the nearest claims; should drive a post or erect a monument of stones at each corner of his surface ground, and at the point of discovery or discovery shaft should fix a post, stake, or board, upon which should be designated the name of the lode, the name or names of the locators, the number of feet claimed, and in which direction from the point of discovery; it being essential that the location notice filed for record, in addition to the foregoing description, should state whether the entire claim of fifteen hundred feet is taken on one side of the point of discovery, or whether it is partly upon one and partly upon the other side thereof, and in the latter case, how many feet are claimed upon each side of such discovery point.

11. The location notice must be filed for record in all respects as required by the state or territorial laws and local rules and regulations, if there be any.

12. In order to hold the possessory title to a mining claim located prior to May 10, 1872, the law requires that ten dollars shall be expended annually in labor or improvements for each one hundred feet in length along the vein or lode. In order to hold the possessory right to a location made since May 10, 1872, not less than one hundred dollars' worth of labor must be performed or improvements made thereon annually. Under the provisions of the act of congress approved January 22, 1880, the first annual expenditure becomes due and must be performed during the calendar year succeeding that in which the location was made. Where a number of continguous claims are held in common, the aggregate expenditure that would be necessary to hold all the claims, may be made upon any one claim. Cornering locations are held not to be contiguous.

13. Failure to make the expenditure or perform the labor required upon a location made before or since May 10, 1872, will subject a claim to relocation, unless the original locator, his heirs, assigns, or legal representatives have resumed work after such failure and before relocation.

14. Annual expenditure is not required subsequent to entry, the date of issuing the patent certificate being the date contemplated by statute.

15. Upon the failure of any one of several co-owners to contribute his proportion of the required expenditures, the co-owners, who have performed the labor or made the improvements as required, may, at the expiration of the year, give such delinquent co-owner personal notice in writing, or notice by publication in the newspaper published nearest the claim for at least once a week for ninety days; and if upon the expiration of ninety days after such notice in writing, or upon the expiration of one hundred and eighty days after the first newspaper publication of notice, the delinquent co-owner shall have failed to contribute his proportion to meet such expenditures or improvements, his interest in the claim by law passes to his co-owners who have made the expenditures

or improvements as aforesaid. Where a claimant alleges ownership of a forfeited interest under the foregoing provision, the sworn statement of the publisher as to the facts of publication, giving dates and a printed copy of the notice published, should be furnished, and the claimant must swear that the delinquent co-owner failed to contribute his proper proportion within the period fixed by the statute.

Tunnels.

16. The effect of section 2323, Revised Statutes, is to give the proprietors of a mining tunnel run in good faith the possessory right to fifteen hundred feet of any blind lodes cut, discovered, or intersected by such tunnel, which were not previously known to exist, within three thousand feet from the face or point of commencement of such tunnel, and to prohibit other parties, after the commencement of the tunnel, from prospecting for and making locations of lodes on the line thereof and within said distance of three thousand feet, unless such lodes appear upon the surface or were previously known to exist. The term "face," as used in said section, is construed and held to mean the first working face formed in the tunnel, and to signify the point at which the tunnel actually enters cover; it being from this point that the three thousand feet are to be counted upon which prospecting is prohibited as aforesaid.

17. To avail themselves of the benefits of this provision of law, the proprietors of a mining tunnel will be required, at the time they enter cover as aforesaid, to give proper notice of their tunnel location by erecting a substantial post, board, or monument at the face or point of commencement thereof, upon which should be posted a good and sufficient notice, giving the names of the parties or company claiming the tunnel right; the actual or proposed course or direction of the tunnel, the height and width thereof, and the course and distance from such face or point of commencement to some permanent well-known objects in the vicinity by which to fix and determine the locus in manner heretofore set forth applicable to locations of veins or lodes, and at the time of posting such notice they shall, in order that miners or prospectors may be enabled to determine whether or not they are within the lines of the tunnel, establish the boundary lines thereof, by stakes or monuments placed along such lines at proper intervals, to the terminus of the three thousand feet from the face or point of commencement of the tunnel, and the lines so marked will define and govern as to specific boundaries within which prospecting for lodes not previously known to exist is prohibited while work on the tunnel is being prosecuted with reasonable diligence.

18. A full and correct copy of such notice of location defining the tunnel claim must be filed for record with the mining recorder of the district, to which notice must be attached the sworn statement or declaration of the owners, claimants,

or projectors of such tunnel, setting forth the facts in the case; stating the amount expended by themselves and their predecessors in interest in prosecuting work thereon; the extent of the work performed, and that it is bona fide their intention to prosecute work on the tunnel so located and described with reasonable diligence for the development of a vein or lode, or for the discovery of mines, or both, as the case may be. This notice of location must be duly recorded, and, with the said sworn statement attached, kept on the recorder's files for future reference.

Placer Claims.

19. But one discovery of mineral is required to support a placer location, whether it be of twenty acres by an individual, or of one hundred and sixty acres or less by an association of persons.

20. The act of August 4, 1892, extends the mineral land laws so as to bring lands chiefly valuable for building stone within the provisions of said law by authorizing a placer entry of such lands. Registers and receivers should make a reference to said act on the entry papers in the case of all placer entries made for lands containing stone chiefly valuable for building purposes. Lands reserved for the benefit of public schools or donated to any state are not subject to entry under said act.

21. The act of February 11, 1897, provides for the location and entry of public lands chiefly valuable for petroleum or other mineral oils, and entries of that nature made prior to the passage of said act are to be considered as though made thereunder.

22. By section 2330 authority is given for subdividing forty-acre legal subdivisions into ten-acre tracts. These ten-acre tracts should be considered and dealt with as legal subdivisions, and an applicant having a placer claim which conforms to one or more of such ten-acre tracts, contiguous in case of two or more tracts, may make entry thereof, after the usual proceedings, without further survey or plat.

23. In subdividing forty-acre legal subdivisions, the ten-acre tracts must be in square form, with lines at right angles with the lines of the public surveys; and the notice given of the application must be specific and accurate in description.

24. A ten-acre subdivision may be described, for instance if situated in the extreme northeast of the section, as the "NE. ¼ of the NE. ¼ of the NE. ¼" of the section, or, in like manner, by appropriate terms, wherever situated; but, in addition to this description, the notice must give all the other data required in a mineral application, by which parties may be put on inquiry as to the land sought to be patented. The proofs submitted with applications must show clearly the character and extent of the improvements upon the premises.

25. The proof of improvements must show their value to be not less than five hundred dollars and that they were made

by the applicant for patent or his grantors. This proof should consist of the affidavit of two or more disinterested witnesses. The annual expenditure to the amount of $100, required by section 2324, Revised Statutes, must be made upon placer claims as well as lode claims.

26.   Applicants for patent to a placer claim, who are also in possession of a known vein or lode included therein, must state in their application that the placer includes such vein or lode. The published and posted notices must also include such statement. If veins or lodes lying within a placer location are owned by other parties, the fact should be distinctly stated in the application for patent and in all the notices. But in all cases, whether the lode is claimed or excluded, it must be surveyed and marked upon the plat, the field notes and plat giving the area of the lode claim or claims and the area of the placer separately. An application which omits to claim such known vein or lode must be construed as a conclusive declaration that the applicant has no right of possession to the vein or lode. Where there is no known lode or vein, the fact must appear by the affidavit of two or more witnesses.

27.   By section 2330 it is declared that no location of a placer claim, made after July 9, 1870, shall exceed one hundred and sixty acres for any one person or association of persons, which location shall conform to the United States surveys.

28.   Section 2331 provides that all placer mining claims located after May 10, 1872, shall conform as nearly as practicable with the United States system of public lands surveys and the rectangular subdivisions of such surveys, and such locations shall not include more than twenty acres for each individual claimant.

29.   The foregoing provisions of law are construed to mean that after the 9th day of July, 1870, no location of a placer claim can be made to exceed one hundred and sixty acres, whatever may be the number of locators associated together, or whatever the local regulations of the district may allow; and that from and after May 10, 1872, no location can exceed twenty acres for each individual participating therein; that is, a location by two persons can not exceed forty acres, and one by three persons can not exceed sixty acres.

30.   The regulations hereinbefore given as to the manner of marking locations on the ground, and placing the same on record, must be observed in the case of placer locations so far as the same are applicable, the law requiring, however, that all placer mining claims located after May 10, 1872, shall conform as near as practicable with the United States system of public land surveys and the rectangular subdivisions of such surveys, whether the locations are upon surveyed or unsurveyed lands.

Regulations Under Saline Act.

31. Under the act approved January 31, 1901, extending the mining laws to saline lands, the provisions of the law relating to placer mining claims are extended to all states and territories and the district of Alaska, so as to permit the location and purchase thereunder of all unoccupied public lands containing salt springs, or deposits of salt in any form, and chiefly valuable therefor, with the proviso, "That the same person shall not locate or enter more than one claim hereunder.

32. Rights obtained by location under the placer mining laws are assignable, and the assignee may make the entry in his own name; so, under this act a person holding as assignee may make entry in his own name: Provided, He has not held under this act, at any time, either as locator or entryman, any other lands; his right is exhausted by having held under this act any particular tract, either as locator or entryman, either as an individual or as a member of an association. It follows, therefore, that no application for patent or entry, made under this act, shall embrace more than one single location.

33. In order that the conditions imposed by the proviso, as set forth in the above paragraph, may duly appear, the notice of location presented for record and the application for patent must each contain a specific statement under oath by each person whose name appears therein that he never has, either as an individual or as a member of an association, located or entered any other lands, under the provisions of this act. Assignments made by persons who are not severally qualified as herein stated will not be recognized.

Procedure to Obtain Patent to Mineral Lands.—Lode Claims.

34. The claimant is required, in the first place, to have a correct survey of his claim made under authority of the surveyor general of the state or territory in which the claim lies, such survey to show with accuracy the exterior surface boundaries of the claim, which boundaries are required to be distinctly marked by monuments on the ground. Four plats and one copy of the original field notes in each case will be prepared by the surveyor general; one plat and the original field notes to be retained in the office of the surveyor general; one copy of the plat to be given the claimant for posting upon the claim; one plat and a copy of the field notes to be given the claimant for filing with the proper register, to be finally transmitted by that officer, with other papers in the case, to this office, and one plat to be sent by the surveyor general to the register of the proper land district, to be retained on his files for future reference. As there is no resident surveyor general for the State of Arkansas, applications for the survey of mineral claims in said state should be made to the commissioner of this office, who, under the law, is ex officio the U. S. surveyor general.

35. The survey and plat of mineral claims required to be filed in the proper land office with application for patent must be made subsequent to the recording of the location of the claim (if the laws of the state or territory or the regulations of the mining district require the notice of location to be recorded), and when the original location is made by survey of a United States mineral surveyor such location survey can not be substituted for that required by the statute, as above indicated.

36. The surveyors general should designate all surveyed mineral claims by a progressive series of numbers, beginning with survey No. 37, irrespective as to whether they are situated on surveyed or unsurveyed lands, the claim to be so designated at date of issuing the order therefor, in addition to the local designation of the claim; it being required in all cases that the plat and field notes of the survey of a claim must, in addition to the reference to permanent objects in the neighborhood, describe the locus of the claim with reference to the lines of public surveys by·a line connecting a corner of the claim with the nearest public corner of the United States surveys, unless such claim be on unsurveyed lands at a distance of more than two miles from such public corner, in which latter case it should be connected with a United States mineral monument. Such connecting line must not be more than two miles in length, and should be measured on the ground direct between the points, or calculated from actually surveyed traverse lines if the nature of the country should not permit direct measurement. If a regularly established survey corner is within two miles of a claim situated on unsurveyed lands, the connection should be made with such corner in preference to a connection with a United States mineral monument. The connecting line or traverse line must be surveyed by the mineral surveyor at the time of his making the particular survey and be made a part hereof.

37. (a) Promptly upon the approval of a mineral survey the surveyor general will advise both this office and the appropriate local land office by letter (Form 4-286), of the date of approval, number of the survey, name and area of the claim, name and survey number of each approved mineral survey with which actually in conflict, name and address of the applicant for survey, and name of the mineral surveyor who made the survey; and will also briefly describe therein the locus of the claim, specifying each legal subdivision or portion thereof, when upon surveyed lands, covered in whole or in part by the survey; but hereafter no segregation of any such claim upon the official township survey records will be made until mineral entry has been made and approved for patent, unless other wise directed by this office.

(b) Upon application to make agricultural entry of the residue of any original lot or legal subdivision of forty acres, reduced by mining claims for which patent applications have been filed and which residue has been already relotted in accordance therewith, the local officers will accept and approve the application as usual, if found to be regular. When such an application is filed for any such original lot or subdivision, reduced in available area by duly asserted mining claims but not yet relotted accordingly, the local officers will promptly advise this office thereof; and will also report and identify any pending application for mineral patent affecting such subdivision which the agricultural applicant does not desire to contest. The surveyor general will thereupon be advised by this office of such mining claims, or portions thereof, as are proper to be segregated, and directed to at once prepare, upon the usual drawing-paper township blank, diagram of amended township survey of such original lot or legal forty-acre subdivision so made fractional by such mineral segregation, designating the agricultural portion by appropriate lot number, beginning with No. 1 in each section and giving the area of each lot, and will forthwith transmit one approved copy to the local land office and one to this office. In the meantime the local officers will accept the agricultural application (if no other objection appears), suspend it with reservation of all rights of the applicant if continuously asserted by him, and upon receipt of amended township diagram will approve the application (if then otherwise satisfactory) as of the date of filing, corrected to describe the tract as designated in the amended survey.

(c) The register and receiver will allow no agricultural claim for any portion of an original lot or legal forty-acre subdivision, where the reduced area is made to appear by reason of approved surveys of mining claims and for which applications for patent have not been filed, until there is submitted by such agricultural applicant a satisfactory showing that such surveyed claims are in fact mineral in character; and applications to have lands asserted to be mineral, or mining locations, segregated by survey, with the view to agricultural appropriation of the remainder, will be made to the register and receiver for submission to the commissioner of the general land office, for his consideration and direction, and must be supported by the affidavit of the party in interest, duly corroborated by two or more disinterested persons, or by such other or further evidence as may be required in any case, that the lands sought to be segregated as mineral are in fact mineral in character; otherwise, in the absence of satisfactory showing in any such case, such original lot or legal subdivision will be subject to agricultural appropriation only. When any such showing shall be found to be satisfactory and the necessary survey is had, amended township diagram will be required and made as prescribed in the preceding section.

38. The following particulars should be observed in the survey of every mining claim:

(1) The exterior boundaries of the claim, the number of feet claimed along the vein, and, as nearly as can be ascer-

tained, the direction of the vein, and the number of feet claimed on the vein in each direction from the point of discovery or other well-defined place on the claim should be represented on the plat of survey and in the field notes.

(2) The intersection of the lines of the survey with the lines of conflicting prior surveys should be noted in the field notes and represented upon the plat.

(3) Conflicts with unsurveyed claims, where the applicant for survey does not claim the area in conflict, should be shown by actual survey.

(4) The total area of the claim embraced by the exterior boundaries should be stated, and also the area in conflict with each intersecting survey, substantially as follows:

	Acres.
Total area of claim	10.50
Area in conflict with survey No. 302	1.56
Area in conflict with survey No. 948	2.33
Area in conflict with Mountain Maid lode mining claim, unsurveyed	1.48

It does not follow that because mining surveys are required to exhibit all conflicts with prior surveys the areas of conflict are to be excluded. The field notes and plat are made a part of the application for patent, and care should be taken that the description does not inadvertently exclude portions intended to be retained. The application for patent should state the portions to be excluded in express terms.

39. The claimant is then required to post a copy of the plat of such survey in a conspicuous place upon the claim, together with notice of his intention to apply for a patent therefor, which notice will give the date of posting, the name of the claimant, the name of the claim, the number of the survey, the mining district and county, and the names of adjoining and conflicting claims as shown by the plat survey. Too much care can not be exercised in the preparation of this notice, inasmuch as the data therein are to be repeated in the other notices required by the statute, and upon the accuracy and completeness of these notices will depend, in a great measure, the regularity and validity of the proceedings for patent.

40. After posting the said plat and notice upon the premises, the claimant will file with the proper register and receiver a copy of such plat and the field notes of survey of the claim, accompanied by the affidavit of at least two credible witnesses that such plat and notice are posted conspicuously upon the claim, giving the date and place of such posting; a copy of the notice so posted to be attached to and form a part of said affidavit.

41. Accompanying the field notes so filed must be the sworn statement of the claimant that he has the possessory right to the premises therein described, in virtue of a compliance by himself (and by his grantors, if he claims by pur-

chase) with the mining rules, regulations, and customs of the mining district, state, or territory in which the claim lies, and with the mining laws of congress; such sworn statement to narrate briefly, but as clearly as possible, the facts constituting such compliance, the origin of his possession, and the basis of his claim to a patent.

42. This sworn statement must be supported by a copy of each location notice, certified by the legal custodian of the record thereof, and also by an abstract of title of each claim, completed to the date of filing said statement and certified by the legal custodian of the records of transfers, or by a duly authorized abstracter of titles. The certificate must state that no conveyances affecting the title to the claim or claims appear of record other than those set forth.

Abstracters will be required to attach to each abstract certified by them a certificate stating that they have filed in the office of the Commissioner of the General Land Office a certified copy of the existing statute by which they are authorized to compile abstracts of title, and evidence in the form of a certificate by the proper state, territorial, or county officer that they have complied with the requirements of such statute.

43. In the event of the mining records in any case having been destroyed by fire or otherwise lost, affidavit of the fact should be made, and secondary evidence of possessory title will be received, which may consist of the affidavit of the claimant, supported by those of any other parties cognizant of the facts relative to his location, occupancy, possession, improvements, &c.; and in such case of lost records, any deeds, certificates of location or purchase, or other evidence which may be in the claimant's possession and tend to establish his claim, should be filed.

44. Before receiving and filing an application for mineral patent local officers will be particular to see that it includes no land which is embraced in a prior or pending application for patent or entry, or for any lands embraced in a railroad selection, or for which publication is pending or has been made by any other claimants, and if, in their opinion, after investigation, it should appear that a mineral application should not, for these or other reasons, be accepted and filed, they should formally reject the same, giving the reasons therefor, and allow the applicant thirty days for appeal to this office under the rules of practice.

Local officers will give prompt and appropriate notice to the railroad grantee of the filing of every application for mineral patent which embraces any portion of an odd-numbered section of surveyed lands within the primary limits of a railroad land grant, and of every such application embracing any portion of unsurveyed lands within such limits (except as to any such application which embraces a portion or portions of those ascertained or prospective odd-numbered sections only, within the limits of the grant in Montana and Idaho to the

Northern Pacific Railroad Company, which have been classified as mineral under the act of February 26, 1895, without protest by the company within the time limited by the statute or the mineral classification whereof has been approved).

Should the railroad grantee file protest and apply for a hearing to determine the character of the land involved in any such application for mineral patent, proceedings thereunder will be had in the usual manner.

Any application for mineral patent, however, which embraces lands previously listed or selected by a railroad company will be disposed of as provided by the first section of this paragraph, and the applicant afforded opportunity to protest and apply for a hearing or to appeal.

Notice should be given to the duly authorized representative of the railroad grantee, in accordance with rule 17 of Practice. When the claims applied for are upon unsurveyed land, the burden of proving that they are situate within prospective odd-numbered sections will rest upon the railroad.

Evidence of service of notice should be filed with the record in each case.

45. Upon the receipt of these papers, if no reason appears for rejecting the application, the register will, at the expense of the claimant (who must furnish the agreement of the publisher to hold applicant for patent alone responsible for charges of publication), publish a notice of such application for the period of sixty days in a newspaper published nearest to the claim, and will post a copy of such notice in his office for the same period. When the notice is published in a weekly newspaper, nine consecutive insertions are necessary; when in a daily newspaper, the notice must appear in each issue for sixty-one consecutive issues. In both cases the first day of issue must be excluded in estimating the period of sixty days.

46. The notices so published and posted must embrace all the data given in the notice posted upon the claim. In addition to such data the published notice must further indicate the locus of the claim by giving the connecting line, as shown by the field notes and plat, between a corner of the claim and a United States mineral monument or a corner of the public survey, and thence the boundaries of the claim by courses and distances.

47. The register shall publish the notice of application for patent in a paper of established character and general circulation, to be by him designated as being the newspaper published nearest the land.

48. The claimant at the time of filing the application for patent, or at any time within the sixty days of publication, is required to file with the register a certificate of the surveyor general that not less than five hundred dollars' worth of labor has been expended or improvements made, by the applicant or his grantors, upon each location embraced in the application, or if the application embraces several contiguous locations held in common, that an amount equal to five hundred dollars

for each location has been so expended upon, and for the benefit of, the entire group; that the plat filed by the claimant is correct; that the field notes of the survey, as filed, furnish such an accurate description of the claim as will, if incorporated in a patent, serve to fully identify the premises, and that such reference is made therein to natural objects or permanent monuments as will perpetuate and fix the locus thereof: Provided, That as to all applications for patents made and passed to entry before July 1, 1898, or which are by protests or adverse claims prevented from being passed to entry before that time, where the application embraces several locations held in common, proof of an expenditure of five hundred dollars upon the group will be sufficient, and an expenditure of that amount need not be shown to have been made upon, or for the benefit of, each location embraced in the application.

49. The surveyor general may derive his information upon which to base his certificate as to the value of labor expended or improvements made from the mineral surveyor who makes the actual survey and examination upon the premises, and such mineral surveyor should specify with particularity and full detail the character and extent of such improvements, but further or other evidence may be required in any case.

50. It will be convenient to have this certificate indorsed by the surveyor general, both upon the plat and field notes of survey filed by the claimant as aforesaid.

51. After the sixty days' period of newspaper publication has expired, the claimant will furnish from the office of publication a sworn statement that the notice was published for the statutory period, giving the first and last day of such publication, and his own affidavit showing that the plat and notice aforesaid remained conspicuously posted upon the claim sought to be patented during said sixty days' publication, giving the dates.

52. Upon the filing of this affidavit the register will, if no adverse claim was filed in his office during the period of publication, and no other objection appears, permit the claimant to pay for the land to which he is entitled at the rate of five dollars for each acre and five dollars for each fractional part of an acre, except as otherwise provided by law, the receiver issuing the usual duplicate receipt therefor. The claimant will also make a sworn statement of all charges and fees paid by him for publication and surveys, together with all fees and money paid the register and receiver of the land office, after which the complete record will be forwarded to the commissioner of the general land office and a patent issued thereon if found regular.

53. At any time prior to the issuance of patent protest may be filed against the patenting of the claim as applied for, upon any ground tending to show that the applicant has failed to comply with the law in any matter essential to a valid entry under the patent proceedings. Such protest can not,

however, be made the means of preserving a surface conflict lost by failure to adverse or lost by the judgment of the court in an adverse suit. One holding a present joint interest in a mineral location included in an application for patent who is excluded from the application, so that his interest would not be protected by the issue of patent thereon, may protest against the issuance of a patent as applied for, setting forth in such protest the nature and extent of his interest in such location, and such a protestant will be deemed a party in interest entitled to appeal. This results from the holding that a co-owner excluded from an application for patent does not have an "adverse" claim within the meaning of sections 2325 and 2326 of the Revised Statutes. (See Turner v. Sawyer, 150 U. S., 578-586.)

54. Any party applying for patent as trustee must disclose fully the nature of the trust and the name of the cestui que trust; and such trustee, as well as the beneficiaries, must furnish satisfactory proof of citizenship; and the names of beneficiaries, as well as that of the trustee, must be inserted in the final certificate of entry.

55. The annual expenditure of one hundred dollars in labor or improvements on a mining claim, required by section 2324 of the Revised Statutes, is solely a matter between rival or adverse claimants to the same mineral land, and goes only to the right of possession, the determination of which is committed exclusively to the courts.

56. The failure of an applicant for patent to a mining claim to prosecute his application to completion, by filing the necessary proofs and making payment for the land, within a reasonable time after the expiration of the period of publication of notice of the application, or after the termination of adverse proceedings in the courts, constitutes a waiver by the applicant of all rights obtained by the earlier proceedings upon the application.

57. The proceedings necessary to the completion of an application for patent to a mining claim, against which an adverse claim or protest has been filed, if taken by the applicant at the first opportunity afforded therefor under the law and departmental practice, will be as effective as if taken at the date when, but for the adverse claim or protest, the proceedings on the application could have been completed.

Placer Claims.

58. The proceedings to obtain patents for placer claims, including all forms of mineral deposits excepting veins of quartz or other rock in place, are similar to the proceedings prescribed for obtaining patents for vein or lode claims; but where a placer claim shall be upon surveyed lands, and conforms to legal subdivisions, no further survey or plat will be required. Where placer claims can not be conformed to legal subdivisions, survey and plat shall be made as on unsurveyed lands.

59. The proceedings for obtaining patents for veins or lodes having already been fully given, it will not be necessary to repeat them here, it being thought that careful attention thereto by applicants and the local officers will enable them to act understandingly in the matter, and make such slight modifications in the notice, or otherwise, as may be necessary in view of the different nature of the two classes of claims; the price of placer claims being fixed, however, at two dollars and fifty cents per acre or fractional part of an acre.

60. In placer applications for patent care must be exercised to determine the proper classification of the lands claimed. To this end the clearest evidence of which the case is capable should be presented.

(1) If the claim be all placer ground, that fact must be stated in the application and corroborated by accompanying proofs; if of mixed placers and lodes, it should be so set out, with a description of all known lodes situated within the boundaries of the claim. A specific declaration, such as is required by section 2333, Revised Statutes, must be furnished as to each lode intended to be claimed. All other known lodes are, by the silence of the applicant, excluded by law from all claim by him, of whatsoever nature, possessory or otherwise.

(2) Mineral surveyors shall, at the expense of the parties, make full examination of all placer claims surveyed by them and duly note the facts as specified in the law, stating the quality and composition of the soil, the kind and amount of timber and other vegetation, the locus and size of streams, and such other matters as may appear upon the surface of the claim. This examination should include the character and extent of all surface and underground workings, whether placer or lode, for mining purposes.

(3) In addition to these data, which the law requires to be shown in all cases, the mineral surveyor should report with reference to the proximity of centers of trade or residence; also of well-known systems of lode deposit or of individual lodes. He should also report as to the use or adaptability of the claim for placer mining; whether water has been brought upon it in sufficient quantity to mine the same, or whether it can be procured for that purpose; and, finally, what works or expenditures have been made by the claimant or his grantors for the development of the claim, and their situation and location with respect to the same as applied for.

(4) This examination should be reported by the mineral surveyor under oath to the surveyor general, and duly corroborated; and a copy of the same should be furnished with the application for patent to the claim, constituting a part thereof, and included in the oath of the applicant.

(5) Applications awaiting entry, whether published or not, must be made to conform to these regulations, with respect to examination as to the character of the land. Entries al-

ready made will be suspended for such additional proofs as may be deemed necessary in each case.

Mill Sites.

61. Land entered as a mill site must be shown to be non-mineral. Mill sites are simply auxiliary to the working of mineral claims, and as section 2337, which provides for the patenting of mill sites, is embraced in the chapter of the Revised Statutes relating to mineral lands, they are therefore included in this circular.

62. To avail themselves of this provision of law parties holding the possessory right to a vein or lode claim, and to a piece of non-mineral land not contiguous thereto for mining or milling purposes, not exceeding the quantity allowed for such purpose by section 2337, or prior laws, under which the land was appropriated, the proprietors of such vein or lode may file in the proper land office their application for a patent, under oath, in manner already set forth herein, which application, together with the plat and field notes, may include, embrace, and describe, in addition to the vein or lode claim, such non-contiguous mill site, and after due proceedings as to notice, etc., a patent will be issued conveying the same as one claim. The owner of a patented lode may, by an independent application, secure a mill site if good faith is manifest in its use or occupation in connection with the lode and no adverse claim exists.

63. Where the original survey includes a lode claim and also a mill site the lode claim should be described in the plat and field notes as "Sur. No. 37, A," and the mill site as "Sur. No. 37, B," or whatever may be its appropriate numerical designation; the course and distance from a corner of the mill site to a corner of the lode claim to be invariably given in such plat and field notes, and a copy of the plat and notice of application for patent must be conspicuously posted upon the mill site as well as upon the vein or lode claim for the statutory period of sixty days. In making the entry no separate receipt or certificate need be issued for the mill site, but the whole area of both lode and mill site will be embraced in one entry, the price being five dollars for each acre and fractional part of an acre embraced by such lode and mill-site claim.

64. In case the owner of a quartz mill or reduction works is not the owner or claimant of a vein or lode claim the law permits him to make application therefor in the same manner prescribed herein for mining claims, and after due notice and proceedings, in the absence of a valid adverse filing, to enter and receive a patent for his mill site at said price per acre.

65. In every case there must be satisfactory proof that the land claimed as a mill site is not mineral in character, which proof may, where the matter is unquestioned, consist of the sworn statement of two or more persons capable, from acquaintance with the land, to testify understandingly.

Citizenship.

66. The proof necessary to establish the citizenship of applicants for mining patents must be made in the following manner: In case of an incorporated company, a certified copy of their charter or certificate of incorporation must be filed In case of an association of persons unincorporated, the affidavit of their duly authorized agent, made upon his own knowledge or upon information and belief, setting forth the residence of each person forming such association, must be submitted. This affidavit must be accompanied by a power of attorney from the parties forming such association, authorizing the person who makes the affidavit of citizenship to act for them in the matter of their application for patent.

67. In case of an individual or an association of individuals who do not appear by their duly authorized agent, the affidavit of each applicant, showing whether he is a native or naturalized citizen, when and where born, and his residence, will be required.

68. In case an applicant has declared his intention to become a citizen or has been naturalized, his affidavit must show the date, place, and the court before which he declared his intention, or from which his certificate of citizenship issued, and present residence.

69. The affidavit of the claimant as to his citizenship may be taken before the register or receiver, or any other officer authorized to administer oaths within the land districts; or, if the claimant is residing beyond the limits of the district, the affidavit may be taken before the clerk of any court of record or before any notary public of any state or territory.

70. If citizenship is established by the testimony of disinterested persons, such testimony may be taken at any place before any person authorized to administer oaths, and whose official character is duly verified.

71. No entry will be allowed until the register has satisfied himself, by careful examination, that proper proofs have been filed upon the points indicated in the law and official regulations. Transfers made subsequent to the filing of the application for patent will not be considered, but entry will be allowed and patent issued in all cases in the name of the applicant for patent, the title conveyed by the patent, of course, in each instance inuring to the transferee of such applicant where a transfer has been made pending the application for patent.

72. The consecutive series of numbers of mineral entries must be continued, whether the same are of lode or placer claims or mill sites.

73. In sending up the papers in a case the register must not omit certifying to the fact that the notice was posted in his office for the full period of sixty days, such certificate to state distinctly when such posting was done and how long continued. The plat forwarded as part of the proof should not be folded, but rolled, so as to prevent creasing, and either

transmitted in a separate package or so enclosed with the other papers that it may pass through the mails without creasing or mutilation. If forwarded separately, the letter transmitting the papers should state the fact.

Possessory Right.

74. The provisions of section 2332, Revised Statutes, will greatly lessen the burden of proof, more especially in the case of old claims located many years since, the records of which, in many cases, have been destroyed by fire, or lost in other ways during the lapse of time, but concerning the possessory right to which all controversy or litigation has long been settled.

75. When an applicant desires to make his proof of possessory right in accordance with this provision of law, he will not be required to produce evidence of location, copies of conveyances, or abstracts of title, as in other cases, but will be required to furnish a duly certified copy of the statute of limitation of mining claims for the state or territory, together with his sworn statement giving a clear and succinct narration of the facts as to the origin of his title, and likewise as to the continuation of his possession of the mining ground covered by his application; the area thereof; the nature and extent of the mining that has been done thereon; whether there has been any opposition to his possession, or litigation with regard to his claim, and if so, when the same ceased; whether such cessation was caused by compromise or by judicial decree, and any additional facts within the claimant's knowledge having a direct bearing upon his possession and bona fides which he may desire to submit in support of his claim.

76. There should likewise be filed a certificate, under seal of the court having jurisdiction of mining cases within the judicial district embracing the claim, that no suit or action of any character whatever involving the right of possession to any portion of the claim applied for is pending, and that there has been no litigation before said court affecting the title to said claim or any part thereof for a period equal to the time fixed by the statute of limitations for mining claims in the state or territory as aforesaid other than that which has been finally decided in favor of the claimant.

77. The claimant should support his narrative of facts relative to his possession, occupancy, and improvements by corroborative testimony of any disinterested person or persons of credibility who may be cognizant of the facts in the case and are capable of testifying understandingly in the premises.

Adverse Claims.

78. An adverse claim must be filed with the register and receiver of the land office where the application for patent is filed or with the register and receiver of the district in which

the land is situated at the time of filing the adverse claim. It must be on the oath of the adverse claimant, or it may be verified by the oath of any duly authorized agent or attorney in fact of the adverse claimant cognizant of the facts stated.

79. Where an agent or attorney in fact verifies the adverse claim, he must distinctly swear that he is such agent or attorney, and accompany his affidavit by proof thereof.

80. The agent or attorney in fact must make the affidavit in verification of the adverse claim within the land district where the claim is situated.

Regulations.

81. The adverse claim so filed must fully set forth the nature and extent of the interference or conflict; whether the adverse party claims as a purchaser for valuable consideration or as a locator. If the former, a certified copy of the original location, the original conveyance, a duly certified copy thereof, or an abstract of title from the office of the proper recorder should be furnished, or if the transaction was a merely verbal one he will narrate the circumstances attending the purchase, the date thereof, and the amount paid, which facts should be supported by the affidavit of one or more witnesses, if any were present at the time, and if he claims as a locator he must file a duly certified copy of the location from the office of the proper recorder.

82. In order that the "boundaries" and "extent" of the claim may be shown, it will be incumbent upon the adverse claimant to file a plat showing his entire claim, its relative situation or position with the one against which he claims, and the extent of the conflict: Provided, however, That if the application for patent describes the claim by legal subdivisions, the adverse claimant, if also claiming by legal subdivisions, may describe his adverse claim in the same manner without further survey or plat. If the claim is not described by legal subdivisions, it will generally be more satisfactory if the plat thereof is made from an actual survey by a mineral surveyor, and its correctness officially certified thereon by him.

83. Upon the foregoing being filed within the sixty days' period of publication, the register, or in his absence the receiver, will immediately give notice in writing to the parties that such adverse claim has been filed, informing them that the party who filed the adverse claim will be required within thirty days from the date of such filing to commence proceedings in a court of competent jurisdiction to determine the question of right of possession, and to prosecute the same with reasonable diligence to final judgment, and that, should such adverse claimant fail to do so, his adverse claim will be considered waived and the application for patent be allowed to proceed upon its merits.

84. When an adverse claim is filed as aforesaid, the register or receiver will indorse upon the same the precise date

of filing, and preserve a record of the date of notifications issued thereon; and thereafter all proceedings on the application for patent will be stayed, with the exception of the completion of the publication and posting of notices and plat and the filing of the necessary proof thereof, until the controversy shall have been finally adjudicated in court or the adverse claim waived or withdrawn.

85. Where an adverse claim has been filed and suit thereon commenced within the statutory period and final judgment rendered determining the right of possession, it will not be sufficient to file with the register a certificate of the clerk of the court setting forth the facts as to such judgment, but the successful party must, before he is allowed to make entry, file a certified copy of the judgment roll, together with the other evidence required by section 2326, Revised Statutes.

86. Where such suit has been dismissed, a certificate of the clerk of the court to that effect or a certified copy of the order of dismissal will be sufficient.

87. After an adverse claim has been filed and suit commenced, a relinquishment or other evidence of abandonment of the adverse claim will not be accepted, but the case must be terminated and proof thereof furnished as required by the last two paragraphs.

88. Where an adverse claim has been filed, but no suit commenced against the applicant for patent within the statutory period, a certificate to that effect by the clerk of the state court having jurisdiction in the case, and also by the clerk of the circuit court of the United States for the district in which the claim is situated, will be required.

Appointment of Surveyors for Survey of Mining Claims— Charges for Surveys and Publications—Fees of Registers and Receivers, Etc.

89. Section 2334 provides for the appointment of surveyors to survey mining claims, and authorizes the commissioner of the general land office to establish the rates to be charged for surveys and for newspaper publications. Under this authority of law the following rates have been established as the maximum charges for newspaper publications in mining cases:

(1) Where a daily newspaper is designated the charge shall not exceed seven dollars for each ten lines of space occupied, and where a weekly newspaper is designated as the medium of publication five dollars for the same space will be allowed. Such charge shall be accepted as full payment for publication in each issue of the newspaper for the entire period required by law.

It is expected that these notices shall not be so abbreviated as to curtail the description essential to a perfect notice, and the said rates established upon the understanding that they are to be in the usual body type used for advertisements.

(2) For the publication of citations in contests or hear-

ings involving the character of lands the charges shall not exceed eight dollars for five publications in weekly newspapers or ten dollars for publications in daily newspapers for thirty days.

90. The surveyors general of the several districts will, in pursuance of said law, appoint in each land district as many competent surveyors for the survey of mining claims as may seek such appointment, it being distinctly understood that all expenses of these notices and surveys are to be borne by the mining claimants and not by the United States. The statute provides that the claimant shall also be at liberty to employ any United States mineral surveyor to make the survey. Each surveyor appointed to survey mining claims before entering upon the duties of his office or appointment shall be required to enter into a bond of not less than $1,000 for the faithful performance of his duties.

91. With regard to the platting of the claim and other office work in the surveyor general's office, that officer will make an estimate of the cost thereof, which amount the claimant will deposit with any assistant United States treasurer or designated depository in favor of the United States treasurer, to be passed to the credit of the fund created by "individual depositors for surveys of the public lands," and file with the surveyor general duplicate certificates of such deposit in the usual manner.

92. The surveyors general will endeavor to appoint surveyors to survey mining claims so that one or more may be located in each mining district for the greater convenience of miners.

93. The usual oaths will be required of these surveyors and their assistants as to the correctness of each survey executed by them.

The duty of the surveyor ceases when he has executed the survey and returned the field notes and preliminary plat thereof with his report to the surveyor general. He will not be allowed to prepare for the mining claimant the papers in support of an application for patent, or otherwise perform the duties of an attorney before the land office in connection with a mining claim.

The surveyors general and local land officers are expected to report any infringement of this regulation to this office.

94. Should it appear that excessive or exorbitant charges have been made by any surveyor or any publisher, prompt action will be taken with the view of correcting the abuse.

95. The fees payable to the register and receiver for filing and acting upon applications for mineral land patents are five dollars to each officer, to be paid by the applicant for patent at the time of filing, and the like sum of five dollars is payable to each officer by an adverse claimant at the time of filing his adverse claim. (Sec. 2238, R. S., Par. 9.)

96. At the time of payment of fee for mining application or adverse claim the receiver will issue his receipt therefor

in duplicate, one to be given the applicant or adverse claimant, as the case may be, and one to be forwarded to the commissioner of the general land office on the day of issue. The receipt for mining application should have attached the certificate of the register that the lands included in the application are subject to such appropriation, as far as shown by the records of his office.

97. The register and receiver will, at the close of each month, forward to this office an abstract of mining applications filed, an abstract of adverse claims filed, an abstract of mineral lands sold, and a report of receipts from such sales.

98. The fees and purchase money received by registers and receivers must be placed to the credit of the United States in the receiver's monthly and quarterly account, charging up in the disbursing account the sums to which the register and receiver may be respectively entitled as fees and commissions, with limitations in regard to the legal maximum.

Hearings to Determine Character of Lands.

99. The Rules of Practice in cases before the United States district land offices, the general land office, and the department of the interior will, so far as applicable, govern in all cases and proceedings arising 'in contests and hearings to determine the character of lands.

100. Public land returned by the surveyor general as mineral shall be withheld from entry as agricultural land until the presumption arising from such a return shall be overcome by testimony taken in the manner hereinafter described.

101. Hearings to determine the character of lands are practically of two kinds, as follows:

(1) Lands returned as mineral by the surveyor general.

When such lands are sought to be entered as agricultural under laws which require the submission of final proof after due notice by publication and posting, the filing of the proper non-mineral affidavit in the absence of allegations that the land is mineral will be deemed sufficient as a preliminary requirement. A satisfactory showing as to character of land must be made when final proof is submitted.

In case of application to enter, locate, or select such lands as agricultural, under laws in which the submission of final proof after due publication and posting is not required, notice thereof must first be given by publication for sixty days and posting in the local office during the same period, and affirmative proof as to the character of the land submitted. In the absence of allegations that the land is mineral, and upon compliance with this requirement, the entry, location, or selection will be allowed, if otherwise regular.

(2) Lands returned as agricultural and alleged to be mineral in character.

Where as against the claimed right to enter such lands as agricultural it is alleged that the same are mineral, or are applied for as mineral lands, the proceedings in this class of cases will be in the nature of a contest, and the practice will be governed by the rules in force in contest cases.

[Paragraphs 102 to 104, inclusive, are omitted from this revision of the regulations, as appropriate instructions relative to non-mineral proofs in railroad, state, and forest lieu selections are contained in separate circulars.]

105. At hearings to determine the character of lands the claimants and witnesses will be thoroughly examined with regard to the character of the land; whether the same has been thoroughly prospected; whether or not there exists within the tract or tracts claimed any lode or vein of quartz or other rock in place bearing gold, silver, cinnabar, lead, tin, or copper, or other valuable deposit which has ever been claimed, located, recorded, or worked; whether such work is entirely abandoned, or whether occasionally resumed; if such lode does exist, by whom claimed, under what designation, and in which subdivision of the land it lies; whether any placer mine or mines exist upon the land; if so, what is the character thereof—whether of the shallow-surface description, or of the deep cement, blue lead, or gravel deposits; to what extent mining is carried on when water can be obtained, and what the facilities are for obtaining water for mining purposes; upon what particular ten-acre subdivisions mining has been done, and at what time the land was abandoned for mining purposes, if abandoned at all.

106. The testimony should also show the agricultural capacities of the land, what kind of crops are raised thereon, and the value thereof; the number of acres actually cultivated for crops of cereals or vegetables, and within which particular ten-acre subdivision such crops are raised; also which of these subdivisions embrace the improvements, giving in detail the extent and value of the improvements, such as house, barn, vineyard, orchard, fencing, etc., and mining improvements.

107. The testimony should be as full and complete as possible; and in addition to the leading points indicated above, where an attempt is made to prove the mineral character of lands which has been entered under the agricultural laws, it should show at what date, if at all, valuable deposits of minerals were first known to exist on the lands.

108. When the case comes before this office, such decision will be made as the law and the facts may justify. In cases where a survey is necessary to set apart the mineral from the agricultural land, the proper party, at his own expense, will be required to have the work done by a reliable and competent surveyor to be designated by the surveyor general. Application therefor must be made to the register and receiver, accompanied by description of the land to be segregated and the evidence of service upon the opposite party of notice of his intention to have such segregation made. The register and receiver will forward the same to this office, when the

necessary instructions for the survey will be given. The survey in such case, where the claims to e segregated are vein or lode claims, must be executed in such manner as will conform to the requirements in section 2320, United States Revised Statutes, as to length and width and parallel end lines.

109. Such survey when executed must be properly sworn to by the surveyor, either before a notary public, officer of a court of record, or before the register or receiver, the deponent's character and credibility to be properly certified to by the officer administering the oath.

110. Upon the filing of the plat and field notes of such survey with the register and receiver, duly sworn to as aforesaid, they will transmit the same to the surveyor general for his verification and approval, who, if he finds the work correctly performed, will furnish authenticated copies of such plat and description both to the proper local land office and to this office, made upon the usual drawing paper township blank.

The copy of plat furnished the local office and this office must be a diagram verified by the surveyor general, showing the claim or claims segregated, and designating the separate fraction agricultural tracts in each 40-acre legal subdivision by the proper lot number, beginning with No. 1 in each section, and giving the area in each lot, the same as provided in paragraph 37 in the survey of mining claims on surveyed lands.

111. The fact that a certain tract of land is decided upon testimony to be mineral in character is by no means equivalent to an award of the land to a miner. In order to secure a patent for such land, he must proceed as in other cases, in accordance with the foregoing regulations.

Blank forms for proofs in mineral cases are not furnished by the general land office.

District of Alaska.

112. Section 13, act of May 14, 1898, according to native-born citizens of Canada "the same mining rights and privileges" in the district of Alaska as are accorded to citizens of the United States in British Columbia and the Northwest Territory by the laws of the Dominion of Canada, is not now and never has been operative, for the reason that the only mining rights and privileges granted to any person by the laws of the Dominion of Canada are those of leasing mineral lands upon the payment of a stated royalty, and the mining laws of the United States make no provision for such leases.

113. For the sections of the act of June 6, 1900, making further provision for a civil government for Alaska, which provide for the establishment of recording districts and the recording of mining locations; for the making of rules and regulations by the miners and for the legalization of mining records; for the extension of the mining laws to the district of Alaska, and for the exploration and mining of tide lands

and lands below low tide; and relating to the rights of Indians and persons conducting schools or missions, see page —— of this circular.

Mineral Lands Within Forest Reserves.

114. The act of June 4, 1897, provides that "any mineral lands in any forest reservation which have been or which may be shown to be such, and subject to entry under the existing mining laws of the United States and the rules and regulations applying thereto, shall continue to be subject to such location and entry," notwithstanding the reservation. This makes mineral lands in the forest reserves subject to location and entry under the general mining laws in the usual manner.

The act also provides that "The secretary of the interior may permit, under regulations to be prescribed by him, the use of timber and stone found upon such reservations, free of charge, by bona fide settlers, miners, residents, and prospectors for minerals, for firewood, fencing, buildings, mining, prospecting, and other domestic purposes, as may be needed by such persons for such purposes; such timber to be used within the state or territory, respectively, where such reservations may be located."

For further instructions under this act see circular of April 4, 1900 (30 L. D., 23, 28-30).

Surveys of Mining Claims.—General Provisions.

115. Under section 2334, U. S. Rev. Stats., the U. S. surveyor general "may appoint in each land district containing mineral lands as many competent surveyors as shall apply for appointment to survey mining claims."

116. Persons desiring such appointment should therefore file their applications with the surveyor general for the district wherein appointment is asked, who will furnish all information necessary.

117. All appointments of mineral surveyors must be submitted to the commissioner of the general land office for approval.

118. The surveyors general have authority to suspend or revoke the commissions of mineral surveyors for cause. Before final action, however, the matter should be submitted to the commissioner of the general land office for approval.

119. Such surveyors will be allowed the right of appeal from the action of the surveyor general in the usual manner. Such appeal should be filed with the surveyor general, who will at once transmit the same, with a full report, to the general land office.

120. Neither the surveyor general nor the commissioner of the general land office has jurisdiction to settle differences, relative to the payment of charges for field work, between mineral surveyors and claimants. These are matters of pri-

vate contract and must be enforced in the ordinary manner, i. e., in the local courts. The department has, however, authority to investigate charges affecting the official actions of mineral surveyors, and will, on sufficient cause shown, suspend or revoke their appointment.

121. The surveyors general should appoint as many competent mineral surveyors as apply for appointment, in order that claimants may have a choice of surveyors, and be enabled to have their work done on the most advantageous terms.

122. The schedule of charges for office work should be as low as is possible. No additional charges should be made for orders for amended surveys, unless the necessity therefor is clearly the fault of the claimant, or considerable additional office work results therefrom.

123. In cases where the error in the original survey is due to the carelessness or neglect of the surveyor who made it, he should be required to make the necessary corrections in the field at his own expense, and the surveyor general should advise him that the penalty for failure to comply with instructions within a specified time will be the suspension or revocation of his appointment.

124. Mineral surveyors will address all official communications to the surveyor general. They will, when a mining claim is the subject of correspondence, give the name and survey number. In replying to letters they will give the subject-matter and date of the letter. They will promptly notify the surveyor general of any change in post office address.

125. Mineral surveyors should keep a complete record of each survey made by them and the facts coming to their knowledge at the time, as well as copies of all their field notes, reports, and official correspondence, in order that such evidence may be readily produced when called for at any future time. Field notes and other reports must be written in a clear and legible hand or typewritten, in non-copying ink, and upon the proper blanks furnished gratuitously by the surveyor general's office upon application therefor. No

126. No return by a mineral surveyor will be recognized as official unless it is over his signature as a United States mineral surveyor, and made in pursuance of a special order from the surveyor general's office. After he has received an order for survey he is required to make the survey or return correct field notes thereof to the surveyor general's office without delay.

127. The claimant is required, in all cases, to make satisfactory arrangements with the surveyor for the payment for his services and those of his assistants in making the survey, as the United States will not be held responsible for the same.

128. A mineral surveyor is precluded from acting, either directly or indirectly, as attorney in mineral claims. His duty in any particular case ceases when he has executed the survey and returned the field notes and preliminary plat, with his report, to the surveyor general. He will not be allowed

to prepare for the mining claimant the papers in support of his application for patent, or other wise perform the duties of an attorney before the land office in connection with a mining claim. He is not permitted to combine the duties of surveyor and notary public in the same case by administering oaths to the parties in interest. It is preferable that both preliminary and final oaths of assistants should be taken before some officer duly authorized to administer oaths, other than the mineral surveyor. In cases, however, where great delay, expense, or inconvenience would result from a strict compliance with this rule, the mineral surveyor is authorized to administer the necessary oaths to his assistants, but in each case where this is done, he will submit to the proper surveyor general a full written report of the circumstances which repuired his stated action; otherwise he must have absolutely nothing to do with the case, except in his official capacity as surveyor. He will make no survey of a mineral claim in which he holds an interest, nor will he employ chainmen interested therein in any manner.

Survey—How Made.

129. The survey made and returned must, in every case, be an actual survey on the ground in full detail, made by the mineral surveyor in person after the receipt of the order, and without reference to any knowledge he may have previously acquired by reason of having made the location survey or otherwise, and must show the actual facts existing at the time. This precludes him from calculating the connections to corners of the public survey and location monuments, or any other lines of his survey through prior surveys made by others and substituting the same for connections or lines of the survey returned by him. The term survey in this paragraph applies not only to the usual field work, but also to the examinations required for the preparation of affidavits of five hundred dollars expenditure, descriptive reports on placer claims, and all other reports.

130. The survey of a mining claim may consist of several contiguous locations, but such survey must, in conformity with statutory requirements, distinguish the several locations, and exhibit the boundaries of each. The survey will be given but one number.

131. The survey must be made in strict conformity with, or be embraced within, the lines of the location upon which the order is based. If the survey and location are identical, that fact must be clearly and distinctly stated in the field notes. If not identical, a bearing and distance must be given from each established corner of survey to the corresponding corner of the location, and the location corner must be fully described, so that it can be identified. The lines of the location, as found upon the ground, must be laid down upon the preliminary plat in such a manner as to contrast and show their relation to the lines of survey.

132. In view of the principle that courses and distances must give way when in conflict with fixed objects and monuments, the surveyor will not, under any circumstances, change the corners of the location for the purpose of making them conform to the description in the record. If the difference from the location be slight, it may be explained in the field notes.

133. No mining claim located subsequent to May 10, 1872, should exceed the statutory limit in width on each side of the center of vein or 1,500 feet in length, and all surveys must close within 50-100 feet in 1,000 feet, and the error must not be such as to make the location exceed the statutory limit, and in absence of other proof the discovery point is held to be the center of the vein on the surface. The course and length of the vein should be marked upon the plat.

134. All mineral surveys must be made with a transit, provided with a solar attachment, by which the meridian can be determined independently of the magnetic needle, and all courses must be referred to the true meridian. The variation should be noted at each corner of the survey. The true course of at least one line of each survey must be ascertained by astronomical observations made at the time of the survey; the data for determining the same and details as to how these data were arrived at must be given. Or, in lieu of the foregoing the survey must be connected with some line the true course of which has been previously established beyond question, and in a similar manner, and, when such lines exist, it is desirable in all cases that they should be used as a proof of the accuracy of subsequent work.

135. Corner No. 1 of each location embraced in a survey must be connected by course and distance with nearest corner of the public survey or with a United States location monument, if the claim lies within two miles of such corner or monument. If both are within the required distance, the connection must be with the corner of the public survey.

136. Surveys and connections of mineral claims may be made in suspended townships in the same manner as though the claims were upon unsurveyed land, except as hereinafter specified, by connecting them with independent mineral monuments. At the same time, the position of any public land corner which may be found in the neighborhood of the claim should be noted, so that, in case of the release of the township from suspension, the position of the claim can be shown on the plat.

137. A mineral survey must not be returned with its connection made only with a corner of the public survey, where the survey of the township within which it is situated is under suspension, nor connected with a mineral monument alone, when situated within the limits of a township the regularity and correctness of the survey of which is unquestioned.

138. In making an official survey, corner No. 1 of each location must be established at the corner nearest the corner

of the public survey or location monument, unless good cause is shown for its being placed otherwise. If connections are given to both a corner of the public survey and location monument, corners Nos. 1 should be placed at the corner nearest the corner of the public survey. When a boundary line of a claim intersects a section line, courses and distances from point of intersection to the government corners at each end of the half mile of section line so intersected must be given.

139. In case a survey is situated in a district where there are no corners of the public survey and no monuments within the prescribed limits, a mineral monument must be established, in the location of which the greatest care must be exercised to insure permanency as to site and construction.

140. The site, when practicable, should be some prominent point, visible for a long distance from every direction, and should be so chosen that the permanency of the monument will not be endangered by snow, rock, or landslides, or other natural causes.

141. The monument should consist of a stone not less than 30 inches long, 20 inches wide, and 6 inches thick, set halfway in the ground, with a conical mound of stone 4 feet high and 6 feet base alongside. The letters U. S. L. M., followed by the consecutive number of the monument in the district, must be plainly chiseled upon the stone. If impracticable to obtain a stone of required dimensions, then a post 8 feet long, 6 inches square, set 3 feet in the ground, scribed as for a stone monument, protected by a well-built conical mound of stone of not less than 3 feet high and 6 feet base around it, may be used. The exact point for connection must be indicated on the monument by an X chiseled thereon; if a post is used, then a tack must be driven into the post to indicate the point.

142. From the monument, connections by course and distance must be taken to two or three bearing trees or rocks, and to any well-known and permanent objects in the vicinity, such as the confluence of streams, prominent rocks, buildings, shafts, or mouths of adits. Bearing trees must be properly scribed B. T. and bearing rocks chiseled B. R., together with the number of the location monument; the exact point on the tree or stone to which the connection is taken should be indicated by a cross or other unmistakable mark. Bearings should also be taken to prominent mountain peaks, and the approximate distance and direction ascertained from the nearest town or mining camp. A detailed description of the locating monument, with a topographical map of its location, should be furnished the office of the surveyor general by the surveyor.

143. Corners may consist of—

First—A stone at least 24 inches long set 12 inches in the ground, with a conical mound of stone 1½ feet high, 2 feet base, alongside.

Second—A post at least 3 feet long by 4 inches square, set

18 inches in the ground and surrounded by a substantial mound of stone or earth.

Third—A rock in place.

A stone should always be used for a corner when possible, and when so used the kind should be stated.

144. All corners must be established in a permanent and workmanlike manner, and the corner and survey number must be neatly chiseled or scribed on the sides facing the claim. The exact corner point must be permanently indicated on the corner. When a rock in place is used, its dimensions above ground must be stated and a cross chiseled at the exact corner point.

145. In case the point for the corner be inaccessible or unsuitable a witness corner, which must be marked with the letters W. C. in addition to the corner and survey number, should be established. The witness corner should be located upon a line of the survey and as near as possible to the true corner, with which it must be connected by course and distance. The reason why it is impossible or impracticable to establish the true corner must always be stated in the field notes, and in running the next course it should be stated whether the start is made from the true place for corner or from witness corner.

146. The identity of all corners should be perpetuated by taking courses and distances to bearing trees, rocks, and other objects, as prescribed in the establishment of location monuments, and when no bearings are given it should be stated that no bearings are available. Permanent objects should be selected for bearings whenever possible.

147. If an official mineral survey has been made in the vicinity, within a reasonable distance, a further connecting line should be run to some corner thereof; and in like manner all conflicting surveys and locations should be so connected, and the corner with which connections is made in each case described. Such connections will be made and conflicts shown according to the boundaries of the neighboring or conflicting claims as each is marked, defined, and actually established upon the ground. The mineral surveyor will fully and specifically state in his return how and by what visible evidences he was able to identify on the ground the several conflicting surveys and those which appear according to their returned tie or boundary lines to conflict, if they were so identified, and report errors or discrepancies found by him in any such surveys. In the survey of contiguous claims which constitute a consolidated group, where corners are common, bearings should be mentioned but once.

148. The mineral surveyor should note carefully all topographical features of the claim, taking distances on his lines to intersections with all streams, gulches, ditches, ravines, mountain ridges, roads, trails, etc., with their widths, courses, and other data that may be required to map them correctly.

All municipal or private improvements, such as blocks, streets, and buildings, should be located.

149.   If, in running the exterior lines of a claim, the survey is found to conflict with the survey of another claim, the distances to the points of intersection, and the courses and distances along the line intersected from an established corner of such conflicting claim to such points of intersection, should be described in the field notes: Provided, That where a corner of the conflicting survey falls within the claim being surveyed, such corner should be selected from which to give the bearing, otherwise the corner nearest the intersection should be taken.   The same rule should govern in the survey of claims embracing two or more locations the lines of which intersect.

150.   A lode and mill site claim in one survey will be distinguished by the letters A and B following the number of the survey.   The corners of the mill site will be numbered independently of those of the lode.   Corner No. 1 of the mill site must be connected with a corner of the lode claim as well as with a corner of the public survey or United States location monument.

151.   When a placer claim includes lodes, or when several contiguous placer or lode locations are included as one claim in one survey, there must be given to the corners of each location constituting the same a separate consecutive numerical designation, beginning with corner No. 1 in each case.

152.   Throughout the description of the survey, after each reference to the lines or corners of a location, the name thereof must be given, and if unsurveyed, the fact stated.   If reference is made to a location included in a prior official survey, the survey number must be given, followed by the name of the location.   Corners should be described once only.

153.   The total area of each location and also the area in conflict with each intersecting survey or claim should be stated; also the total area claimed.   But when locations embraced in one survey conflict with each other such conflicts should only be stated in connection with the location from which the conflicting area is excluded.

154.   It should be stated particularly whether the claim is upon surveyed or unsurveyed public lands, giving in the former case the quarter section, township, and range in which it is located, and the section lines should be indicated by full lines and the quarter-section lines by dotted lines.

155.   The title page of the field notes must contain the post office address of the claimant or his authorized agent.

156.   In the mineral surveyor's report of the value of the improvements all actual expenditures and mining improvements made by the claimant or his grantors, having a direct relation to the development of the claim, must be included in the estimate.

157.   The expenditures required may be made from the surface or in running a tunnel, drifts, or crosscuts for the

development of the claim. Improvements of any other character, such as buildings, machinery, or roadways, must be excluded from the estimate, unless it is shown clearly that they are associated with actual excavations, such as cuts, tunnels, shafts, etc., are essential to the practical development of and actually facilitate the extraction of mineral from the claim.

158. All mining and other improvements claimed will be located by courses and distances from corners of the survey, or from points on the center or side lines, specifying with particularity and detail the dimensions and character of each, and the improvements upon each location should be numbered consecutively, the point of discovery being always No. 1. Improvements made by a former locator who has abandoned his claim can not be included in the estimate, but should be described and located in the notes and plat.

159. In case of a lode and mill site claim in the same survey the expenditure of five hundred dollars must be shown upon the lode claim.

160. If the value of the labor and improvements upon a mineral claim is less than five hundred dollars at the time of survey, the mineral surveyor may file with the surveyor general supplemental proof showing five hundred dollars expenditure made prior to the expiration of the period of publication.

161. The mineral surveyor will return with his field notes a preliminary plat on blank sent to him for that purpose, protracted on a scale of two hundred feet to an inch, if practicable. In preparing plats the top is north. Copy of the calculations of areas by double meridian distances and of all triangulations or traverse lines must be furnished. The lines of the claim surveyed should be heavier than the lines of conflicting claims.

162. Whenever a survey has been reported in error the surveyor who made it will be required to promptly make a thorough examination upon the premises and report the result, under oath, to the surveyor general's office. In case he finds his survey in error he will report in detail all discrepancies with the original survey and submit any explanation he may have to offer as to the cause. If, on the contrary, he should report his survey correct, a joint survey will be ordered to settle the differences with the surveyor who reported the error. A joint survey must be made within ten days after the date of order unless satisfactory reasons are submitted, under oath, for a postponement. The field work must in every sense of the term be a joint and not a separate survey, and the observations and measurements taken with the same instrument and chain, previously tested and agreed upon.

163. The mineral surveyor found in error, or, if both are in error, the one who reported the same, will make out the field notes of the joint survey, which, after being duly signed

and sworn to by both parties, must be transmitted to the surveyor general's office.

164. Inasmuch as amended surveys are ordered only by special instructions from the general land office, and the conditions and circumstances peculiar to each separate case and the object sought by the required amendment, alone govern all special matters relative to the manner of making such survey and the form and subject-matter to be embraced in the field notes thereof, but few general rules applicable to all cases can be laid down.

165. The amended survey must be made in strict conformity with, or be embraced within, the lines of the original survey. If the amended and original surveys are identical, that fact must be clearly and distinctly stated in the field notes. If not identical, a bearing and distance must be given from each established corner of the amended survey to the corresponding corner of the original survey. The lines of the original survey, as found upon the ground, must be laid down upon the preliminary plat in such manner as to contrast and show their relation to the lines of the amended survey.

166. The field notes of the amended survey must be prepared on the same size and form of blanks as are the field notes of the original survey, and the word "amended" must be used before the word "survey" wherever it occurs in the field notes.

167. Mineral surveyors are required to make full examinations of all placer claims at the time of survey and file with the field notes a descriptive report, in which will be described—

(a) The quality and composition of the soil, and the kind and amount of timber and other vegetation.

(b) The locus and size of streams, and such other matter as may appear upon the surface of the claims.

(c) The character and extent of all surface and underground workings, whther placer or lode, for mining purposes, locating and describing them.

(d) The proximity of centers of trade or residence.

(e) The proximity of well-known systems of lode deposits or of individual lodes.

(f) The use or adaptability of the claim for placer mining, and whether water has been brought upon it in sufficient quantity to mine the same, or whether it can be procured for that purpose.

(g) What works or expenditures have been made by the claimant or his grantors for the development of the claim, and their situation and location with respect to the same as applied for.

(h) The true situation of all mines, salt licks, salt springs, and mill sites which come to the surveyor's knowledge, or a report by him that none exist on the claim, as the facts may warrant.

(i)　Said report must be made under oath and duly corroborated by one or more disinterested persons.

168.　The employing of claimants, their attorneys, or parties in interest, as assistants in making surveys of mineral claims will not be allowed.

169.　The field work must be accurately and properly performed and returns made in conformity with the foregoing instructions. Errors in the survey must be corrected at the surveyor's own expense, and if the time required in the examination of the returns is increased by reason of neglect or carelessness, he will be required to make an additional deposit for office work. He will be held to a strict accountability for the faithful discharge of his duties, and will be required to observe fully the requirements and regulations in force as to making mineral surveys. If found incompetent as a surveyor, careless in the discharge of his duties, or guilty of a violation of said regulations, his appointment will be promptly revoked.

R. A. BALLINGER,
Commissioner.

Approved May 21, 1907.
JAMES RUDOLPH GARFIELD,
Secretary.

INDEX.

—

(References are to pages.)

INDEX.

www.ingramcontent.com/pod-product-compliance
Lightning Source LLC
Chambersburg PA
CBHW081720220526
45468CB00008B/1917

* 9 7 8 1 7 2 4 3 8 3 3 8 9 *